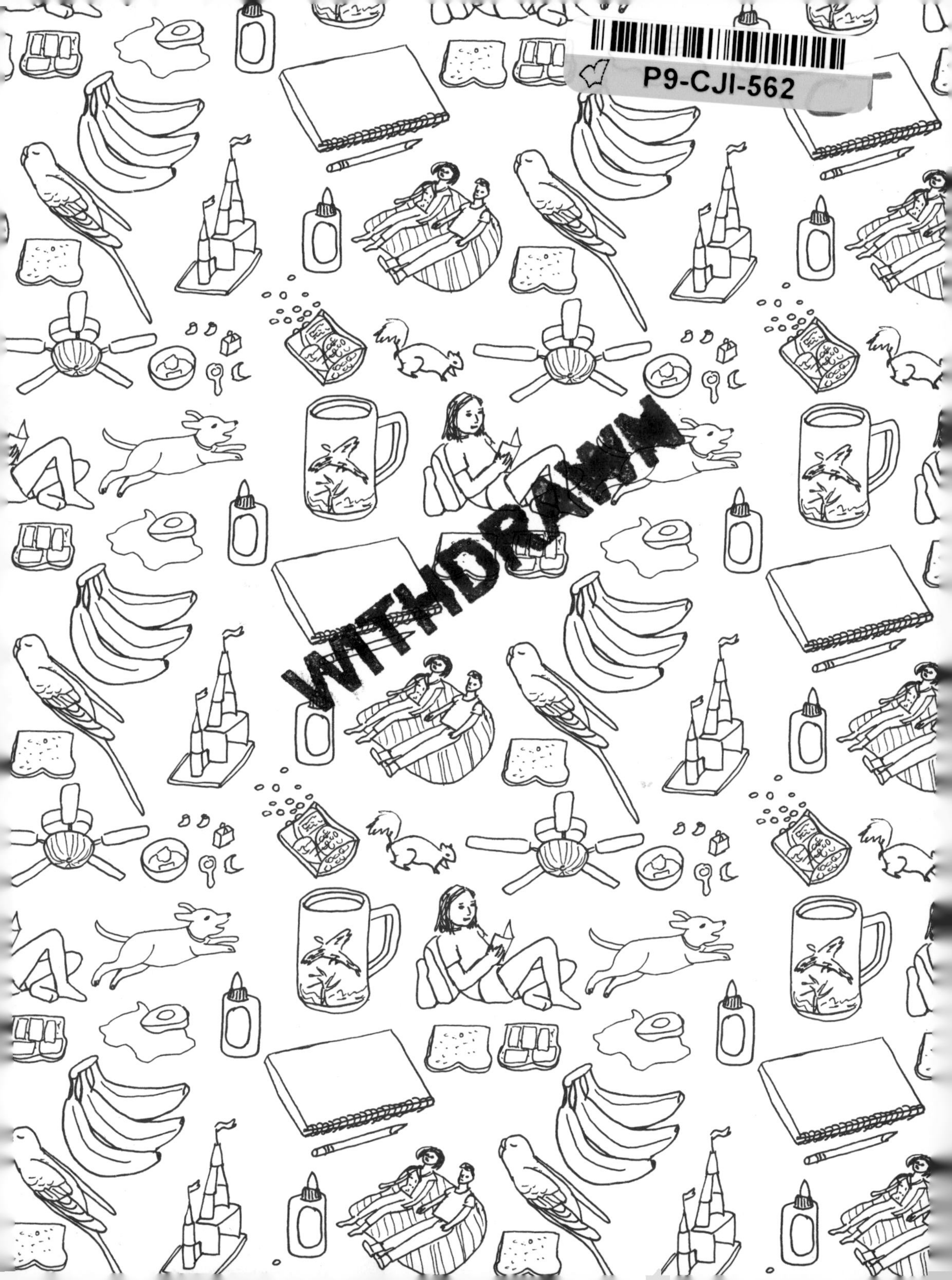

Dedicated to Scott and Xia

Thank you to everyone at Drawn & Quarterly!

Thank you Mom and Dad for all the love, food, conversations, and the new patio chair.

Thank you friends for making life fun.

Thank you Crooky for all the times you did make it outside, or at least chose a spot on the hardwood floor instead of the carpet.

Thank you Xia for providing most of the content of my work and life. Thank you for being a willing participant, and for being so funny.

Thank you Scott for all of it.

Entire contents copyright © 2021 Keiler Roberts. All rights reserved. No part of this book (except small portions for review purposes) may be reproduced in any form without written permission from Keiler Roberts or Drawn & Quarterly.

drawnandquarterly.com
keilerroberts.com

ISBN 978-1-77046-458-2
First edition: May 2021
Printed in China
10 9 8 7 6 5 4 3 2 1

Cataloguing data available from Library and Archives Canada.

Published in the USA by Drawn & Quarterly, a client publisher of Farrar, Straus and Giroux. Published in Canada by Drawn & Quarterly, a client publisher of Raincoast Books. Published in the United Kingdom by Drawn & Quarterly, a client publisher of Publishers Group UK.

MY BEGGING CHART

keiler roberts

3 1336 11332 4009

Drawn & Quarterly

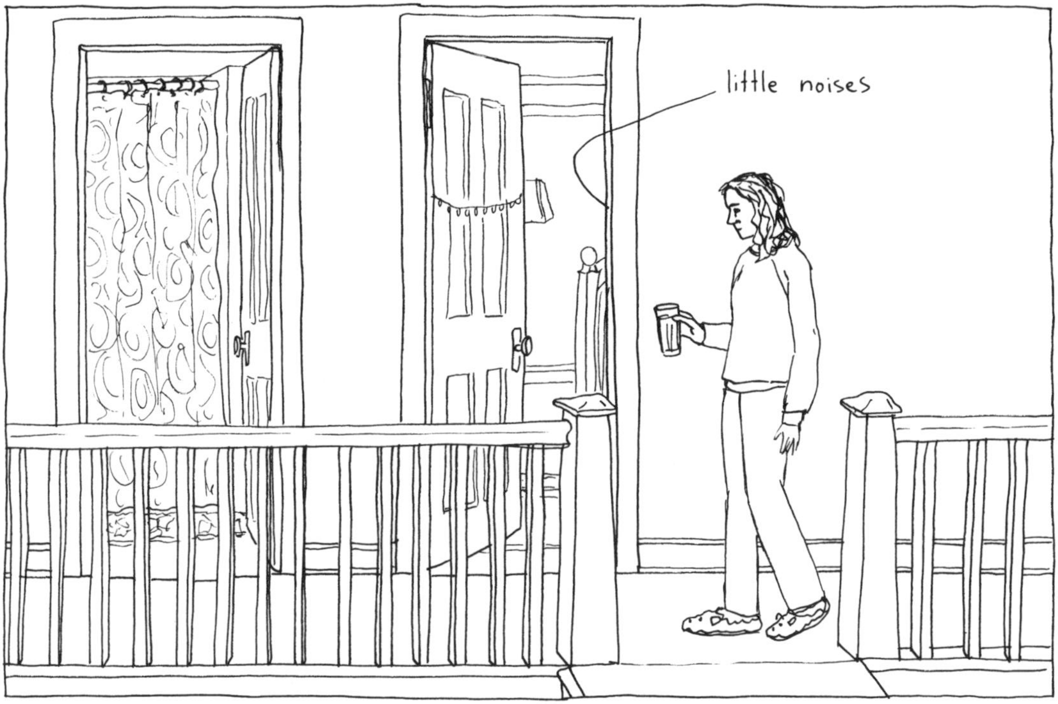
little noises

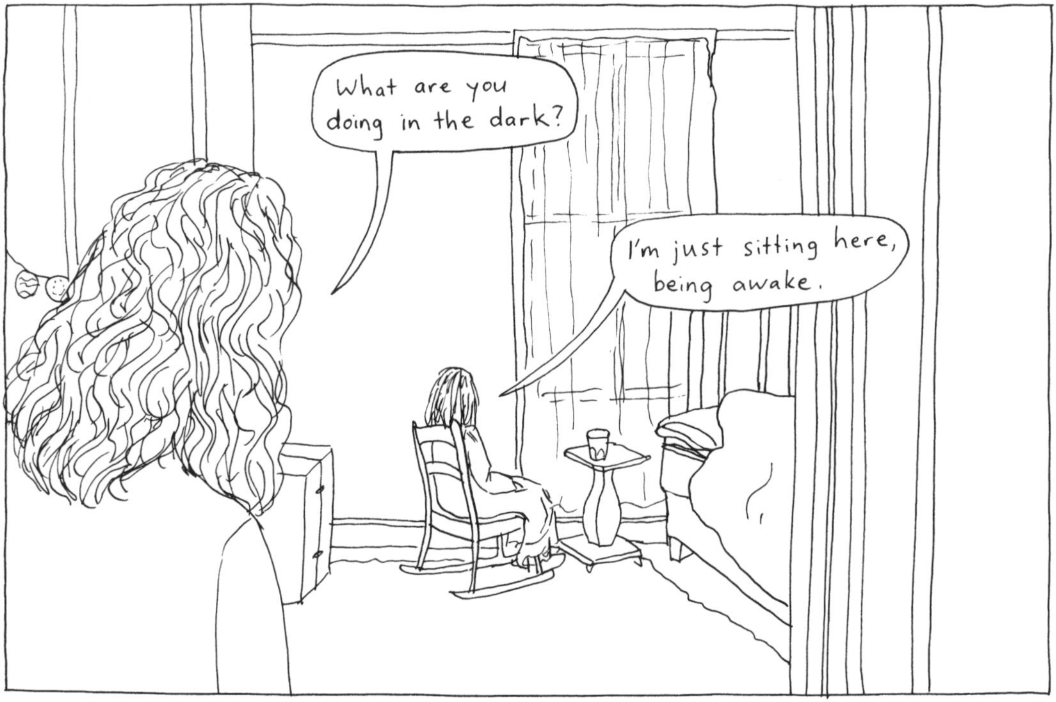
What are you doing in the dark?
I'm just sitting here, being awake.

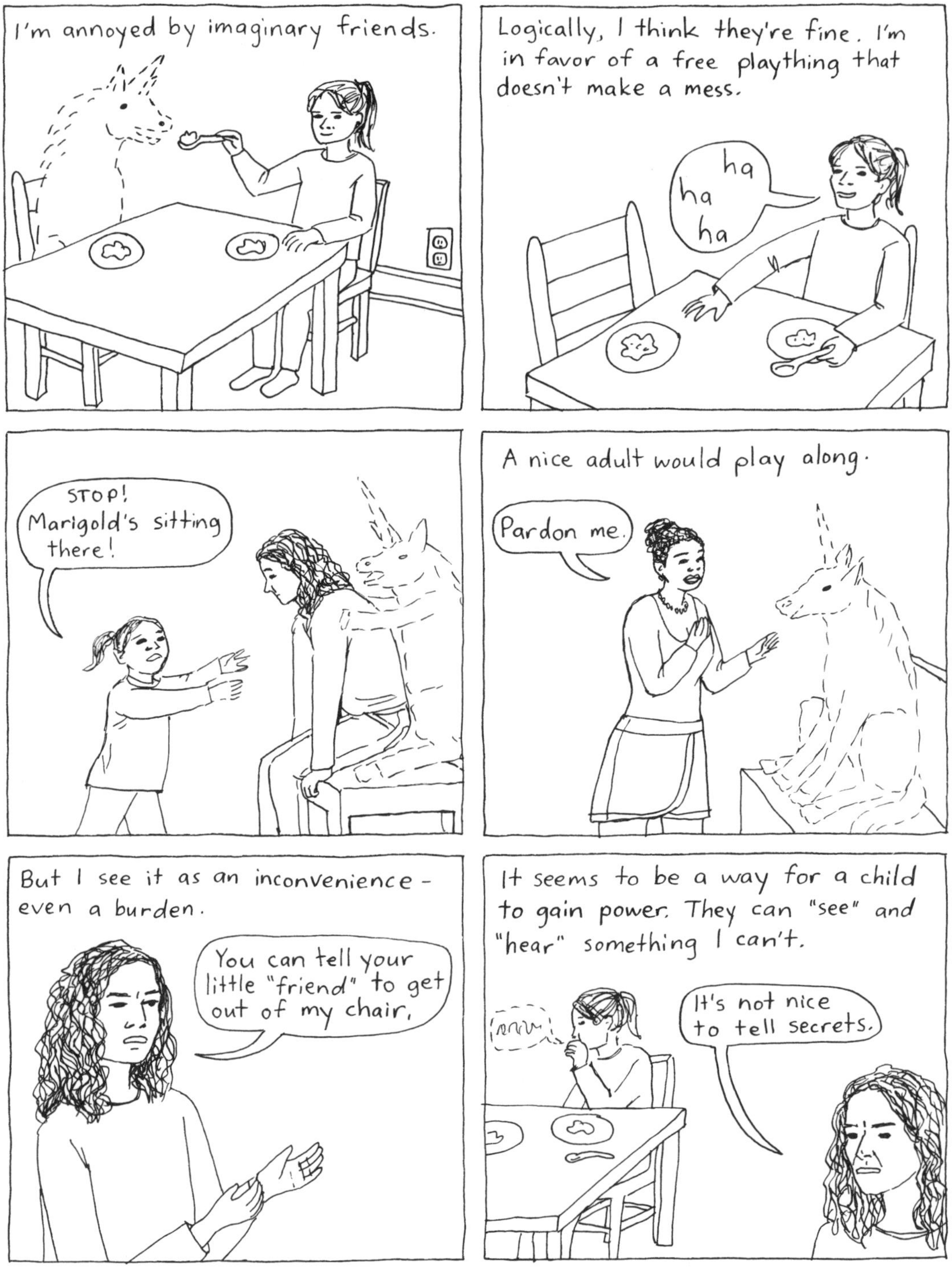
I'm annoyed by imaginary friends.
Logically, I think they're fine. I'm in favor of a free plaything that doesn't make a mess.
ha ha ha
STOP! Marigold's sitting there!
A nice adult would play along.
Pardon me.
But I see it as an inconvenience - even a burden.
You can tell your little "friend" to get out of my chair.
It seems to be a way for a child to gain power. They can "see" and "hear" something I can't.
It's not nice to tell secrets.

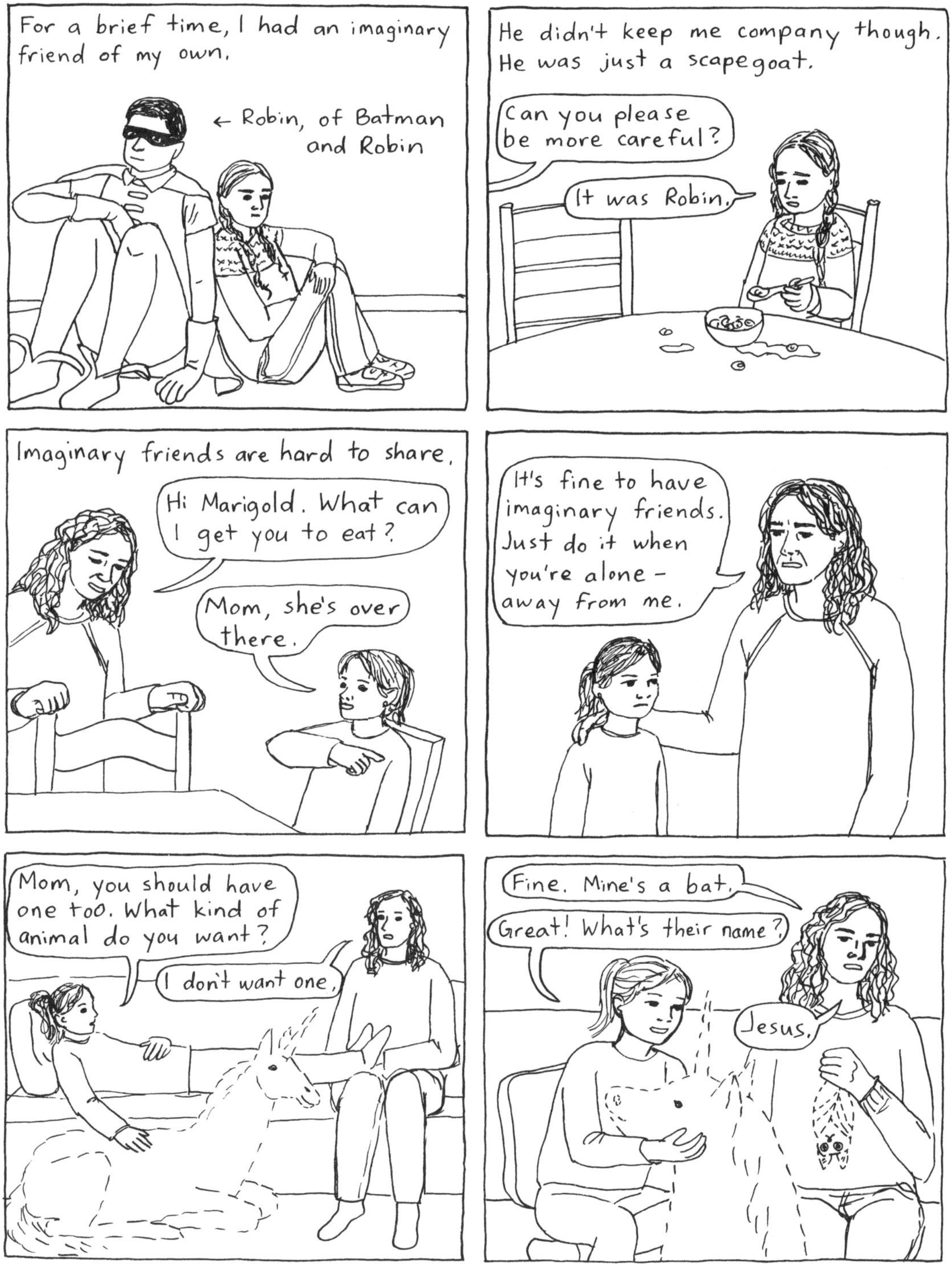
For a brief time, I had an imaginary friend of my own.
← Robin, of Batman and Robin
He didn't keep me company though. He was just a scapegoat.
Can you please be more careful?
It was Robin.
Imaginary friends are hard to share.
Hi Marigold. What can I get you to eat?
Mom, she's over there.
It's fine to have imaginary friends. Just do it when you're alone - away from me.
Mom, you should have one too. What kind of animal do you want?
I don't want one.
Fine. Mine's a bat.
Great! What's their name?
Jesus.

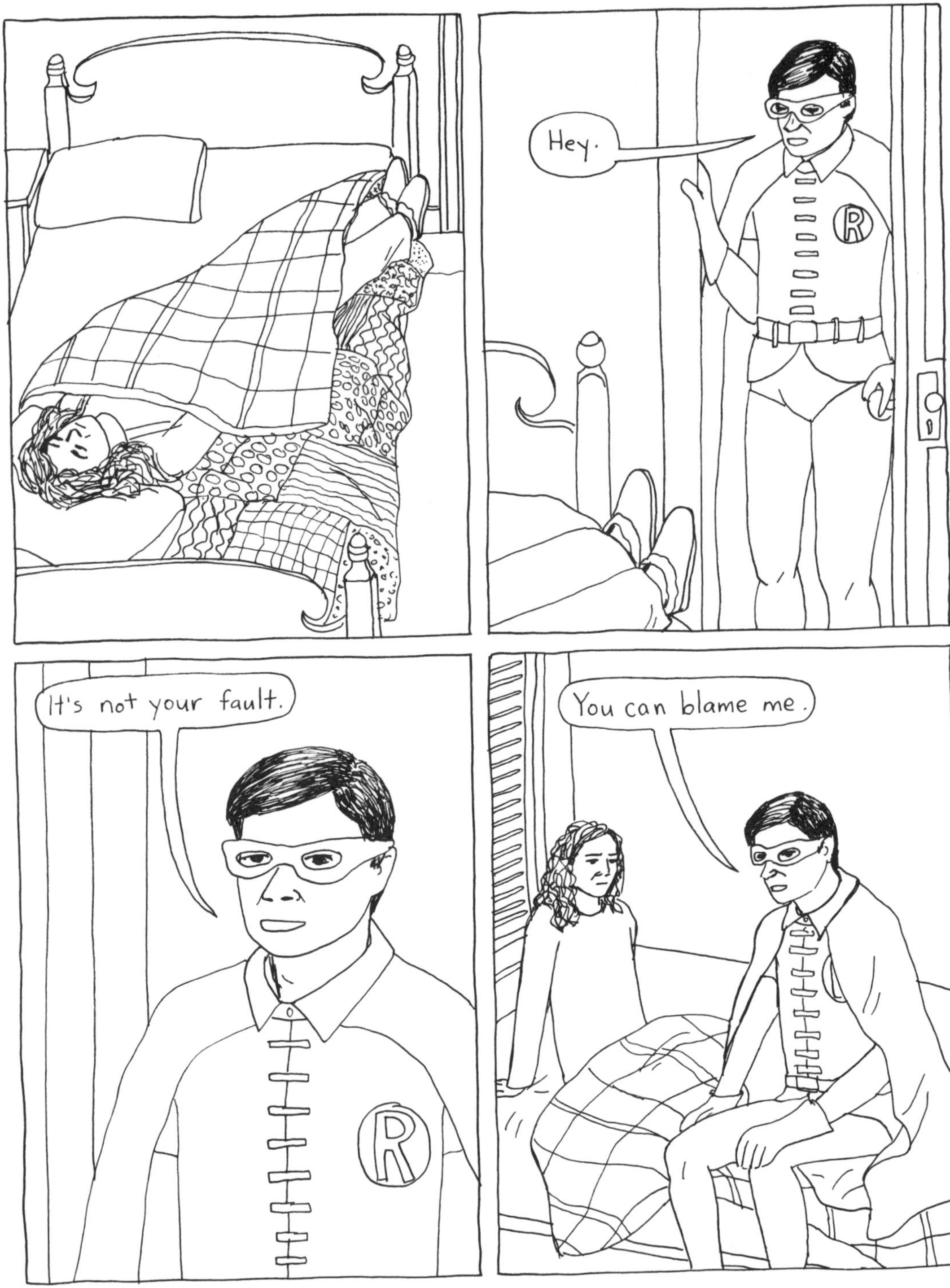
Hey.
It's not your fault.
You can blame me.

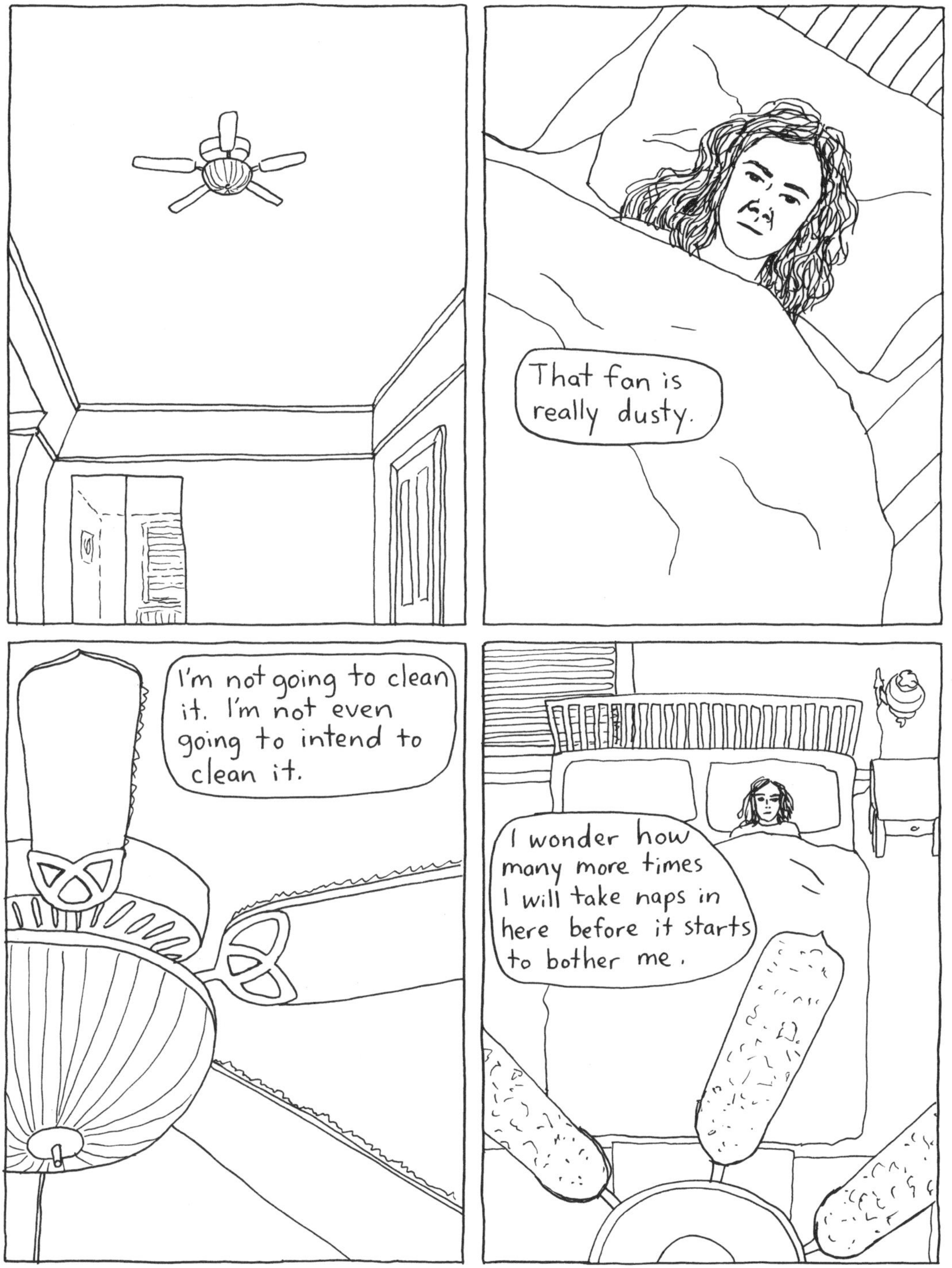
That fan is really dusty.
I'm not going to clean it. I'm not even going to intend to clean it.
I wonder how many more times I will take naps in here before it starts to bother me.

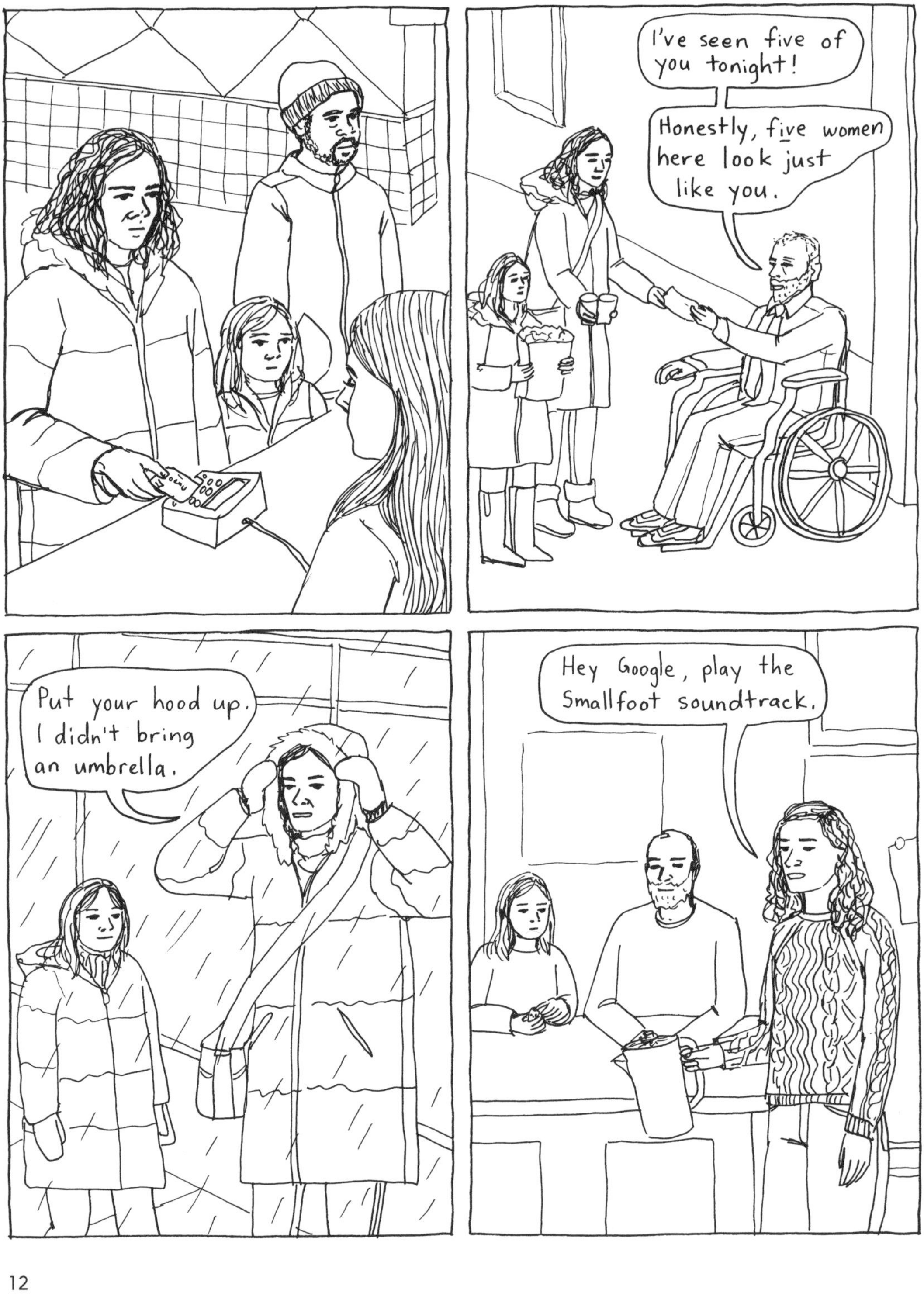
I've seen five of you tonight!
Honestly, five women here look just like you.
Put your hood up. I didn't bring an umbrella.
Hey Google, play the Smallfoot soundtrack.

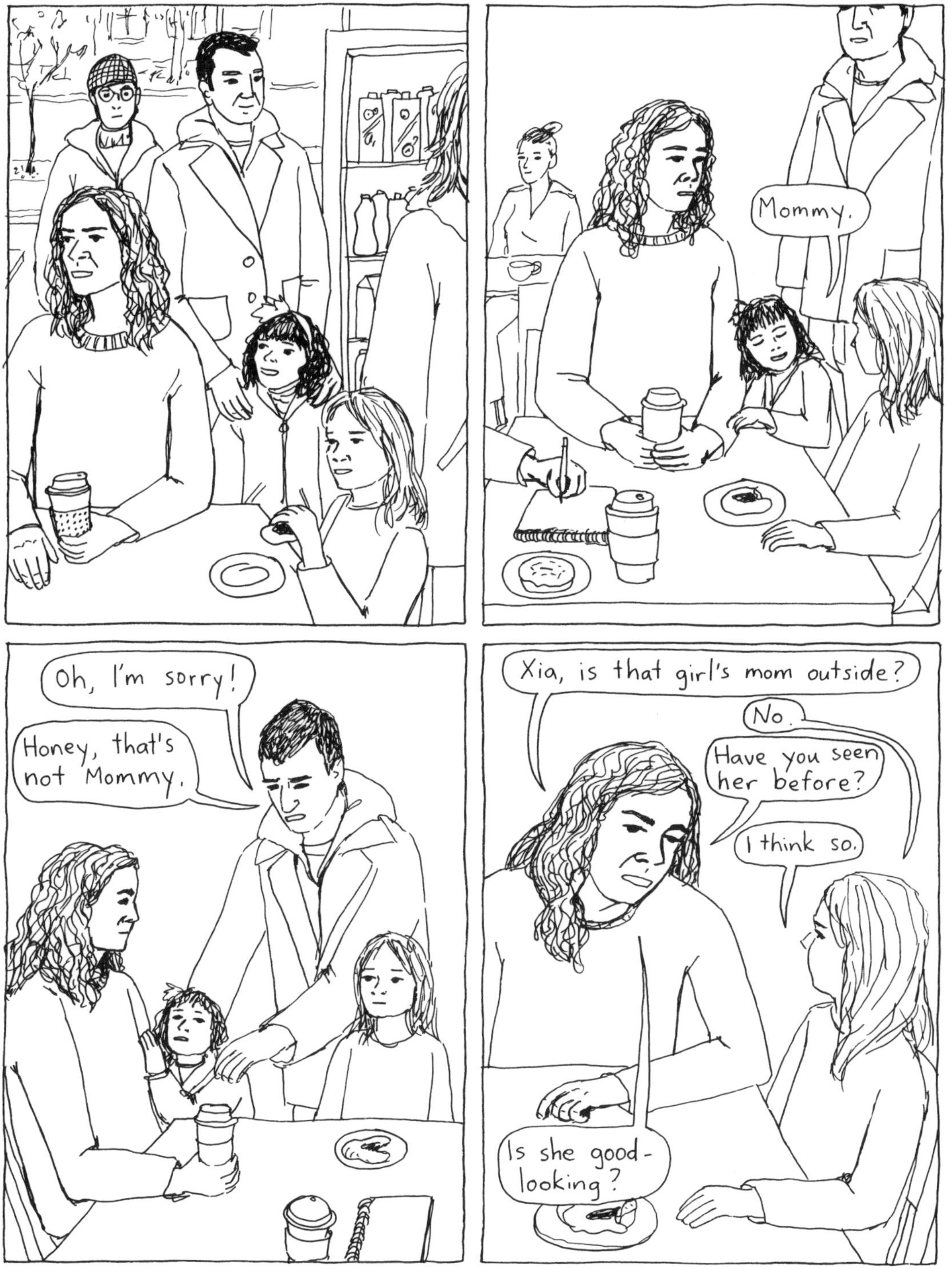
Mommy.
Oh, I'm sorry!
Honey, that's not Mommy.
Xia, is that girl's mom outside?
No.
Have you seen her before?
I think so.
Is she good-looking?

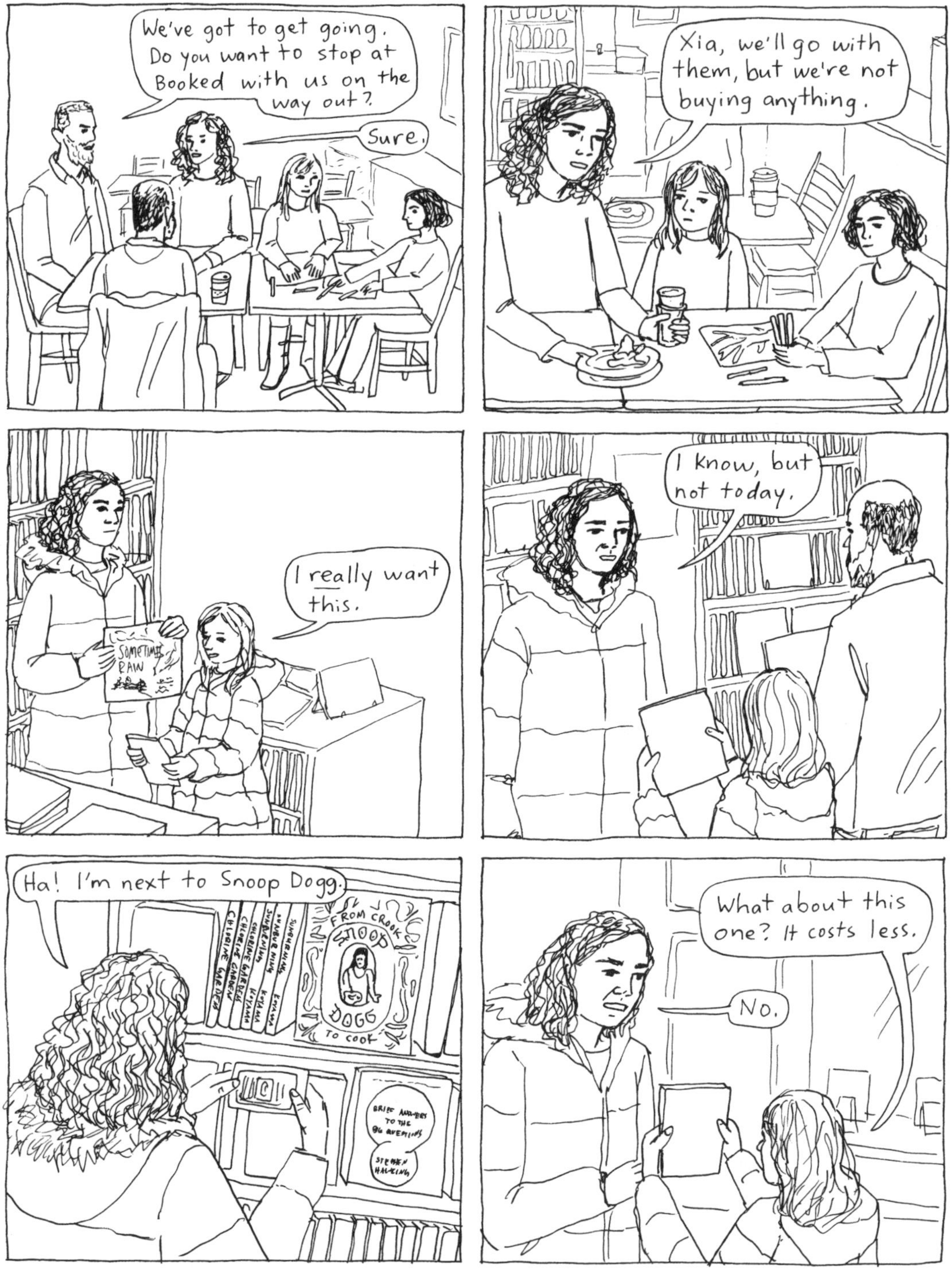
We've got to get going. Do you want to stop at Booked with us on the way out?
Sure.
Xia, we'll go with them, but we're not buying anything.
SOMETIMES RAIN
I really want this.
I know, but not today.
Ha! I'm next to Snoop Dogg.
FROM CROOK TO COOK SNOOP DOGG
BRIEF ANSWERS TO THE BIG QUESTIONS
STEPHEN HAWKING
What about this one? It costs less.
No.

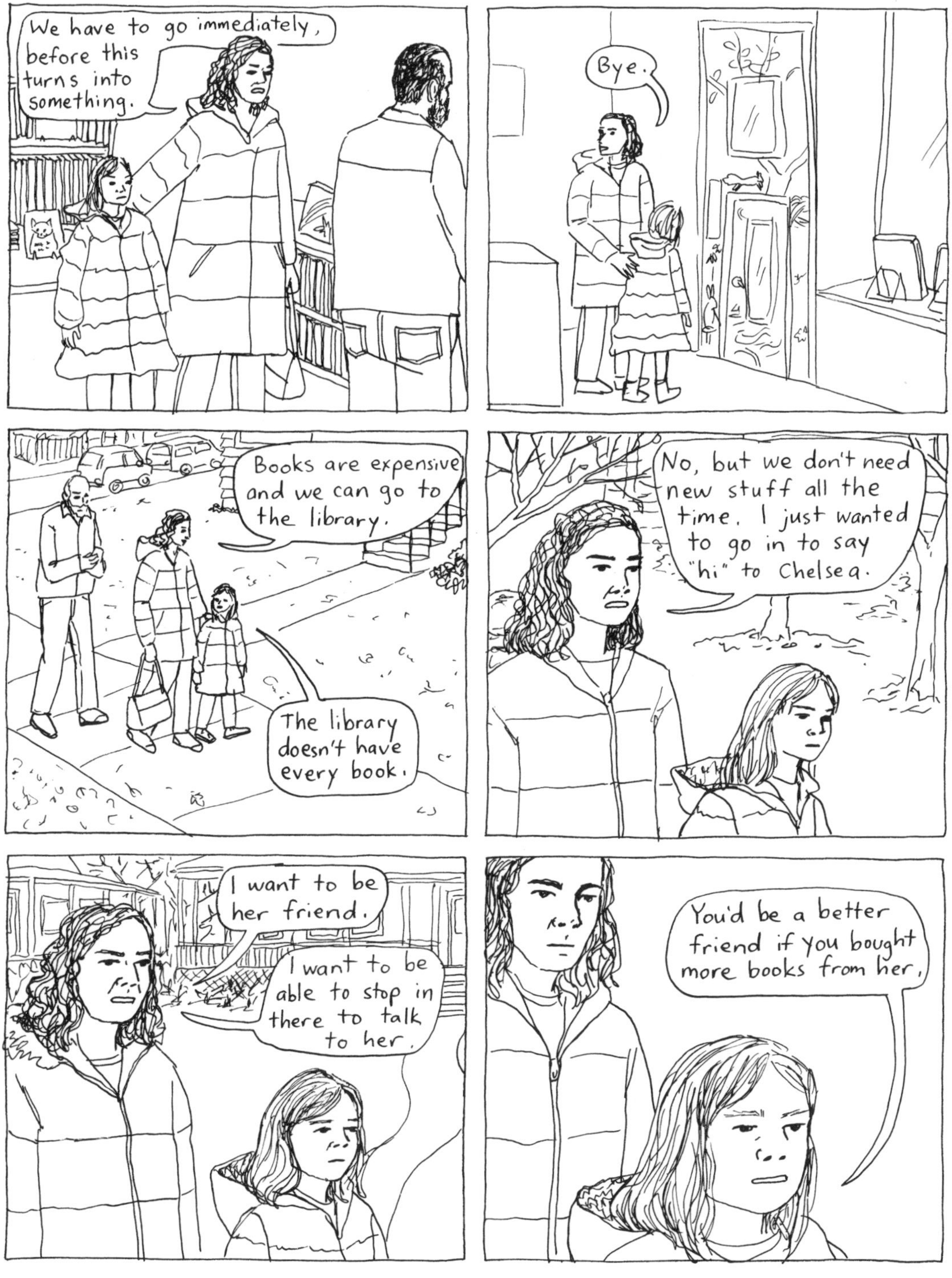
We have to go immediately, before this turns into something.
Bye.
Books are expensive and we can go to the library.
The library doesn't have every book.
No, but we don't need new stuff all the time. I just wanted to go in to say "hi" to Chelsea.
I want to be her friend.
I want to be able to stop in there to talk to her.
You'd be a better friend if you bought more books from her.

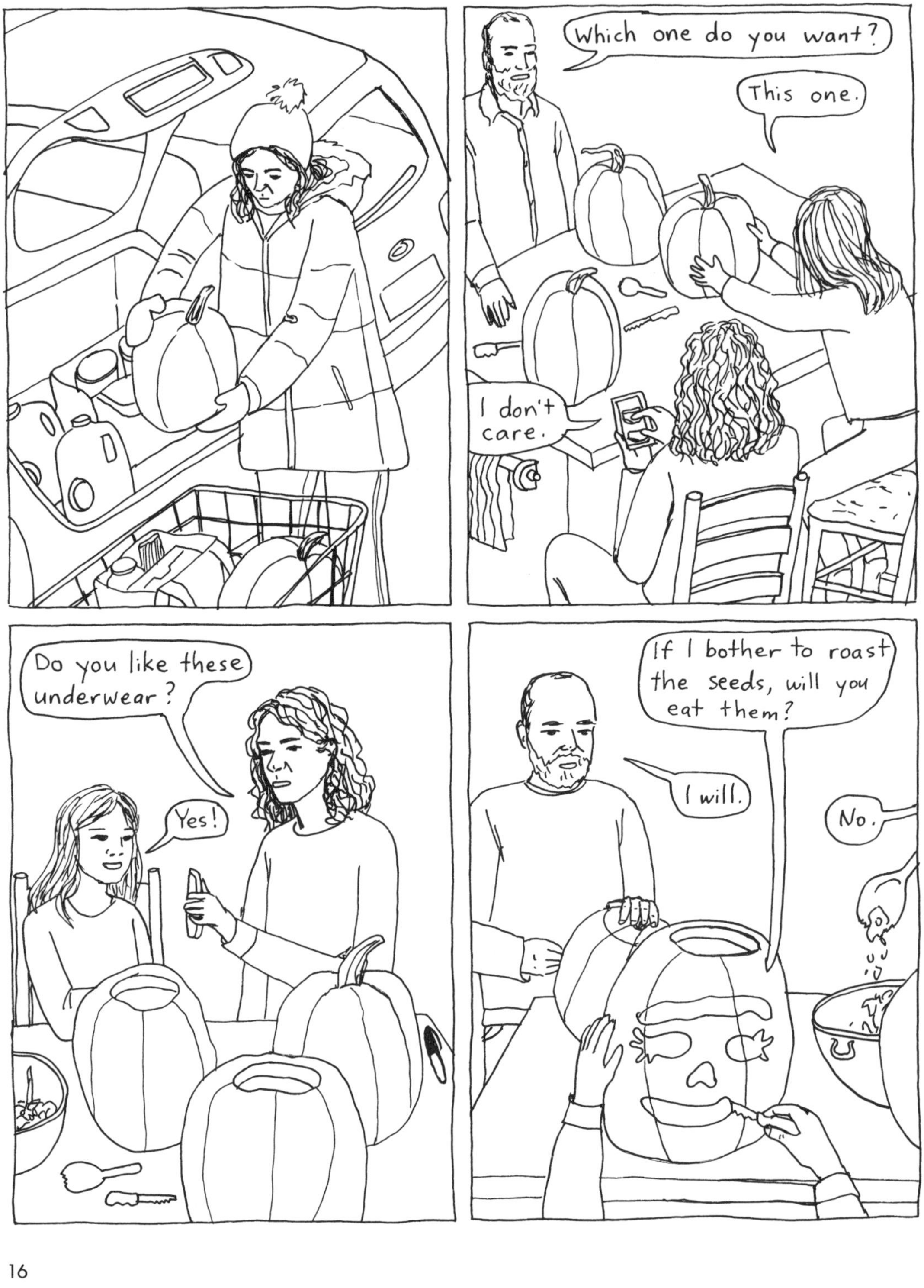
Which one do you want?
This one.
I don't care.
Do you like these underwear?
Yes!
If I bother to roast the seeds, will you eat them?
I will.
No.

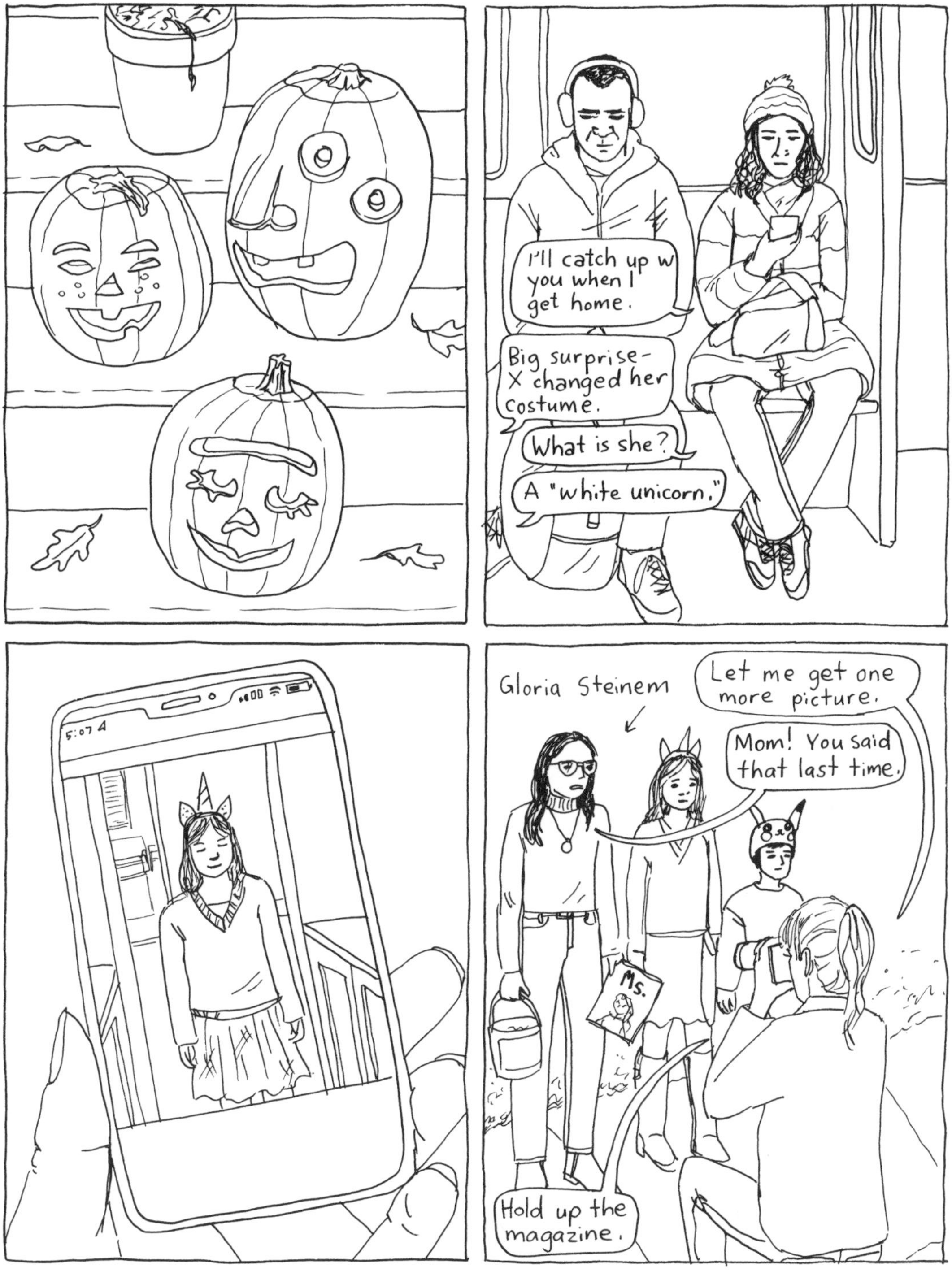
I'll catch up w you when I get home.
Big surprise- X changed her costume.
What is she?
A "white unicorn."
5:07
Gloria Steinem
Let me get one more picture.
Mom! You said that last time.
Ms.
Hold up the magazine.

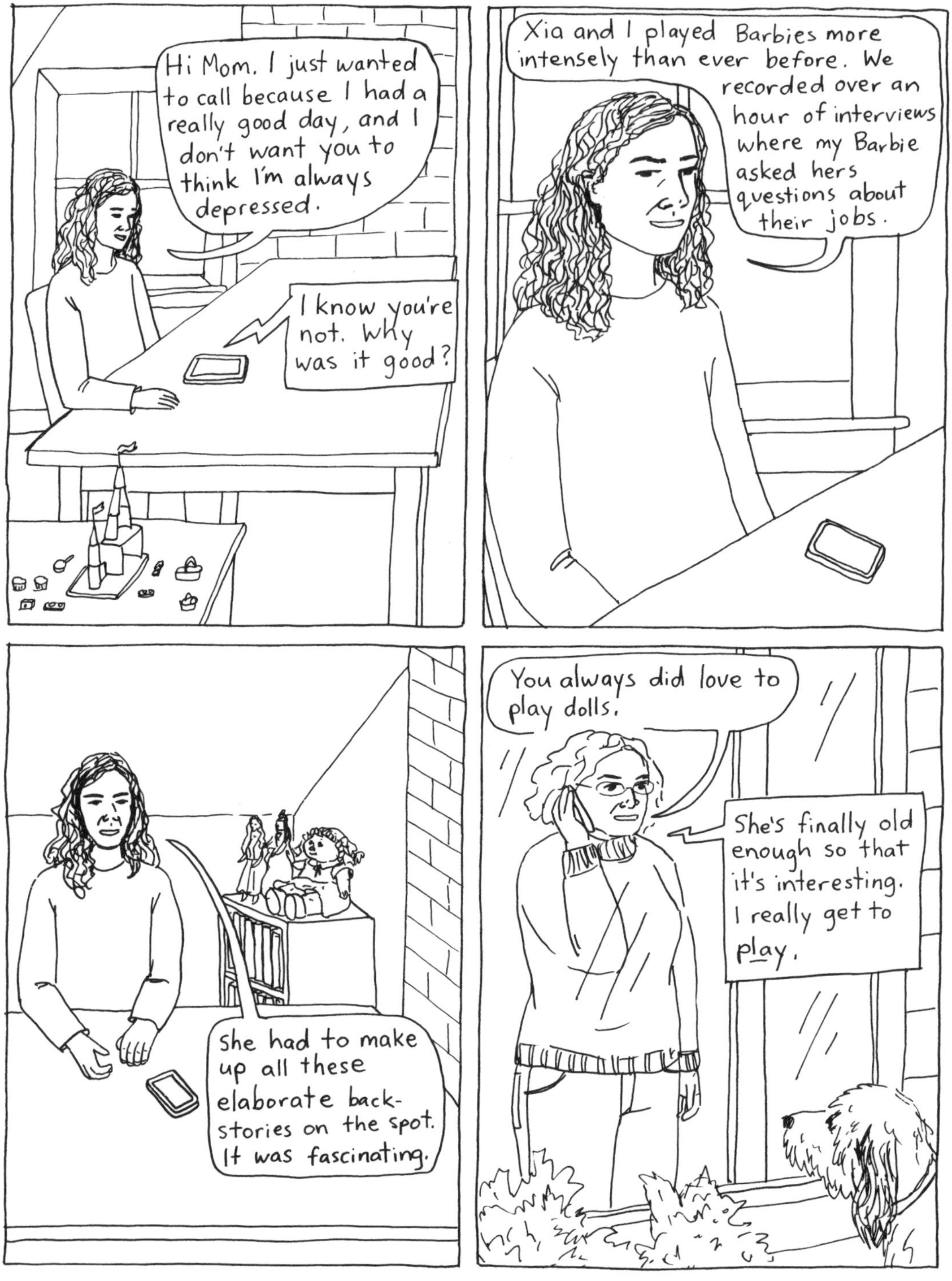
Hi Mom. I just wanted to call because I had a really good day, and I don't want you to think I'm always depressed.
I know you're not. Why was it good?
Xia and I played Barbies more intensely than ever before. We recorded over an hour of interviews where my Barbie asked hers questions about their jobs.
She had to make up all these elaborate back-stories on the spot. It was fascinating.
You always did love to play dolls.
She's finally old enough so that it's interesting. I really get to play.

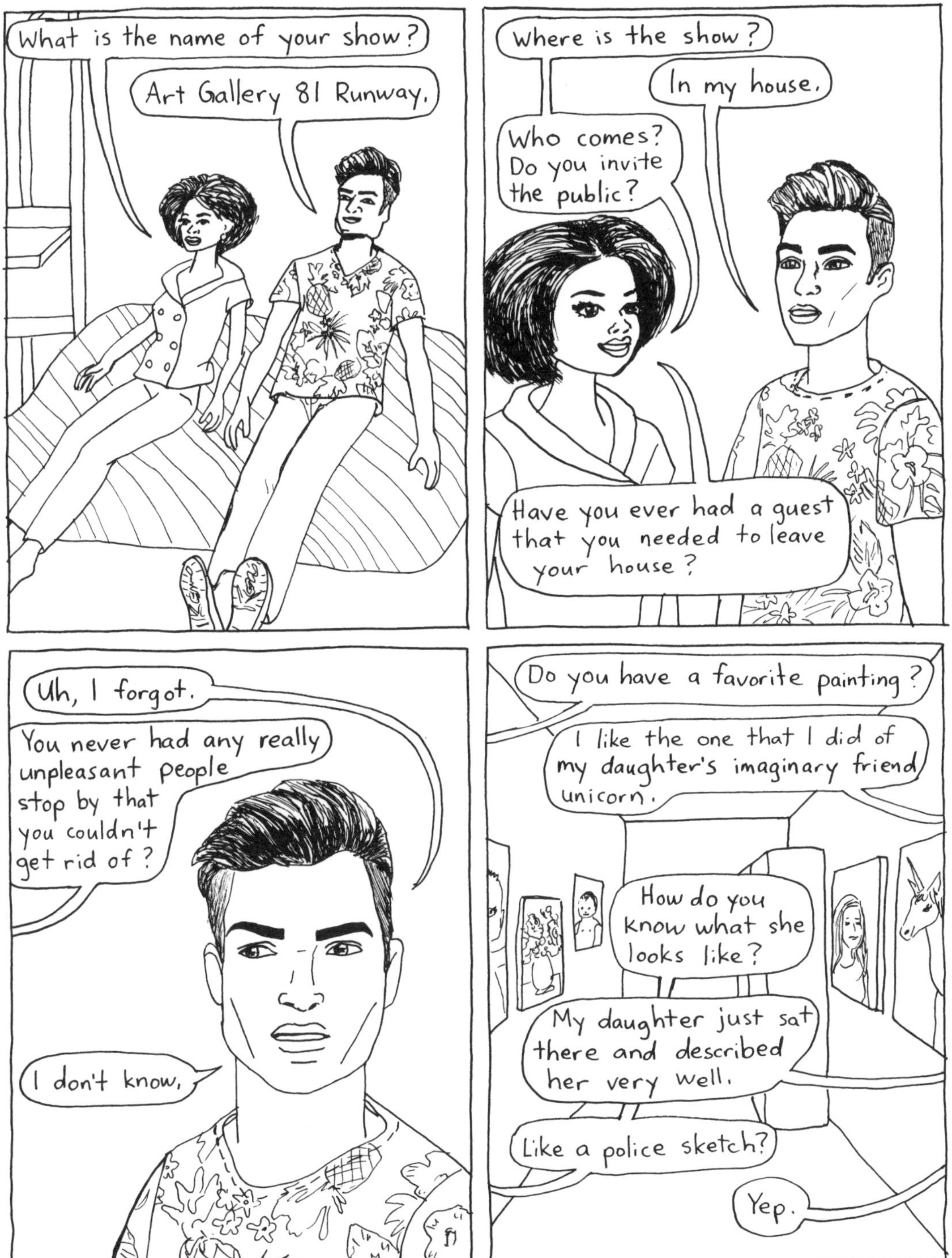
What is the name of your show?
Art Gallery 81 Runway.
Where is the show?
In my house.
Who comes? Do you invite the public?
Have you ever had a guest that you needed to leave your house?
Uh, I forgot.
You never had any really unpleasant people stop by that you couldn't get rid of?
I don't know.
Do you have a favorite painting?
I like the one that I did of my daughter's imaginary friend unicorn.
How do you know what she looks like?
My daughter just sat there and described her very well.
Like a police sketch?
Yep.

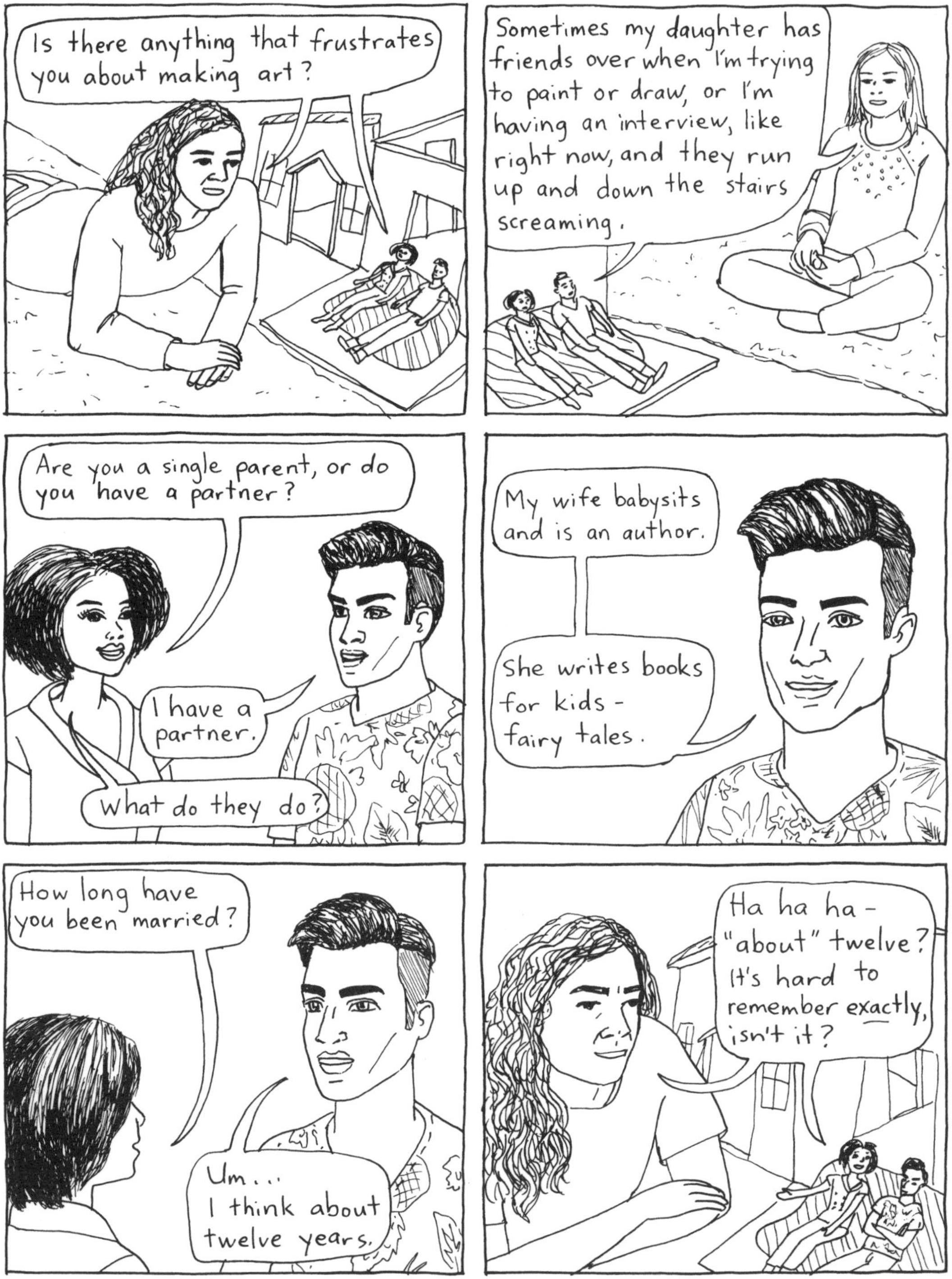
Is there anything that frustrates you about making art?
Sometimes my daughter has friends over when I'm trying to paint or draw, or I'm having an interview, like right now, and they run up and down the stairs screaming.
Are you a single parent, or do you have a partner?
I have a partner.
What do they do?
My wife babysits and is an author.
She writes books for kids - fairy tales.
How long have you been married?
Um... I think about twelve years.
Ha ha ha - "about" twelve? It's hard to remember exactly, isn't it?

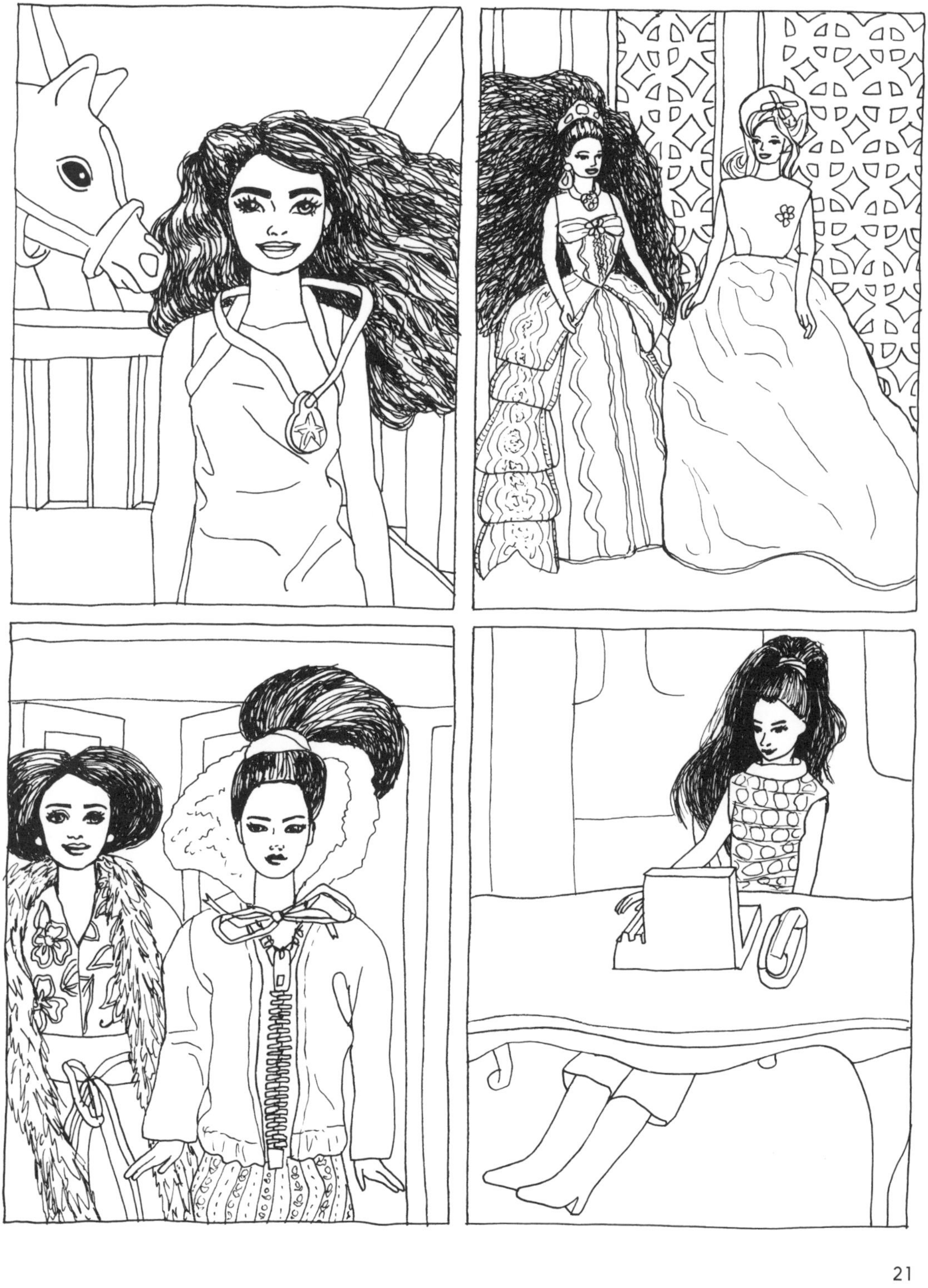

I've been increasingly aware of how unfulfilling life is right now.
I'm sorry.
I put up the decorations and baked cookies, but I never felt cozy.
That's the problem with Christmas. We think those are the activities that bring on that feeling of warmth and relaxation, but you could feel that way anywhere at any time - like at the grocery store.
I would never ever feel that good while grocery shopping.
Well, it won't happen in the frozen foods section. And I mean, after the panic attack - when you're coming down.

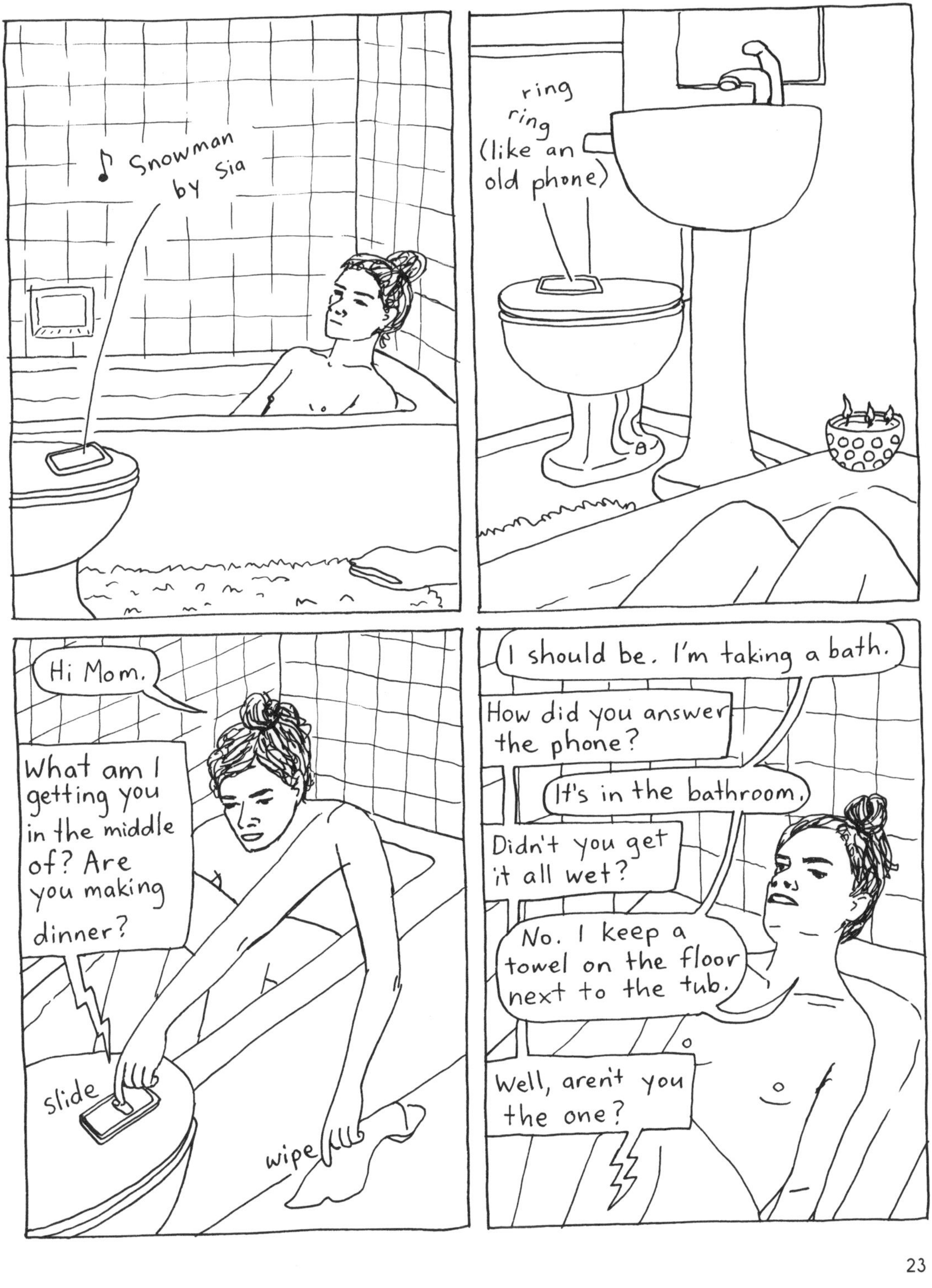

♪ Snowman by Sia
ring ring (like an old phone)
Hi Mom.
What am I getting you in the middle of? Are you making dinner?
slide
wipe
I should be. I'm taking a bath.
How did you answer the phone?
It's in the bathroom.
Didn't you get it all wet?
No. I keep a towel on the floor next to the tub.
Well, aren't you the one?

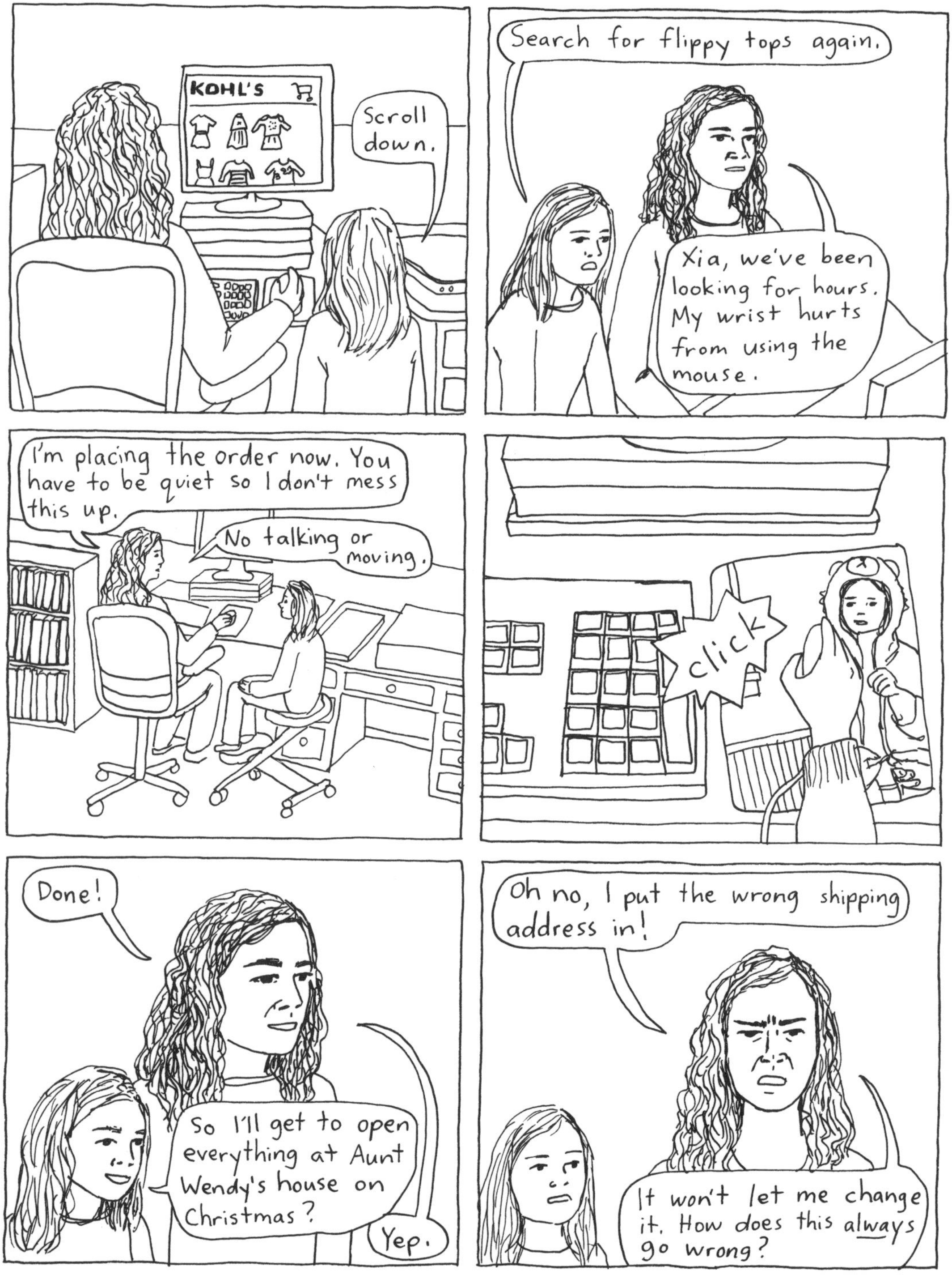
KOHL'S
Scroll down.
Search for flippy tops again.
Xia, we've been looking for hours. My wrist hurts from using the mouse.
I'm placing the order now. You have to be quiet so I don't mess this up.
No talking or moving.
click
Done!
So I'll get to open everything at Aunt Wendy's house on Christmas?
Yep.
Oh no, I put the wrong shipping address in!
It won't let me change it. How does this always go wrong?

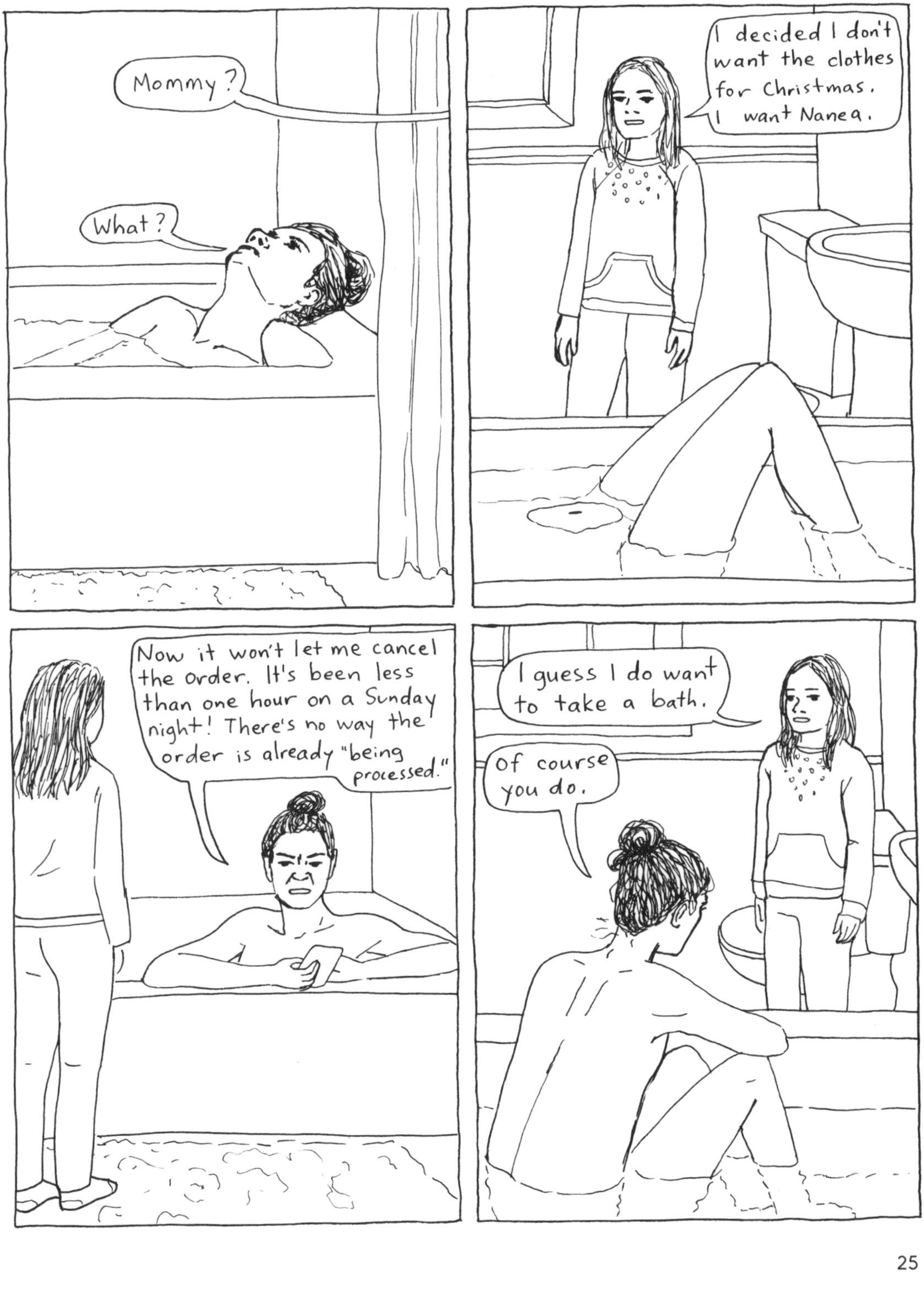
Mommy?
What?
I decided I don't want the clothes for Christmas. I want Nanea.
Now it won't let me cancel the order. It's been less than one hour on a Sunday night! There's no way the order is already "being processed."
I guess I do want to take a bath.
Of course you do.

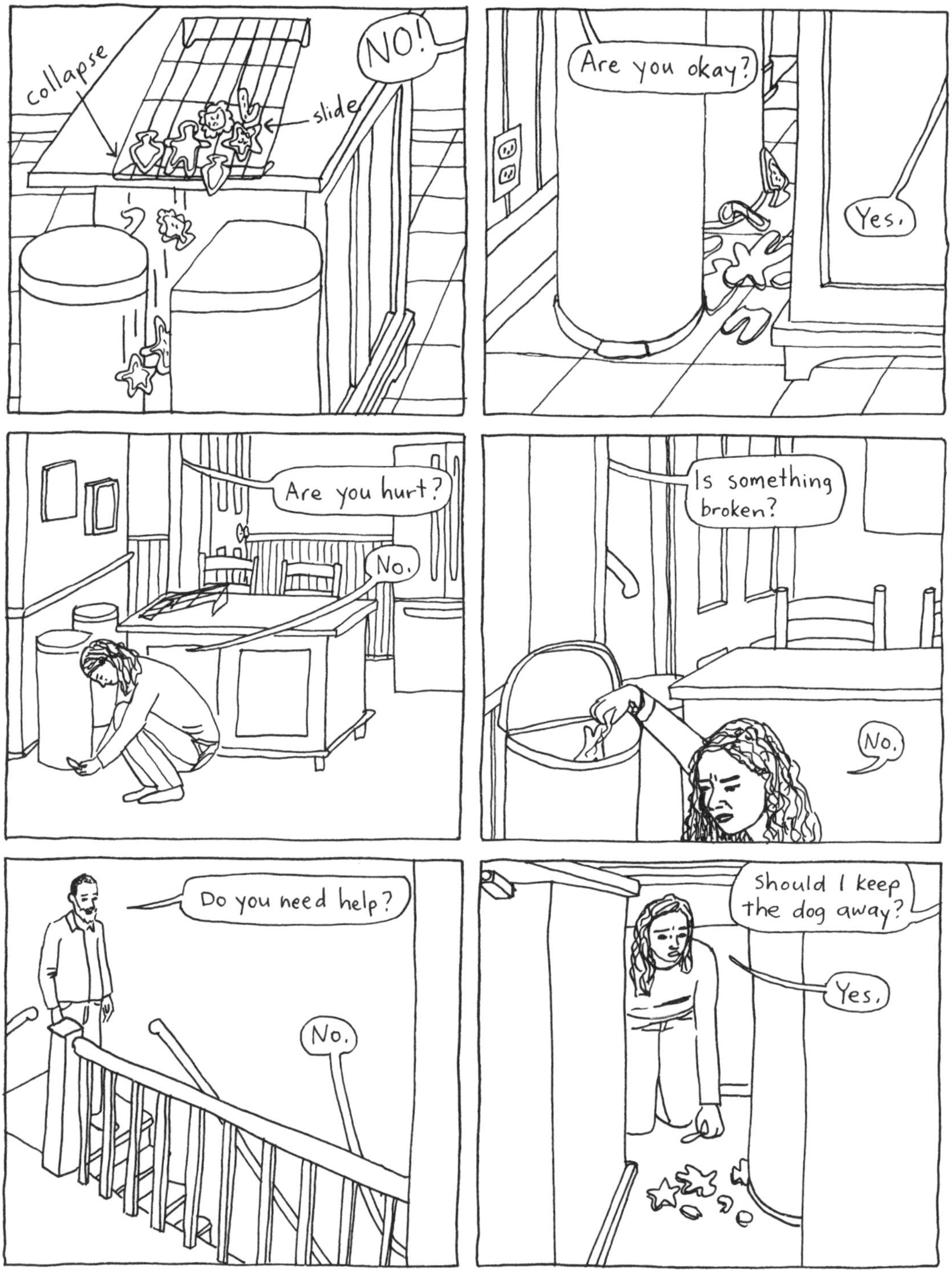
collapse
slide
NO!
Are you okay?
Yes.
Are you hurt?
No.
Is something broken?
No.
Do you need help?
No.
Should I keep the dog away?
Yes.

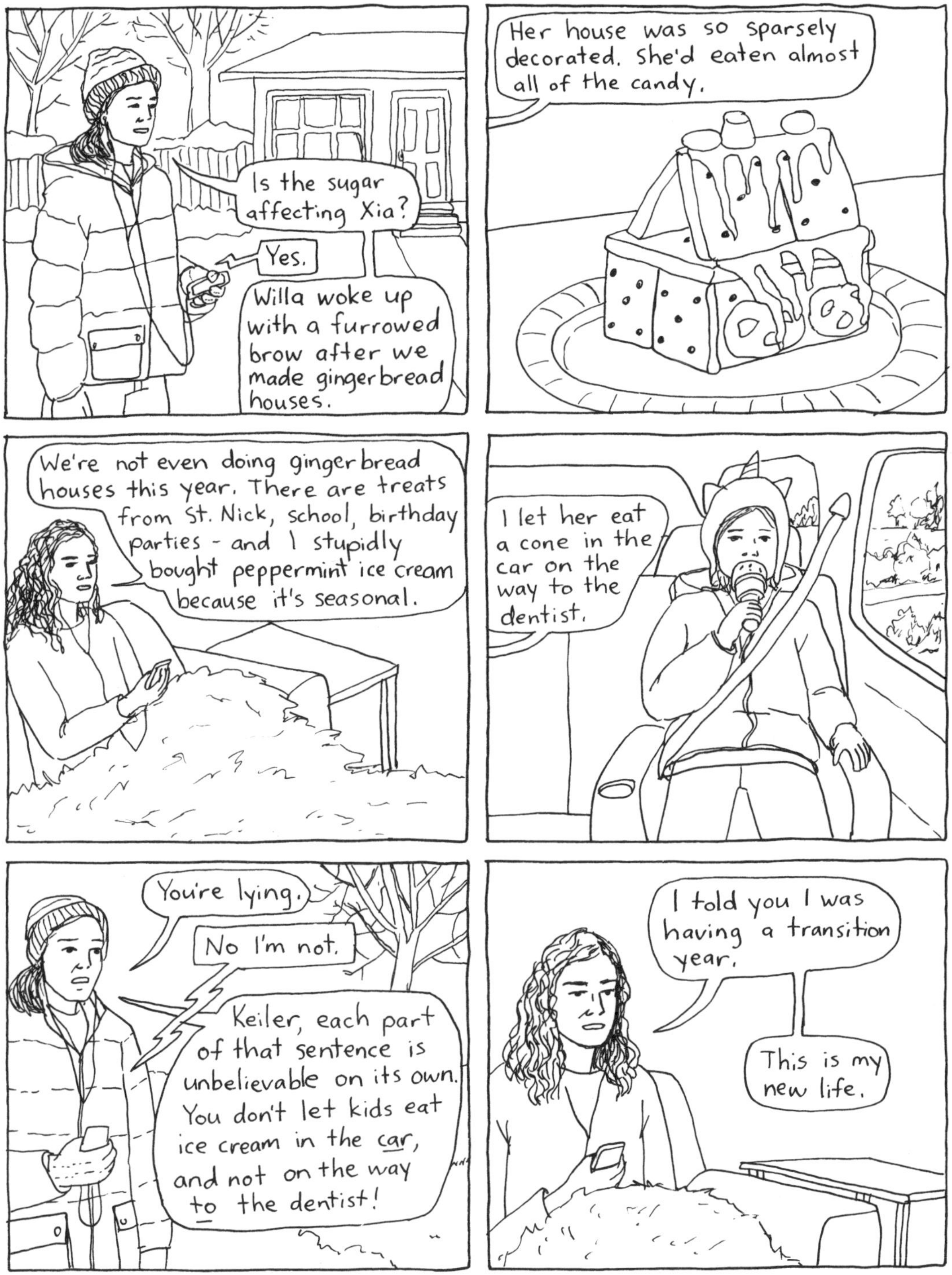

Is the sugar affecting Xia?
Yes.
Willa woke up with a furrowed brow after we made gingerbread houses.
Her house was so sparsely decorated. She'd eaten almost all of the candy.
We're not even doing gingerbread houses this year. There are treats from St. Nick, school, birthday parties - and I stupidly bought peppermint ice cream because it's seasonal.
I let her eat a cone in the car on the way to the dentist.
You're lying.
No I'm not.
Keiler, each part of that sentence is unbelievable on its own. You don't let kids eat ice cream in the car, and not on the way to the dentist!
I told you I was having a transition year.
This is my new life.

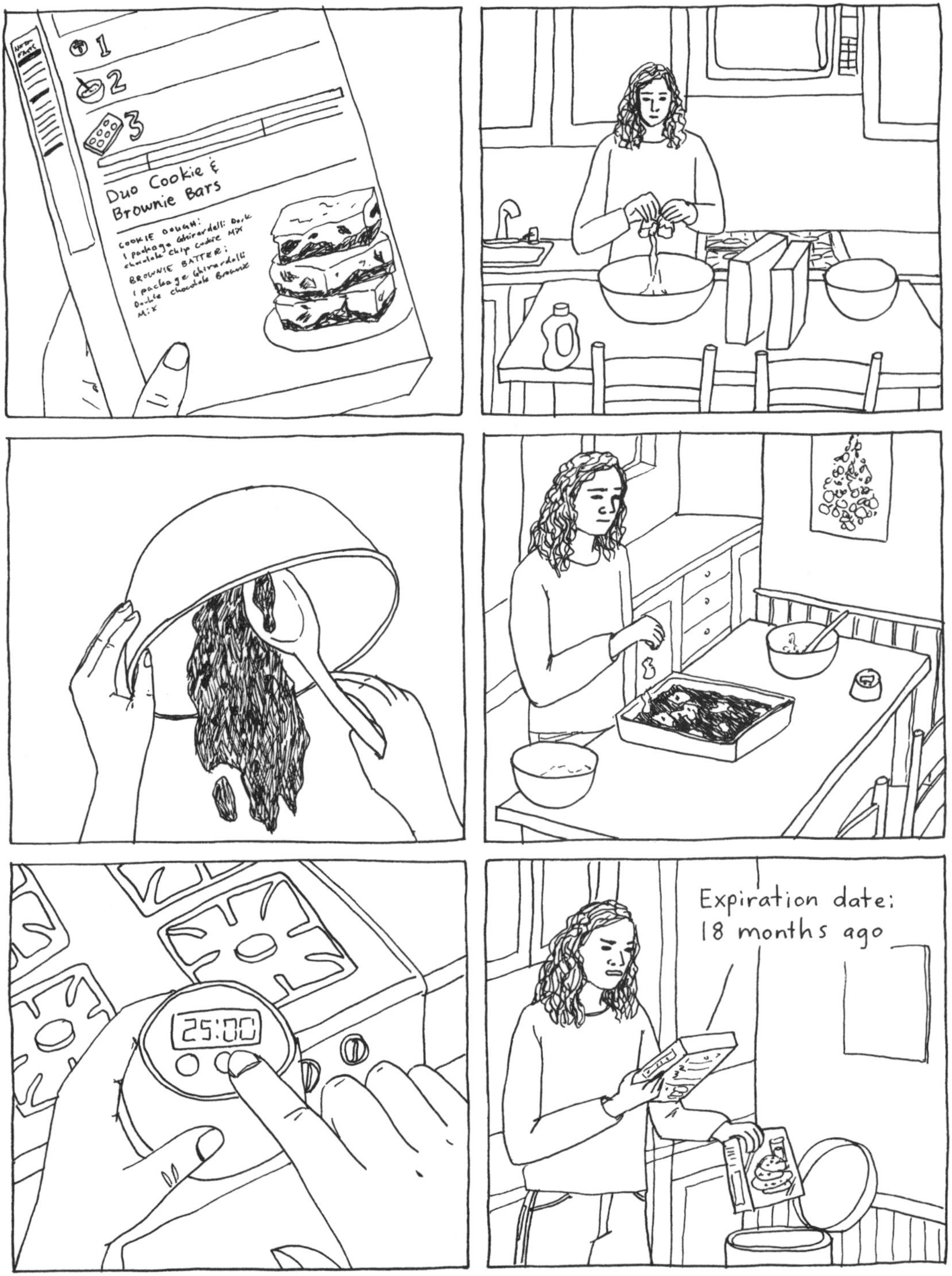
1
2
3
Duo Cookie & Brownie Bars
COOKIE DOUGH: 1 package Ghirardelli Dark chocolate chip cookie mix
BROWNIE BATTER: 1 package Ghirardelli Double chocolate Brownie Mix
25:00
Expiration date: 18 months ago

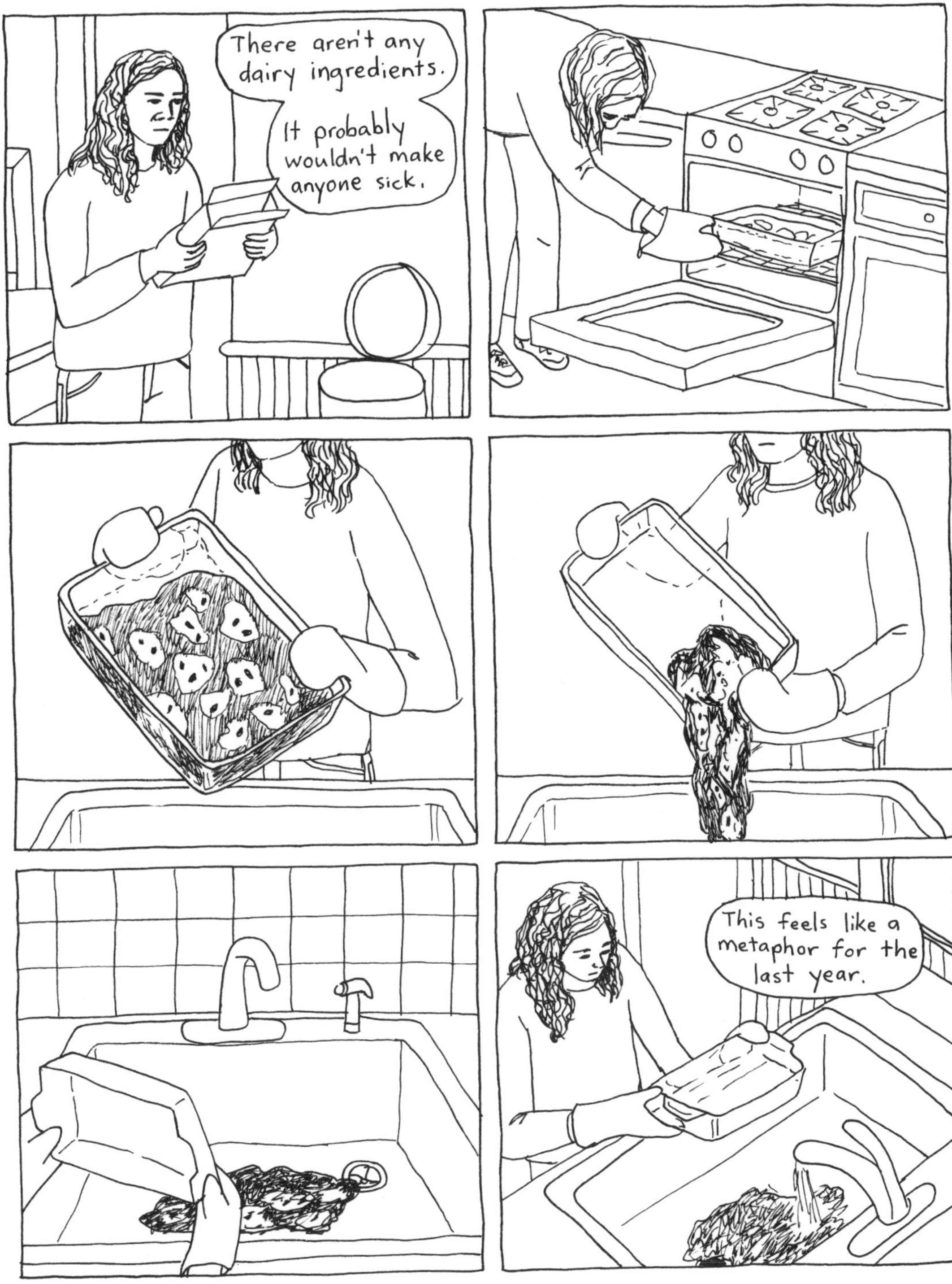
There aren't any dairy ingredients.
It probably wouldn't make anyone sick.
This feels like a metaphor for the last year.

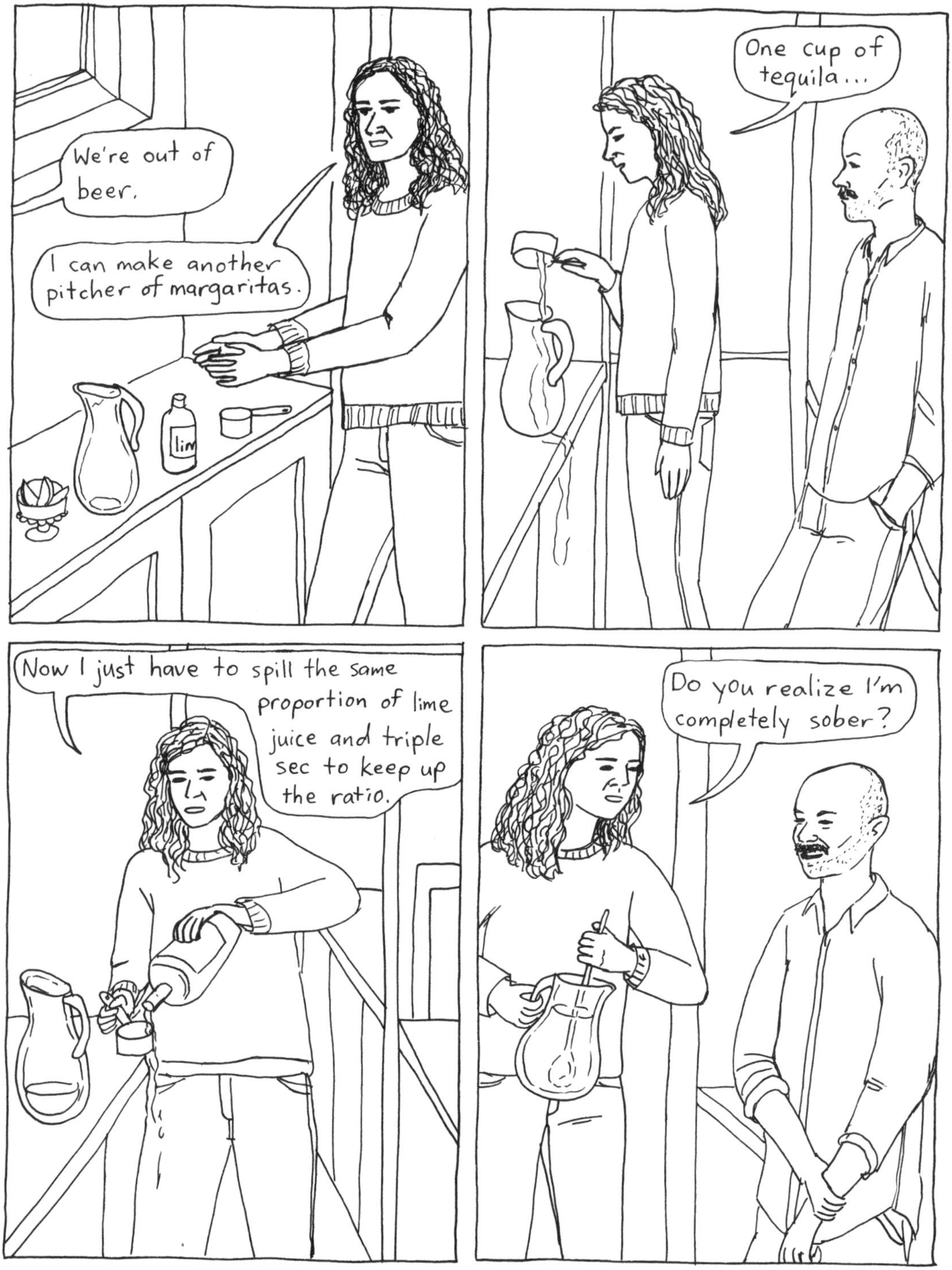
We're out of beer.
I can make another pitcher of margaritas.
lim
One cup of tequila...
Now I just have to spill the same proportion of lime juice and triple sec to keep up the ratio.
Do you realize I'm completely sober?

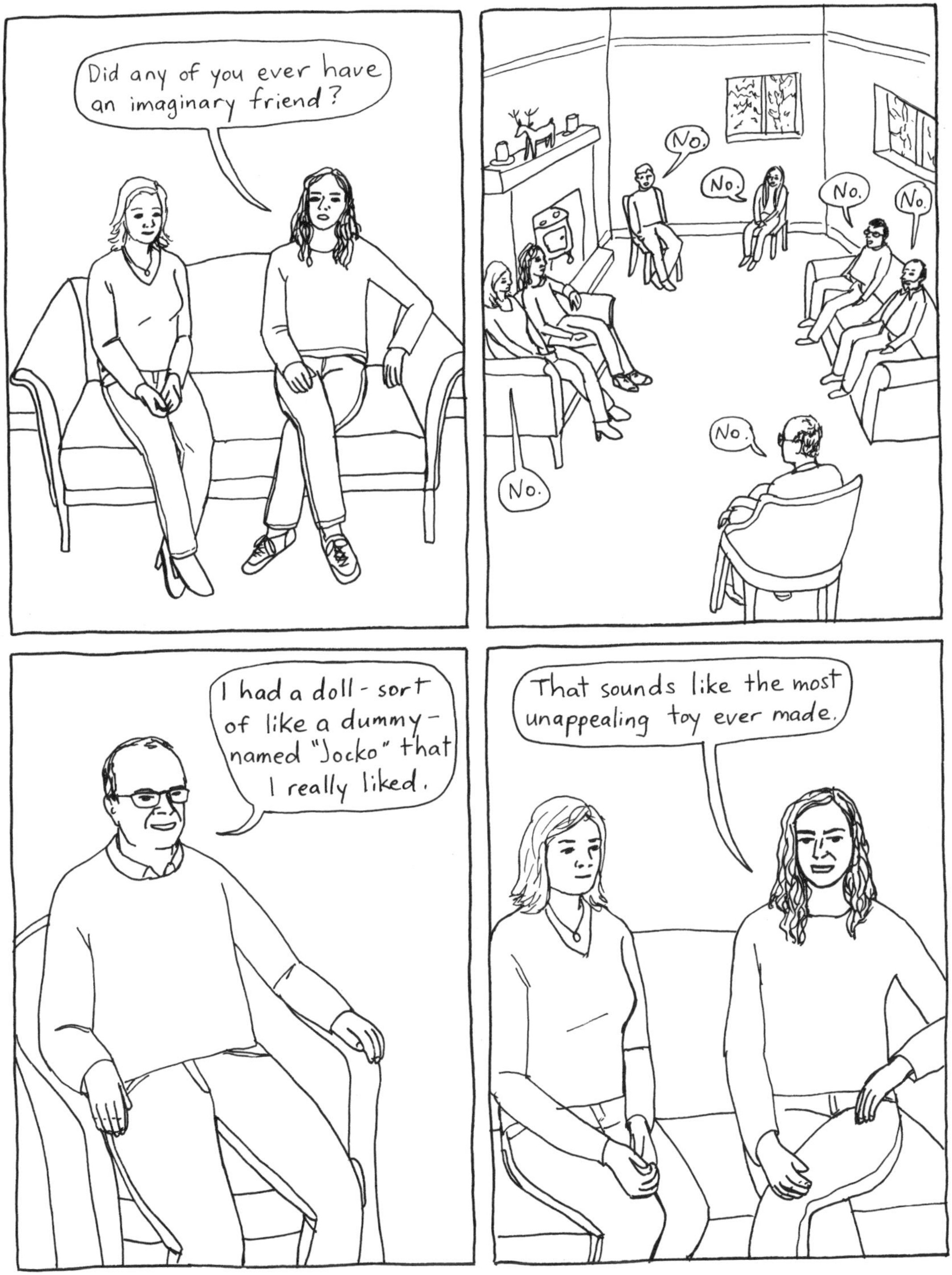
Did any of you ever have an imaginary friend?
No.
No.
No.
No.
No.
No.
I had a doll - sort of like a dummy - named "Jocko" that I really liked.
That sounds like the most unappealing toy ever made.

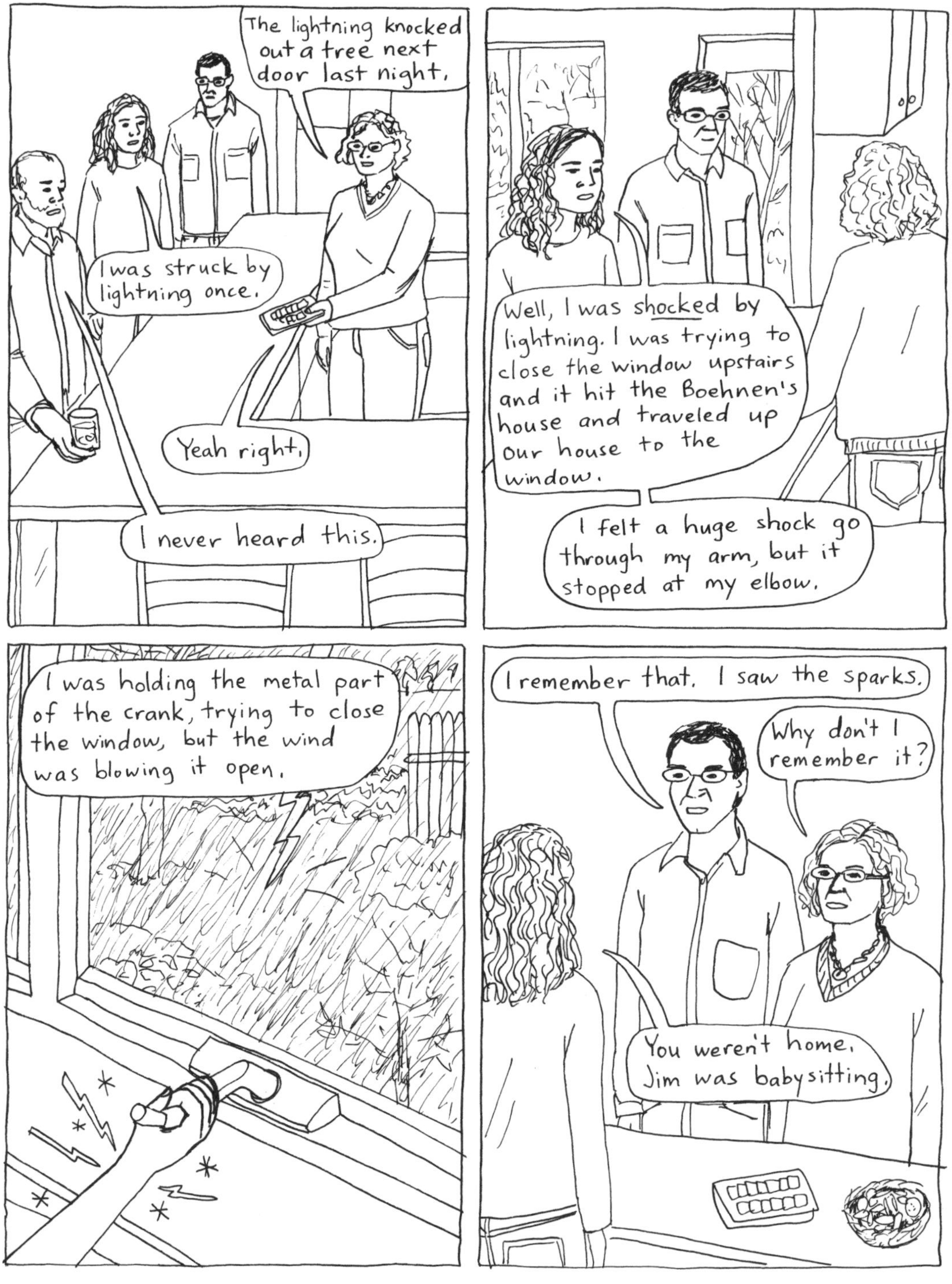
The lightning knocked out a tree next door last night.
I was struck by lightning once.
Yeah right.
I never heard this.
Well, I was shocked by lightning. I was trying to close the window upstairs and it hit the Boehnen's house and traveled up our house to the window.
I felt a huge shock go through my arm, but it stopped at my elbow.
I was holding the metal part of the crank, trying to close the window, but the wind was blowing it open.
I remember that. I saw the sparks.
Why don't I remember it?
You weren't home. Jim was babysitting.

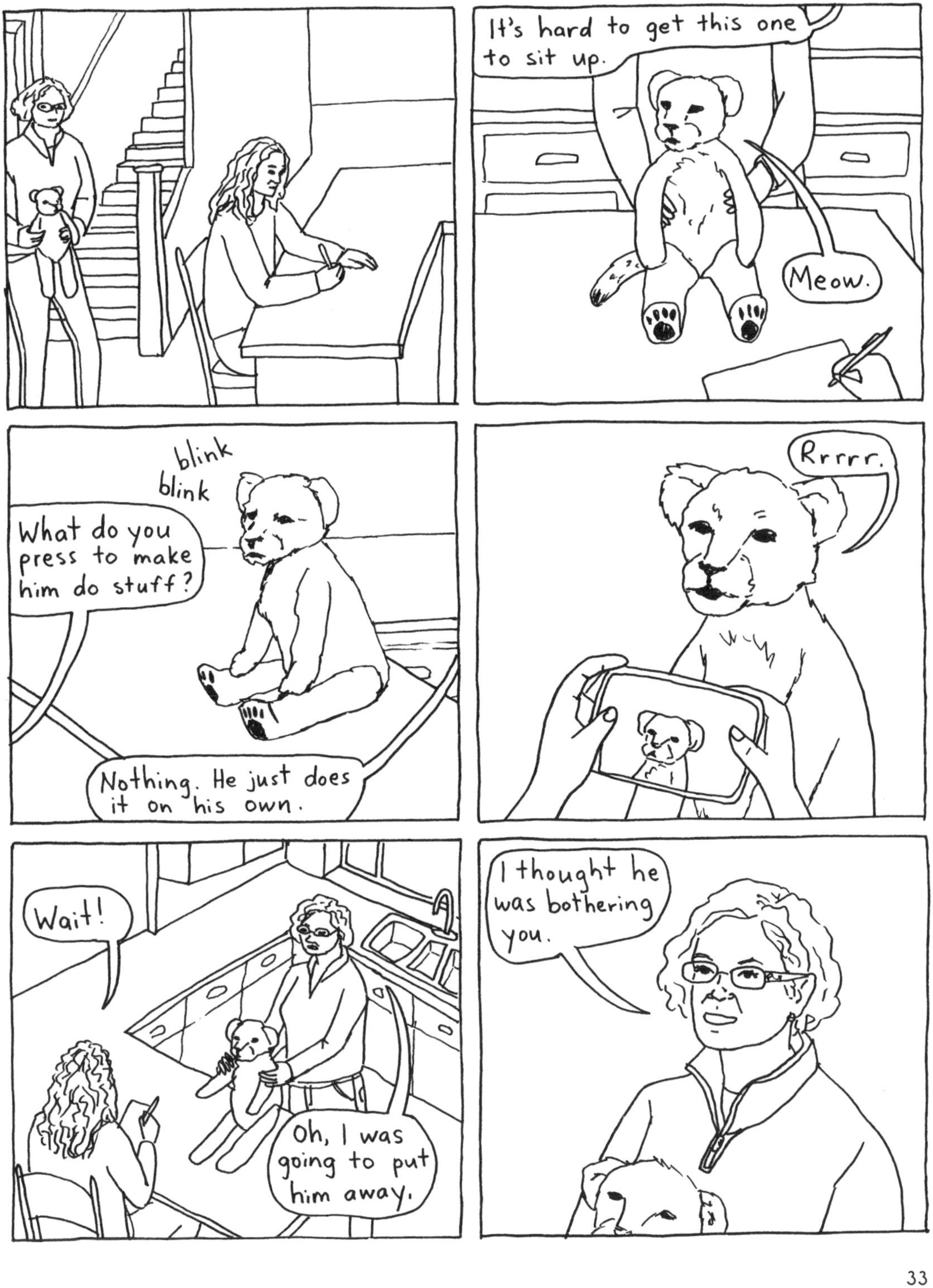
It's hard to get this one to sit up.
Meow.
blink blink
What do you press to make him do stuff?
Nothing. He just does it on his own.
Rrrrr.
Wait!
Oh, I was going to put him away.
I thought he was bothering you.

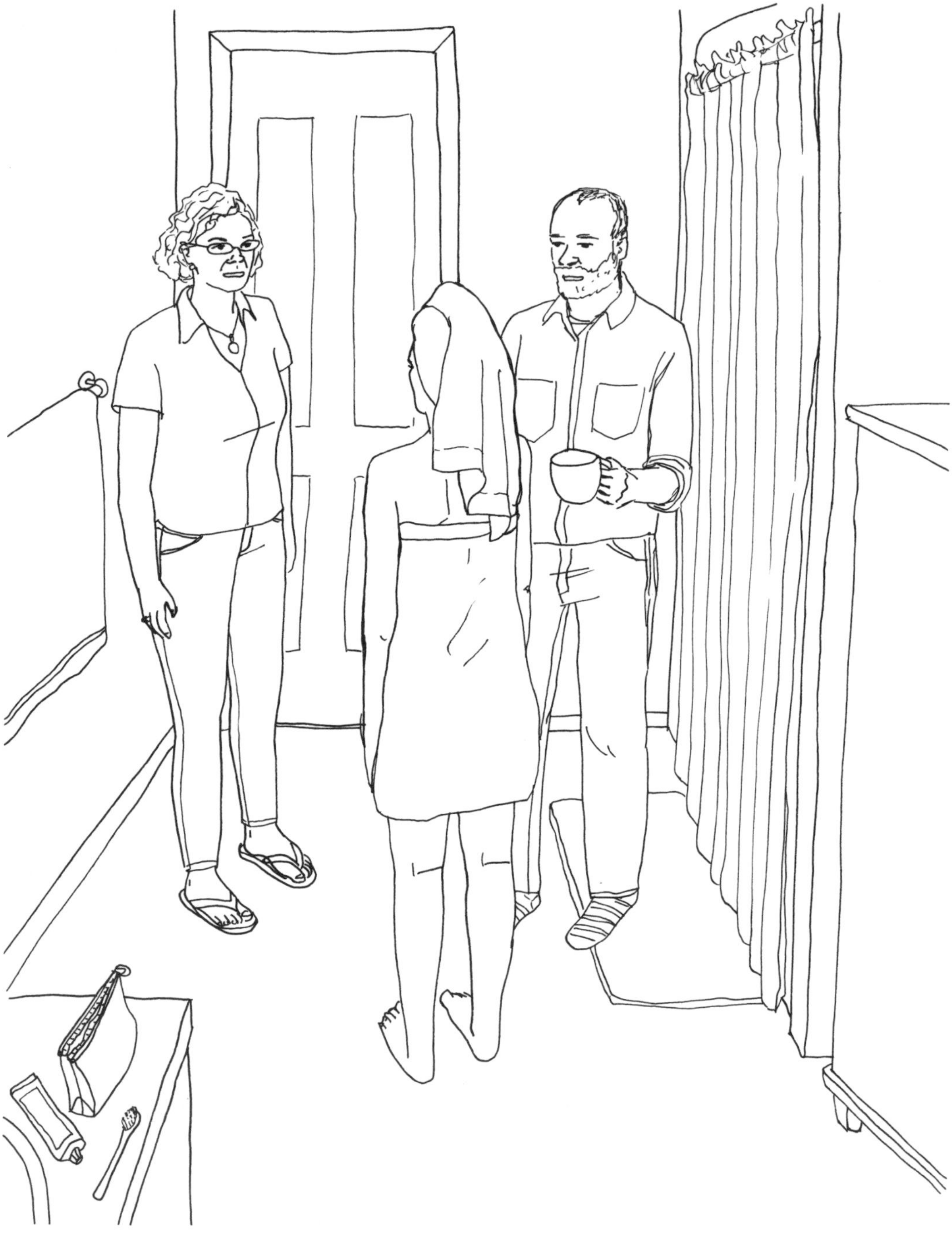

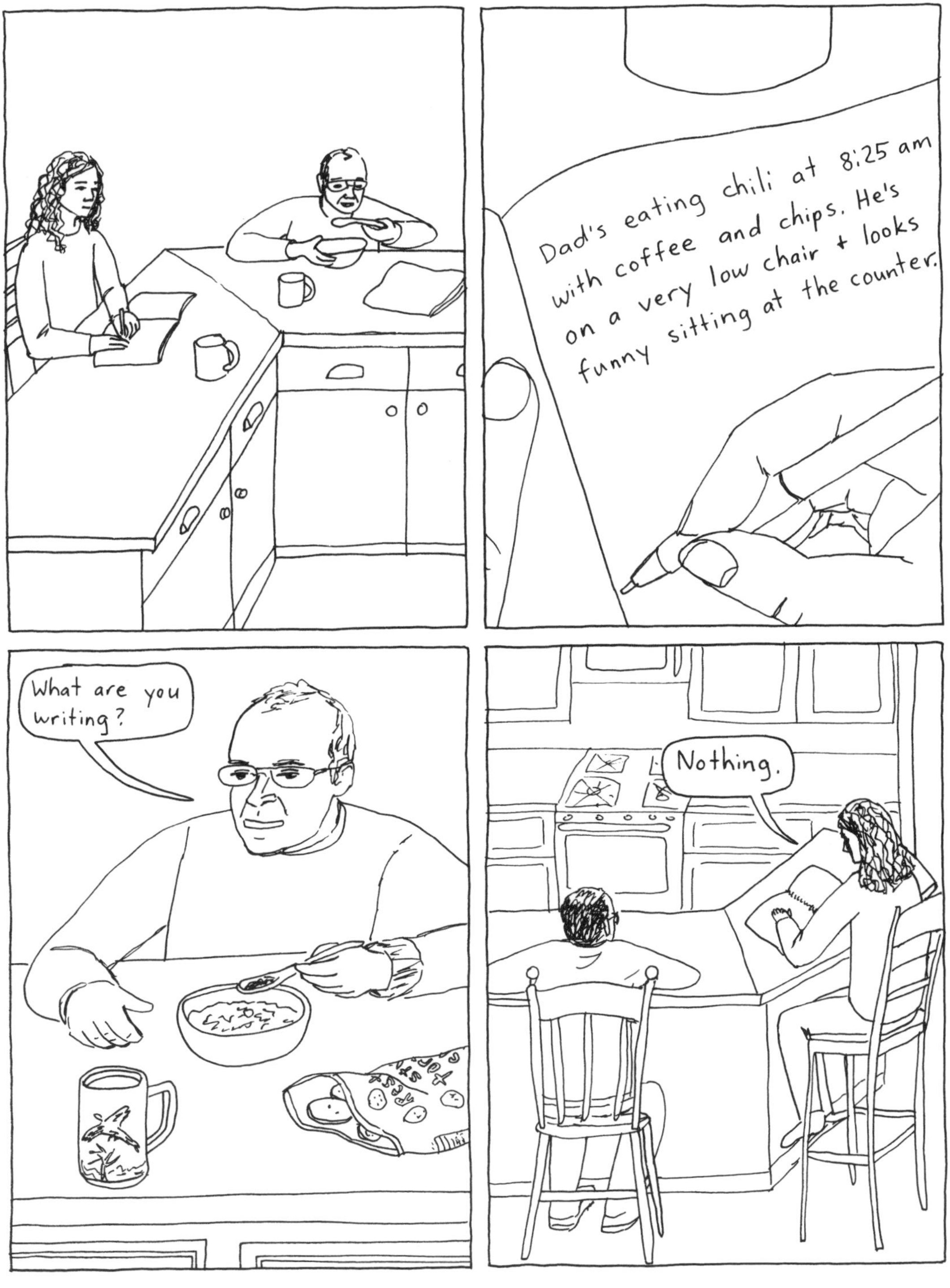
Dad's eating chili at 8:25 am with coffee and chips. He's on a very low chair + looks funny sitting at the counter.
What are you writing?
Nothing.

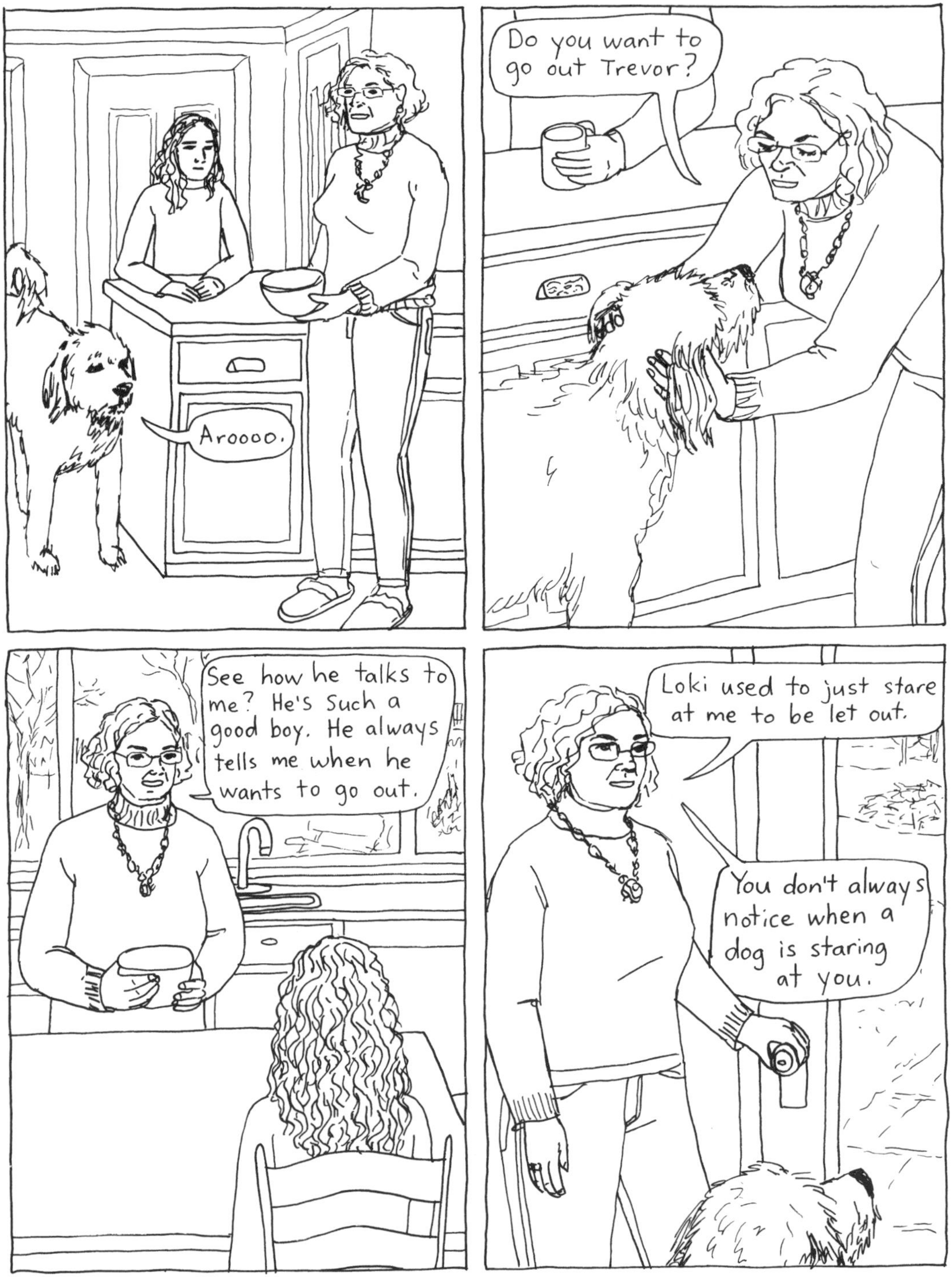
Aroooo.
Do you want to go out Trevor?
See how he talks to me? He's Such a good boy. He always tells me when he wants to go out.
Loki used to just stare at me to be let out.
You don't always notice when a dog is staring at you.

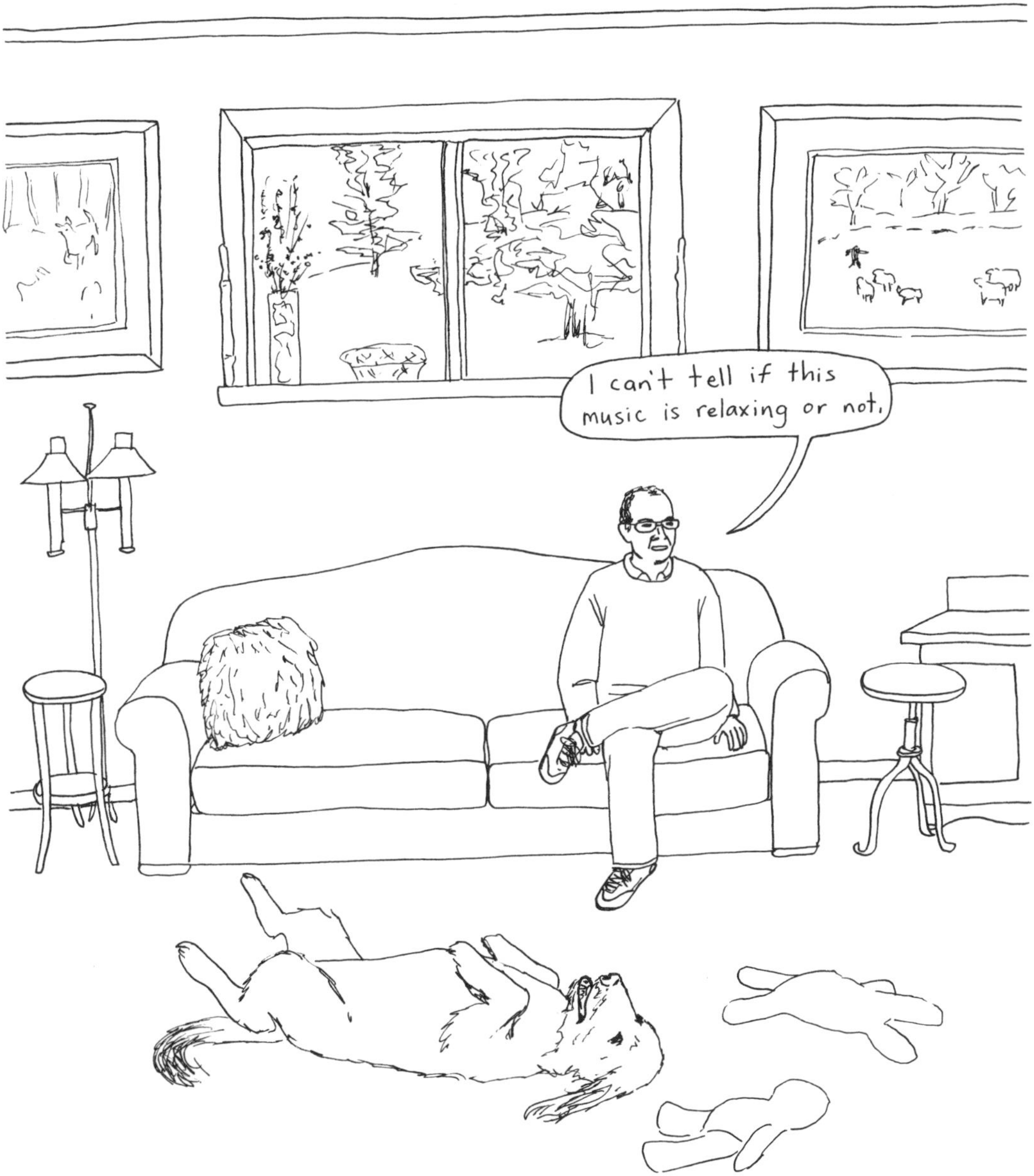
I can't tell if this music is relaxing or not.

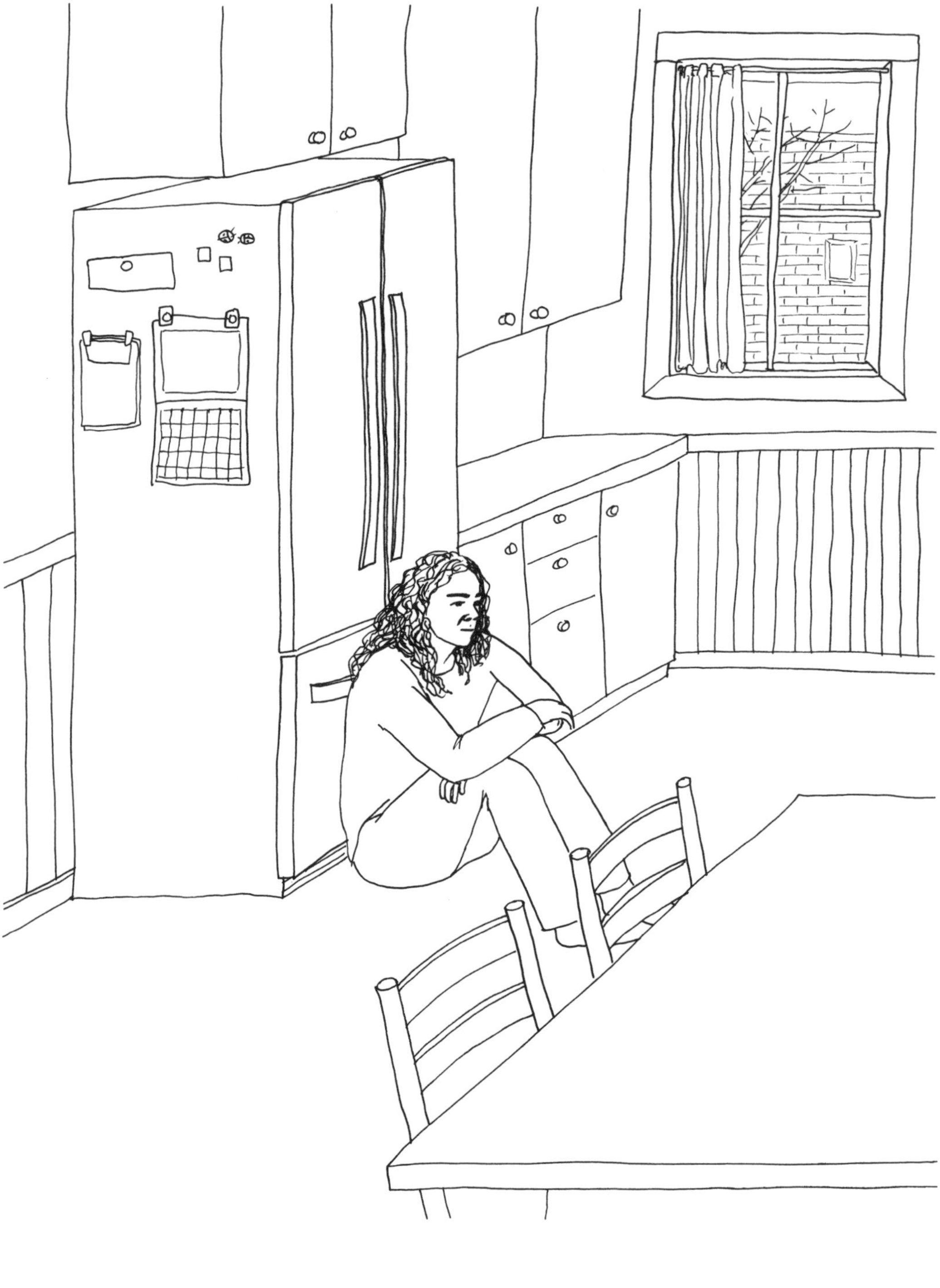

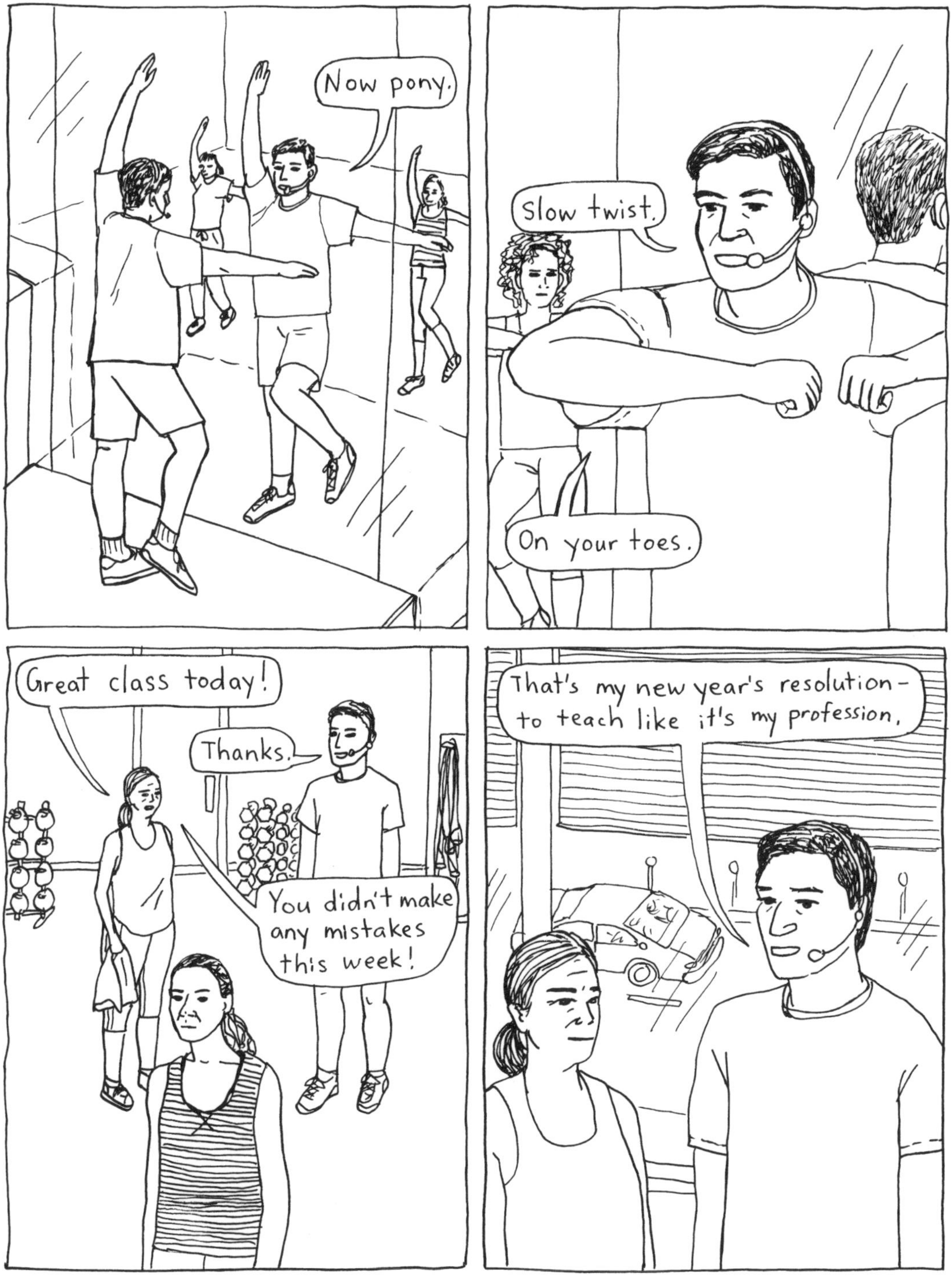
Now pony.
Slow twist.
On your toes.
Great class today!
Thanks.
You didn't make any mistakes this week!
That's my new year's resolution- to teach like it's my profession.

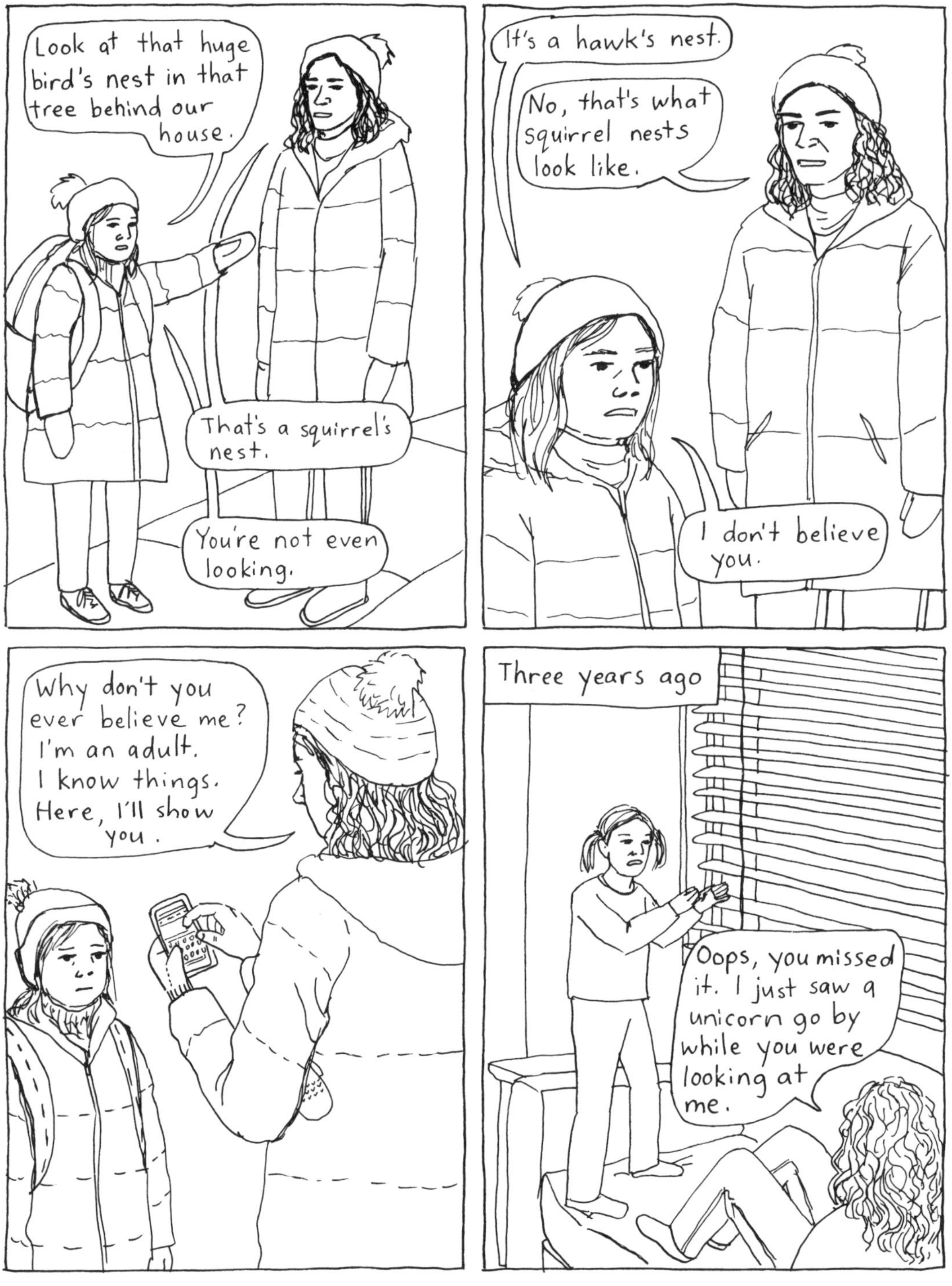
Look at that huge bird's nest in that tree behind our house.
That's a squirrel's nest.
You're not even looking.
It's a hawk's nest.
No, that's what squirrel nests look like.
I don't believe you.
Why don't you ever believe me? I'm an adult. I know things. Here, I'll show you.
Three years ago
Oops, you missed it. I just saw a unicorn go by while you were looking at me.

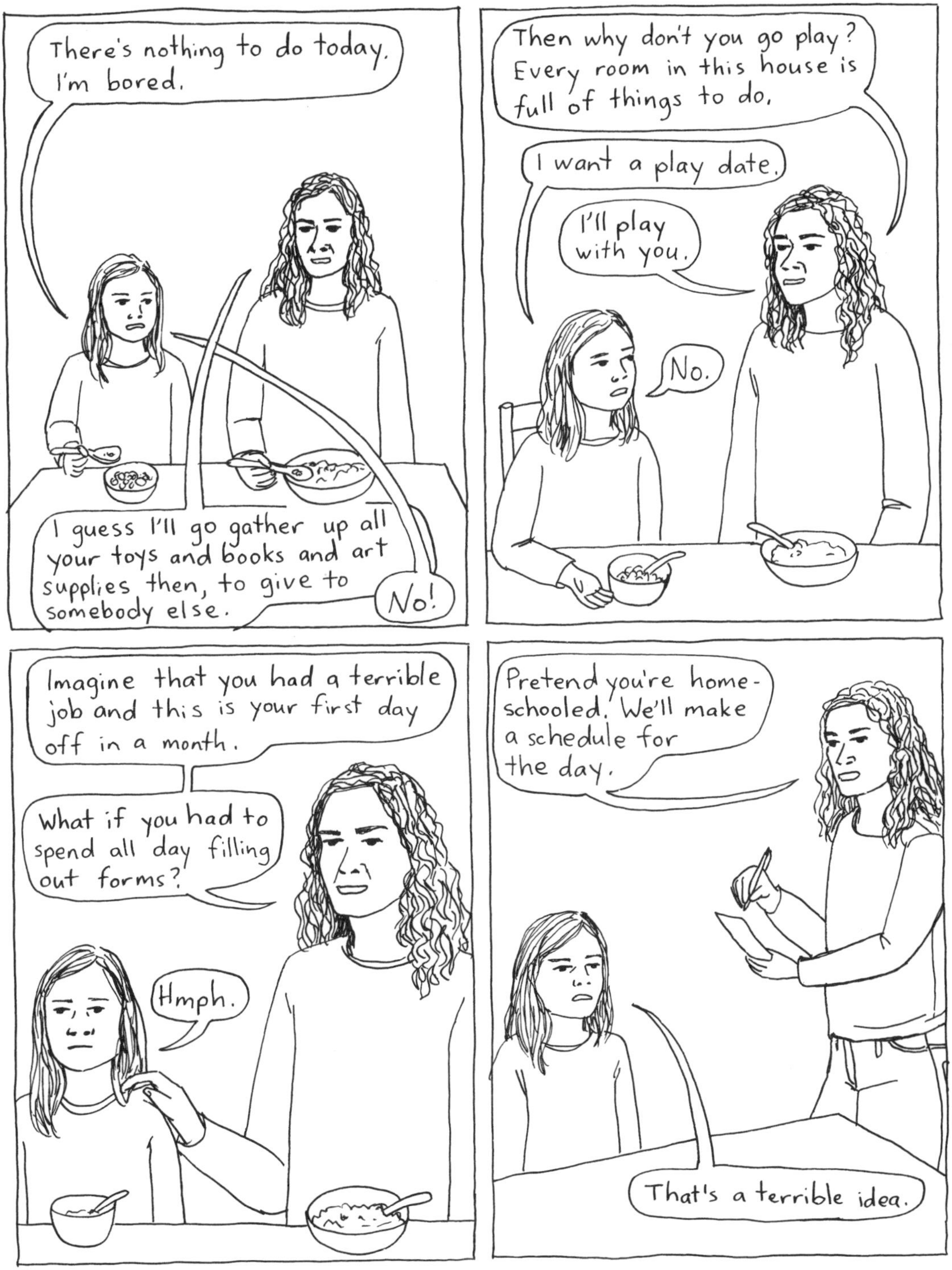
There's nothing to do today. I'm bored.
Then why don't you go play? Every room in this house is full of things to do.
I want a play date.
I'll play with you.
No.
I guess I'll go gather up all your toys and books and art supplies then, to give to somebody else.
No!
Imagine that you had a terrible job and this is your first day off in a month.
What if you had to spend all day filling out forms?
Hmph.
Pretend you're home-schooled. We'll make a schedule for the day.
That's a terrible idea.

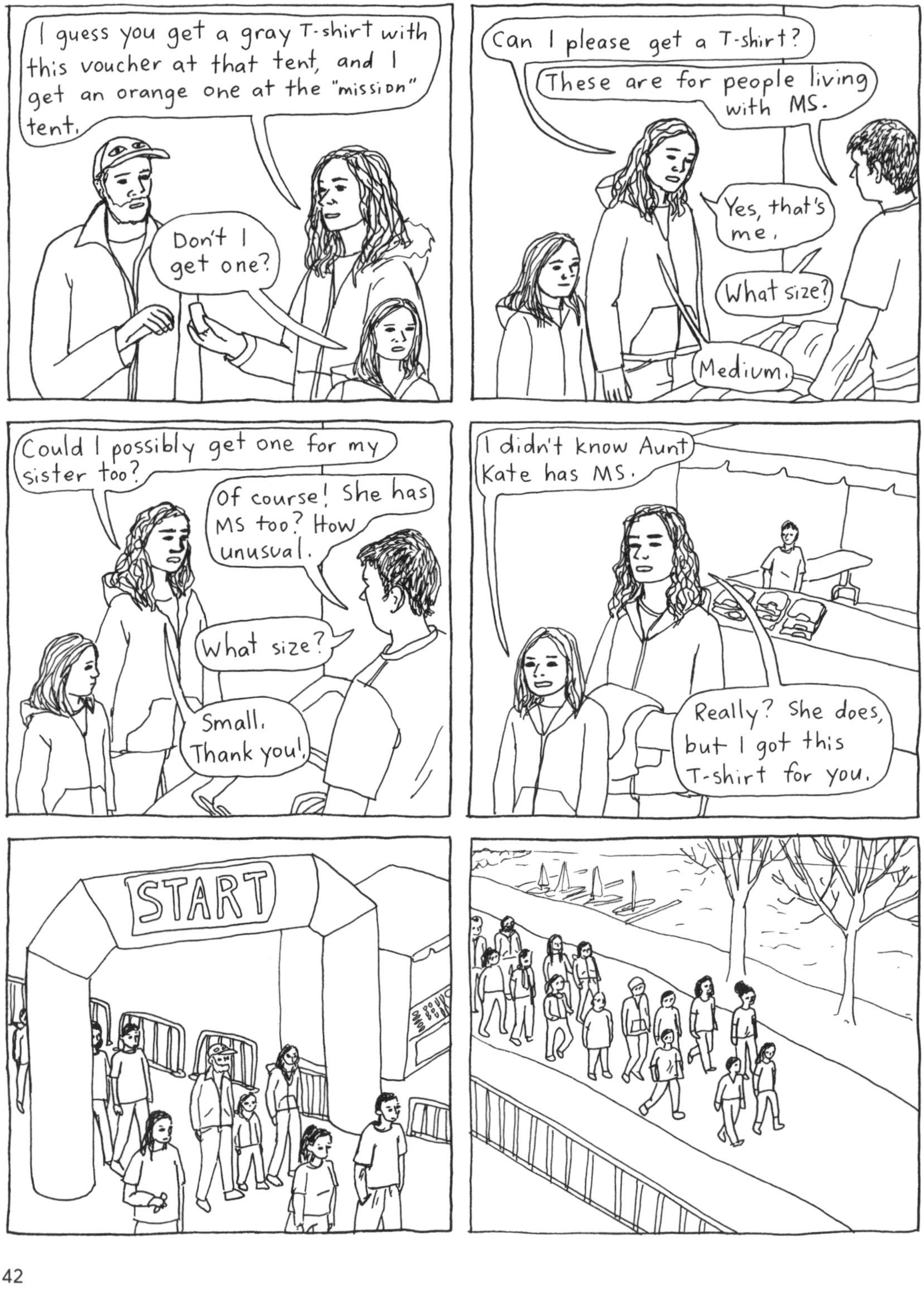
I guess you get a gray T-shirt with this voucher at that tent, and I get an orange one at the "mission" tent.
Don't I get one?
Can I please get a T-shirt?
These are for people living with MS.
Yes, that's me.
What size?
Medium.
Could I possibly get one for my sister too?
Of course! She has MS too? How unusual.
What size?
Small. Thank you!
I didn't know Aunt Kate has MS.
Really? She does, but I got this T-shirt for you.
START

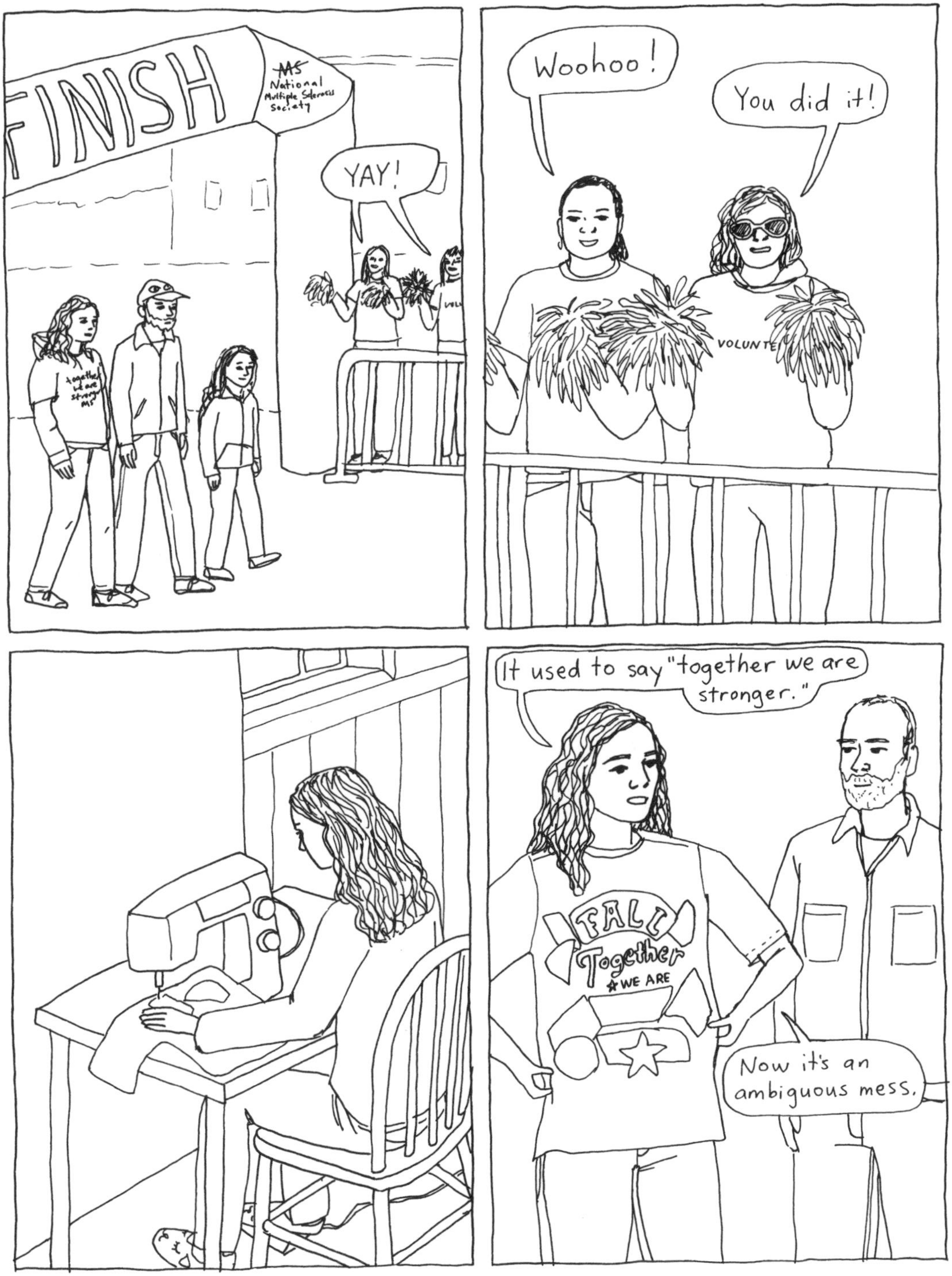
FINISH
MS
National
Multiple Sclerosis
Society
YAY!
together
we are
stronger
MS
VOLU
Woohoo!
You did it!
VOLUNTE
It used to say "together we are stronger."
FALL
Together
WE ARE
Now it's an ambiguous mess.

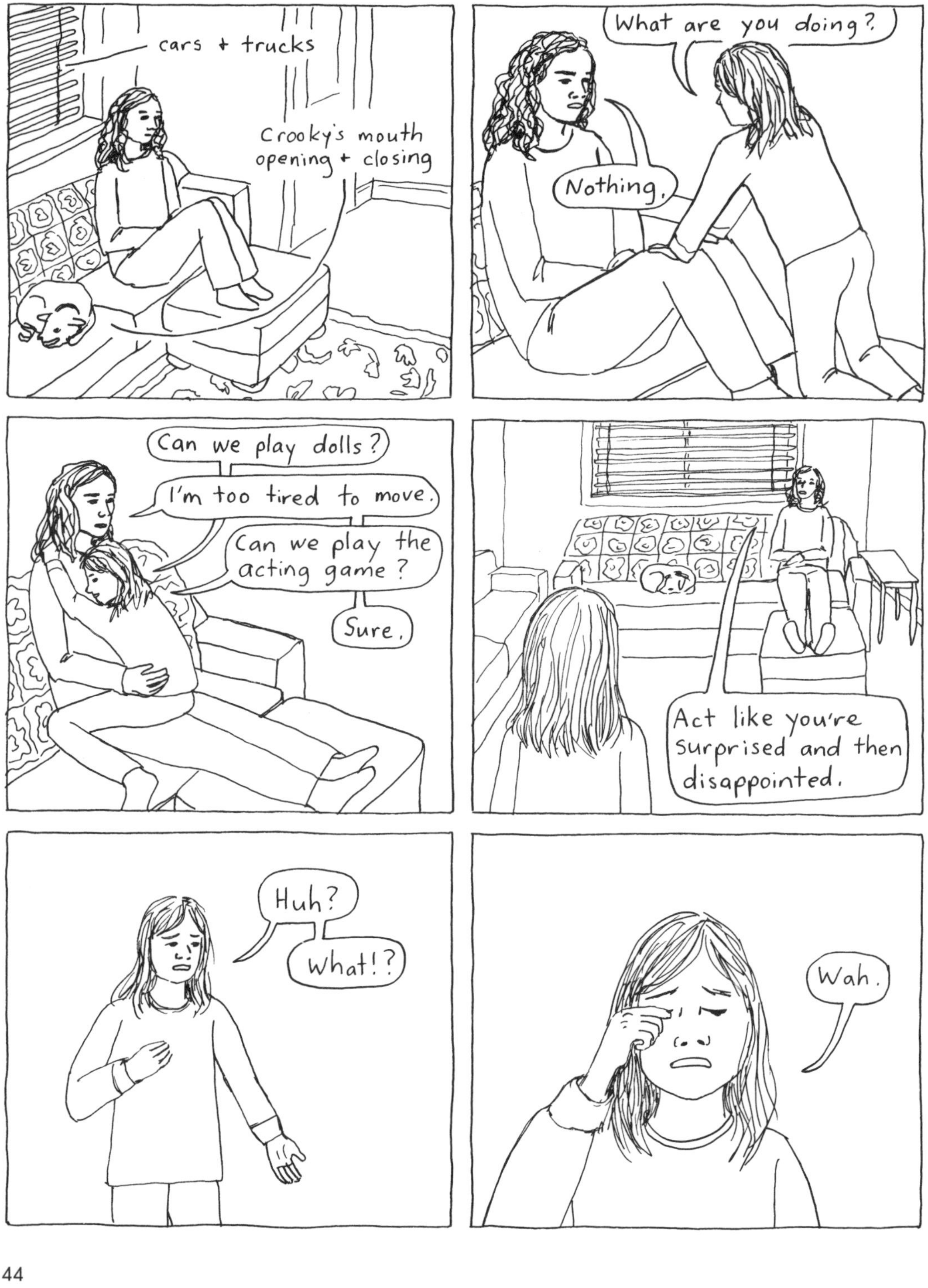
cars + trucks
Crooky's mouth opening + closing
What are you doing?
Nothing.
Can we play dolls?
I'm too tired to move.
Can we play the acting game?
Sure.
Act like you're surprised and then disappointed.
Huh?
What!?
Wah.

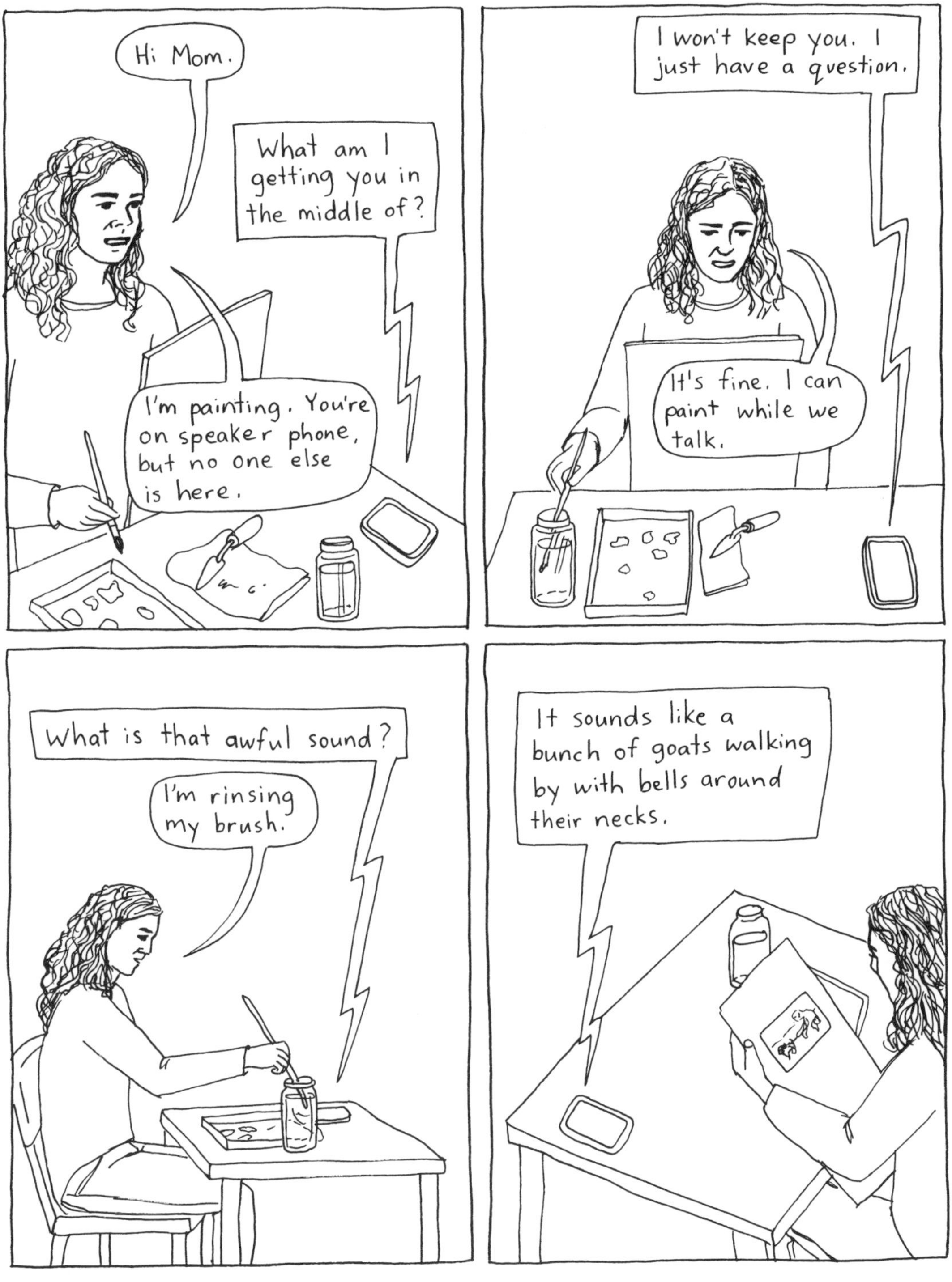

Hi Mom.
What am I getting you in the middle of?
I'm painting. You're on speaker phone, but no one else is here.
I won't keep you. I just have a question.
It's fine. I can paint while we talk.
What is that awful sound?
I'm rinsing my brush.
It sounds like a bunch of goats walking by with bells around their necks.

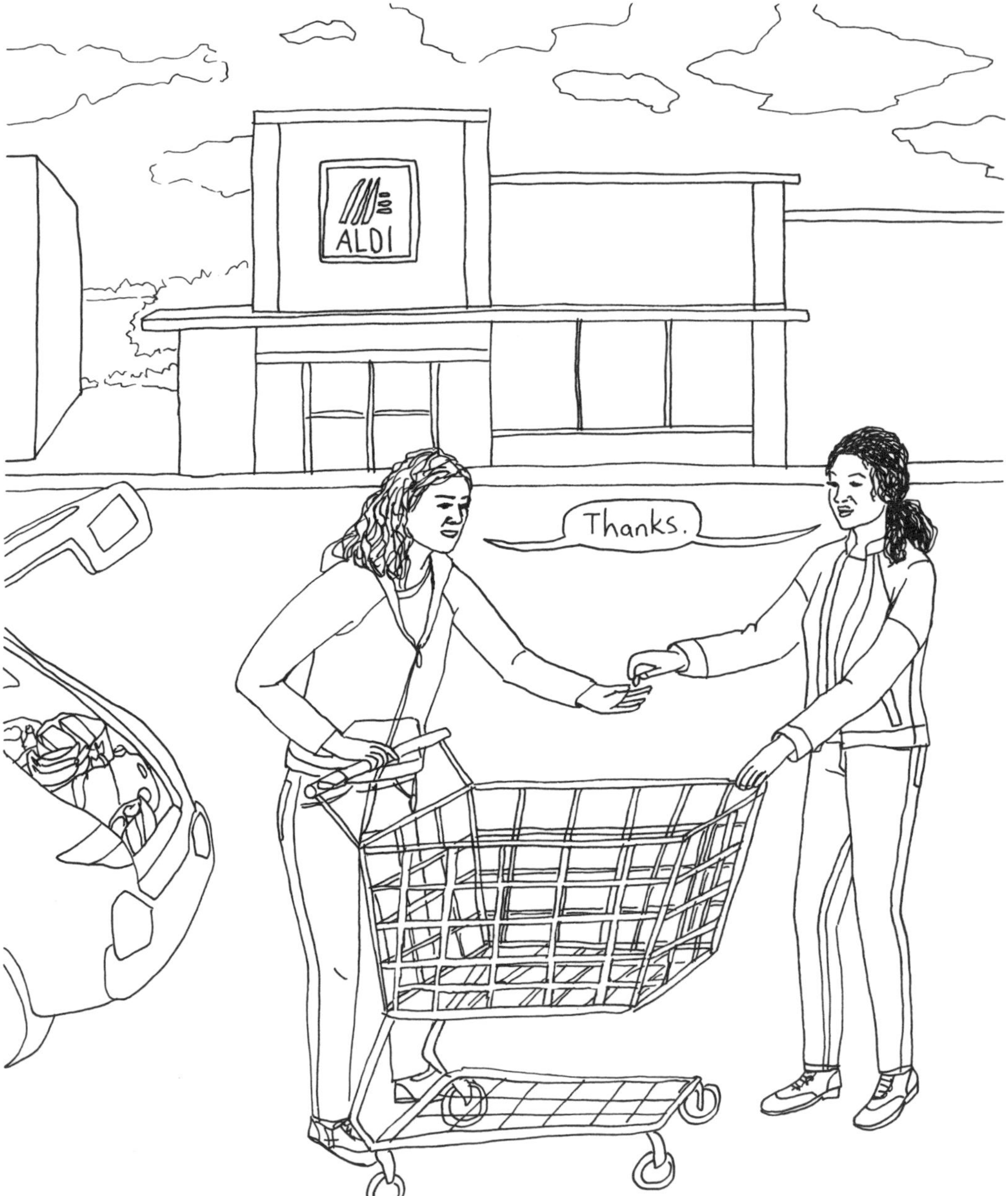
ALDI
Thanks.

A visualization can help you let go of your thoughts. You might see them as clouds passing by. Watch the thought without being consumed by it.

I like to picture my thoughts as cicadas that are clinging to me.

I gently unhook their little claws and let them go.

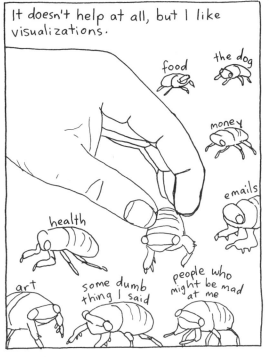

It doesn't help at all, but I like visualizations.

food

the dog

money

emails

health

art

some dumb thing I said

people who might be mad at me

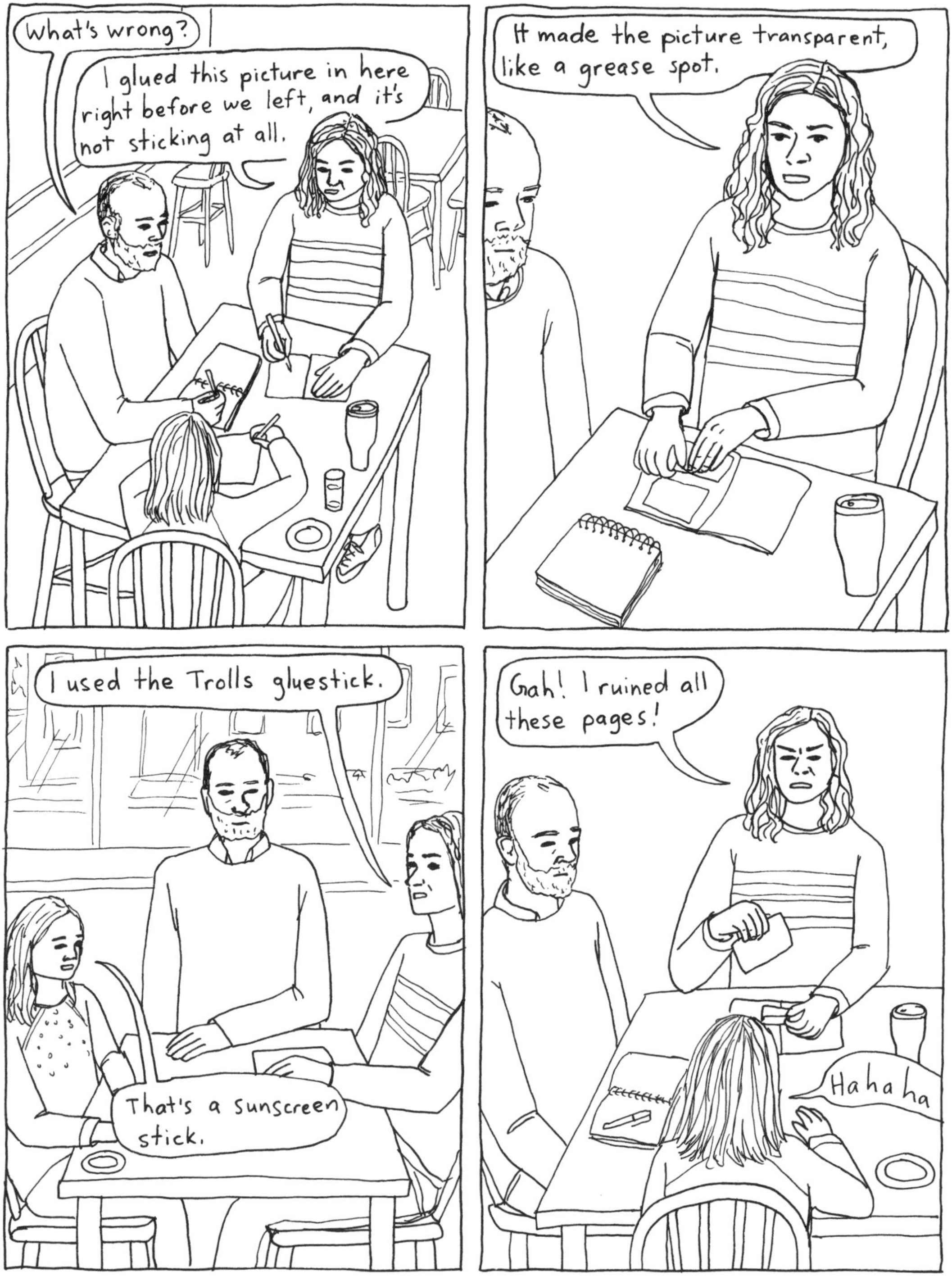
What's wrong?
I glued this picture in here right before we left, and it's not sticking at all.
It made the picture transparent, like a grease spot.
I used the Trolls gluestick.
That's a sunscreen stick.
Gah! I ruined all these pages!
Hahaha

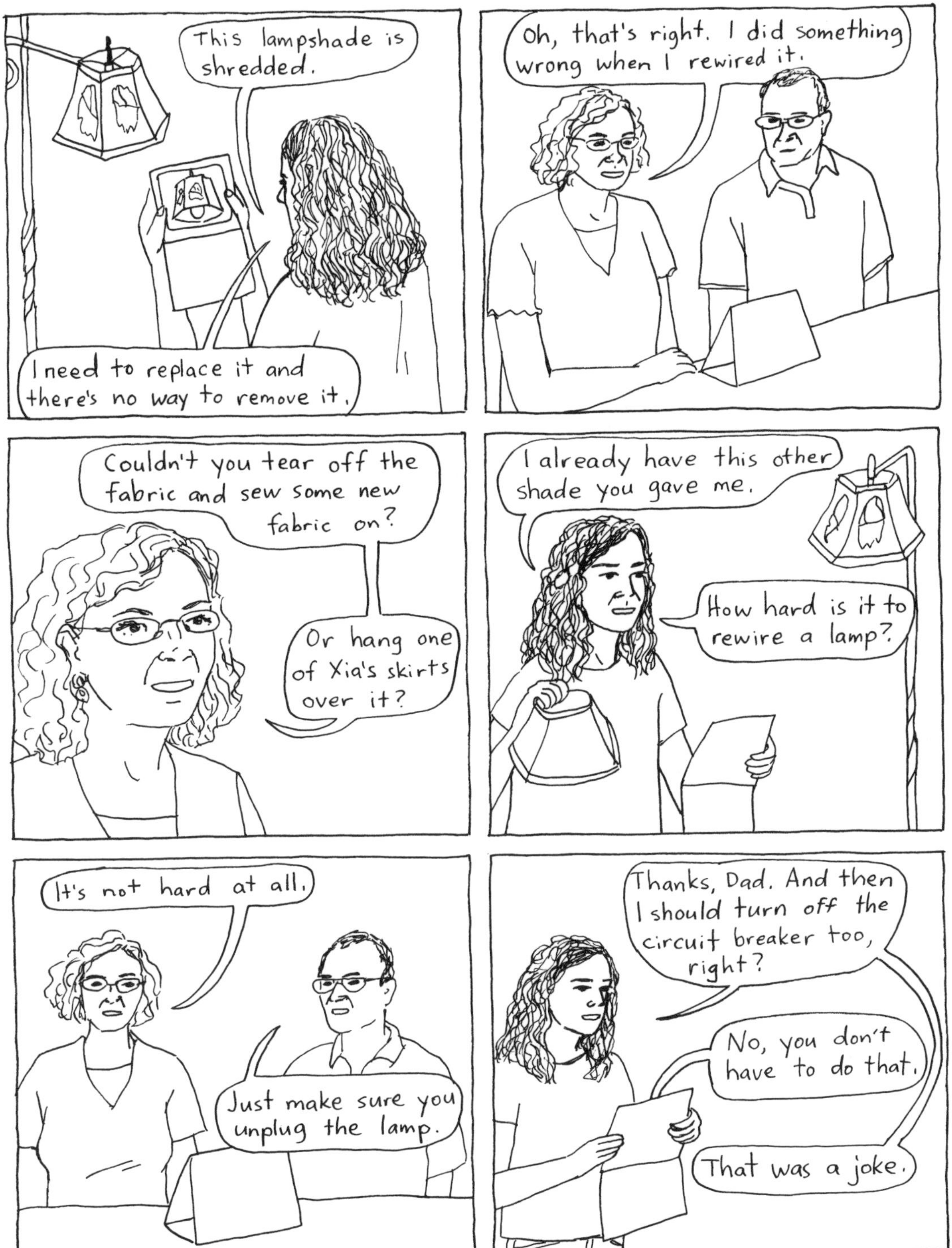
This lampshade is shredded.
I need to replace it and there's no way to remove it.
Oh, that's right. I did something wrong when I rewired it.
Couldn't you tear off the fabric and sew some new fabric on?
Or hang one of Xia's skirts over it?
I already have this other shade you gave me.
How hard is it to rewire a lamp?
It's not hard at all.
Just make sure you unplug the lamp.
Thanks, Dad. And then I should turn off the circuit breaker too, right?
No, you don't have to do that.
That was a joke.

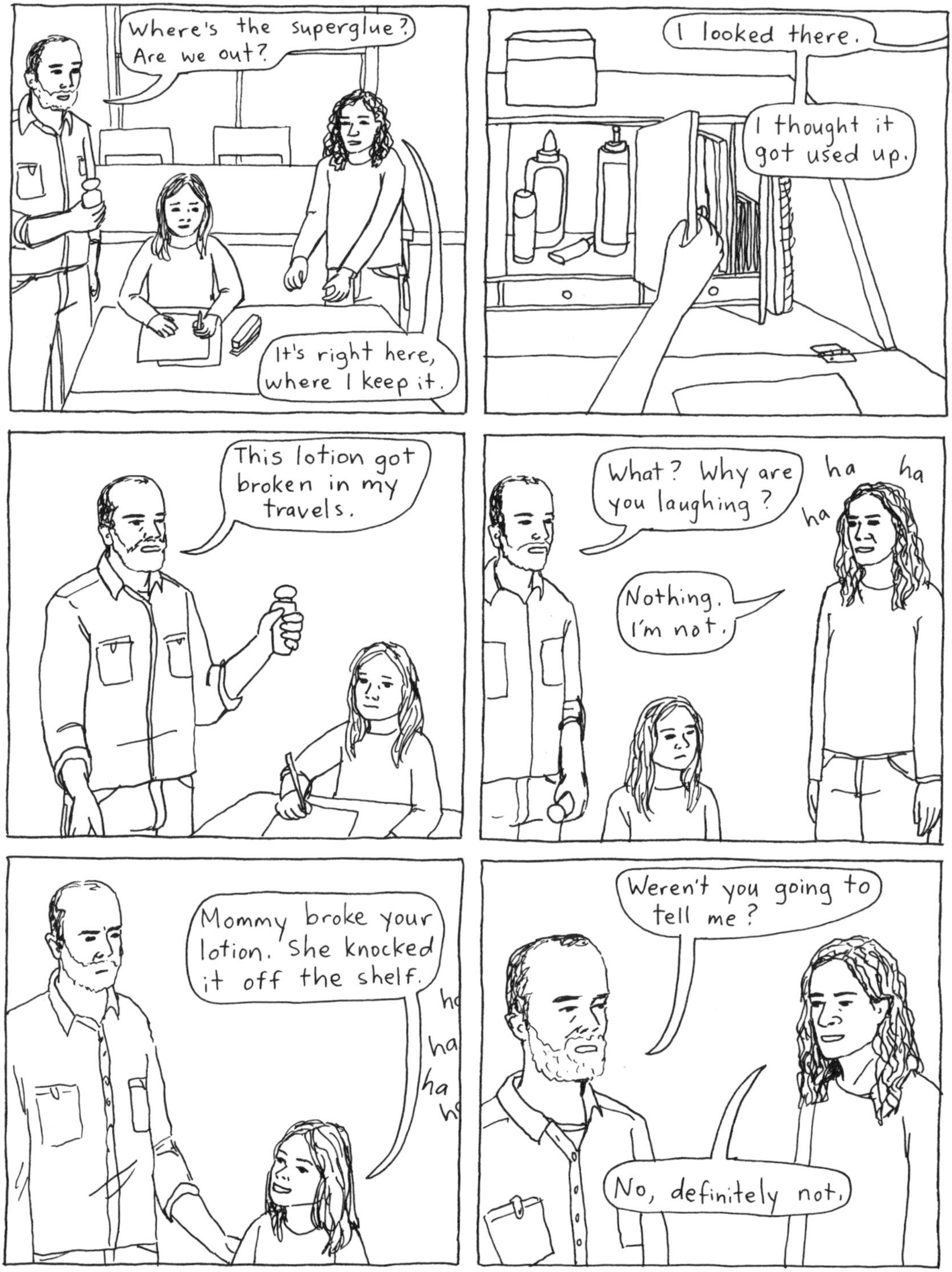
Where's the superglue? Are we out?
It's right here, where I keep it.
I looked there.
I thought it got used up.
This lotion got broken in my travels.
What? Why are you laughing?
ha ha
ha
Nothing. I'm not.
Mommy broke your lotion. She knocked it off the shelf.
ha
ha
Weren't you going to tell me?
No, definitely not.

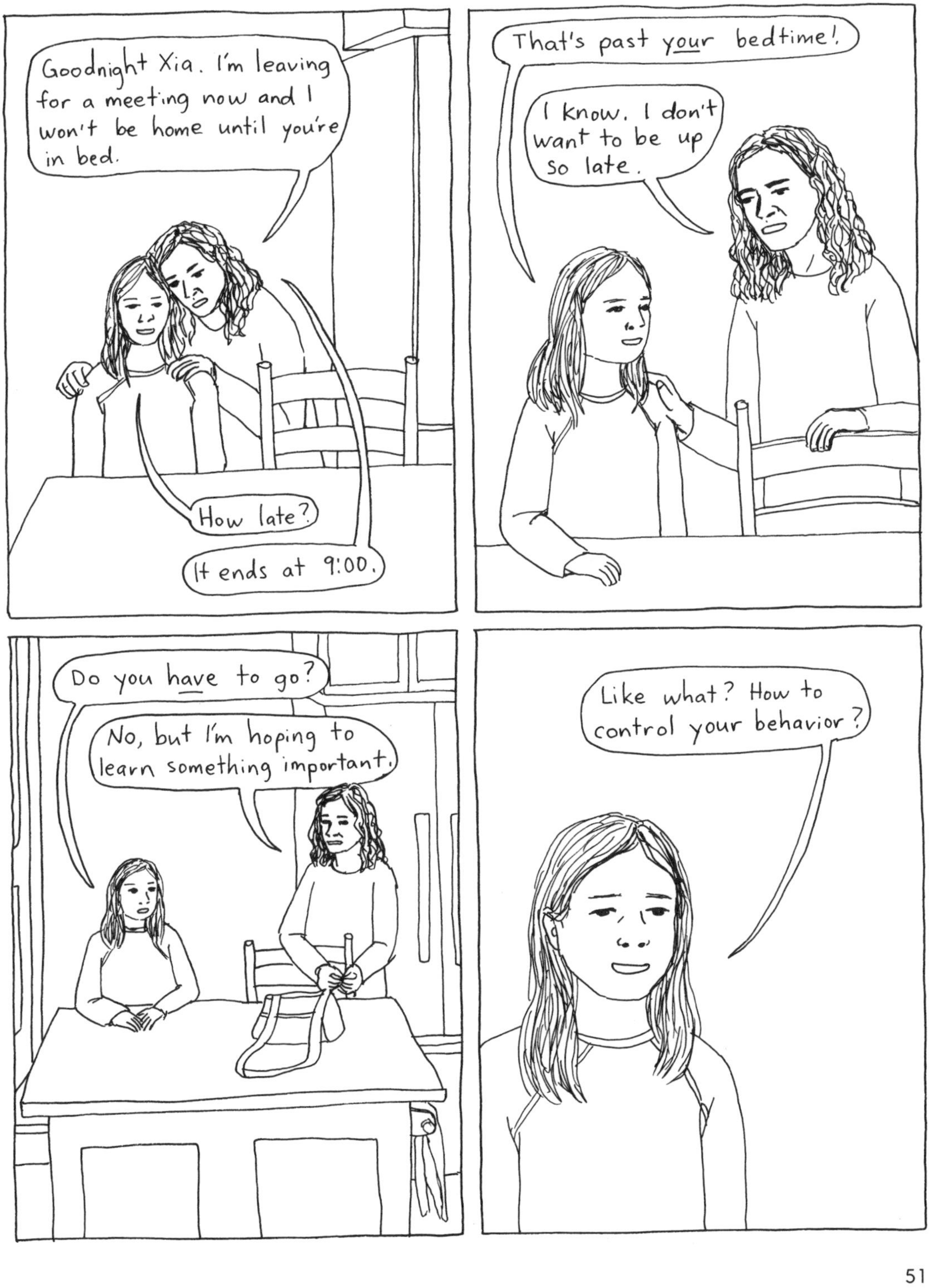
Goodnight Xia. I'm leaving for a meeting now and I won't be home until you're in bed.
How late?
It ends at 9:00.
That's past your bedtime!
I know. I don't want to be up so late.
Do you have to go?
No, but I'm hoping to learn something important.
Like what? How to control your behavior?

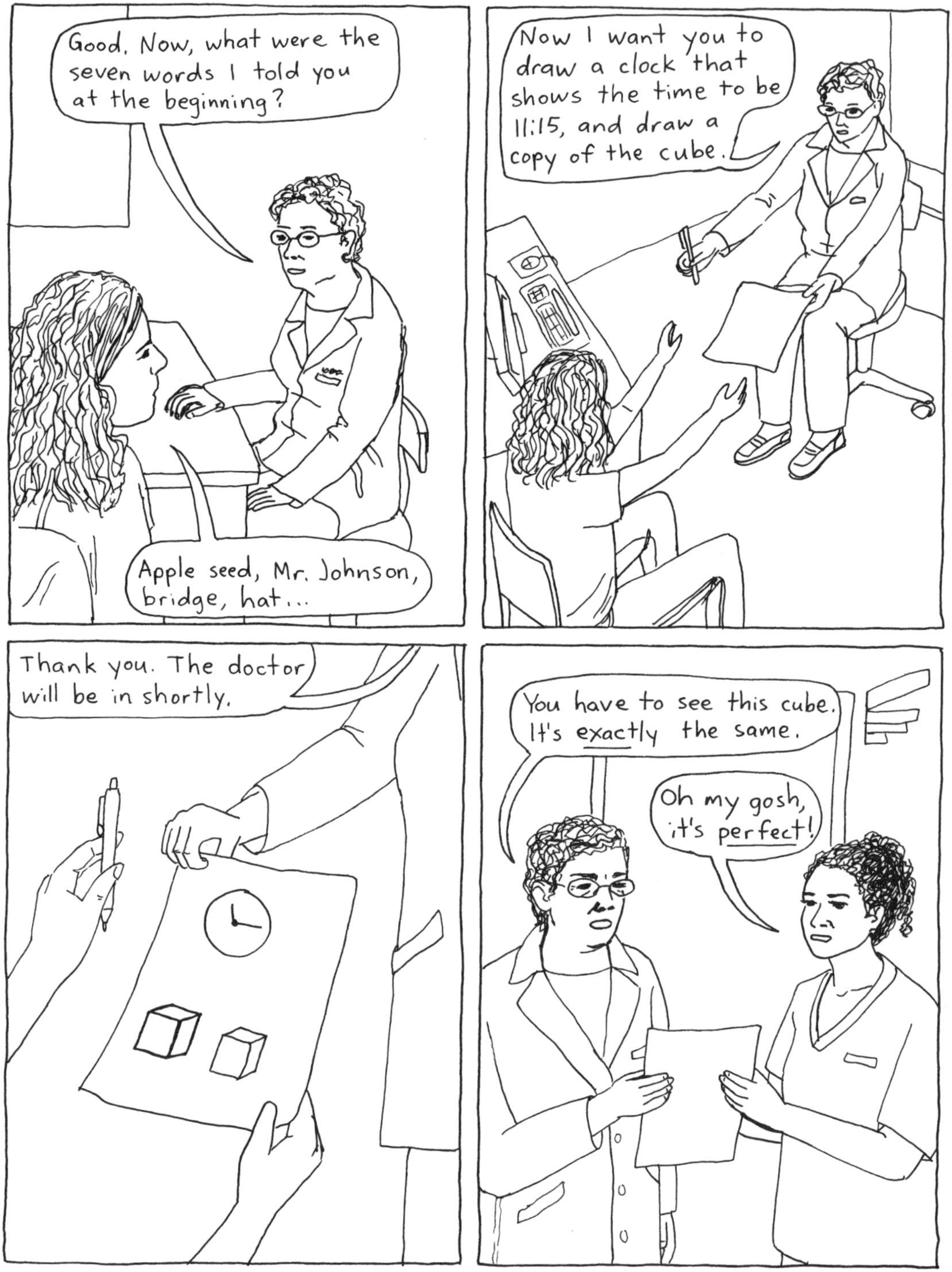
Good. Now, what were the seven words I told you at the beginning?
Apple seed, Mr. Johnson, bridge, hat...
Now I want you to draw a clock that shows the time to be 11:15, and draw a copy of the cube.
Thank you. The doctor will be in shortly.
You have to see this cube. It's exactly the same.
Oh my gosh, it's perfect!

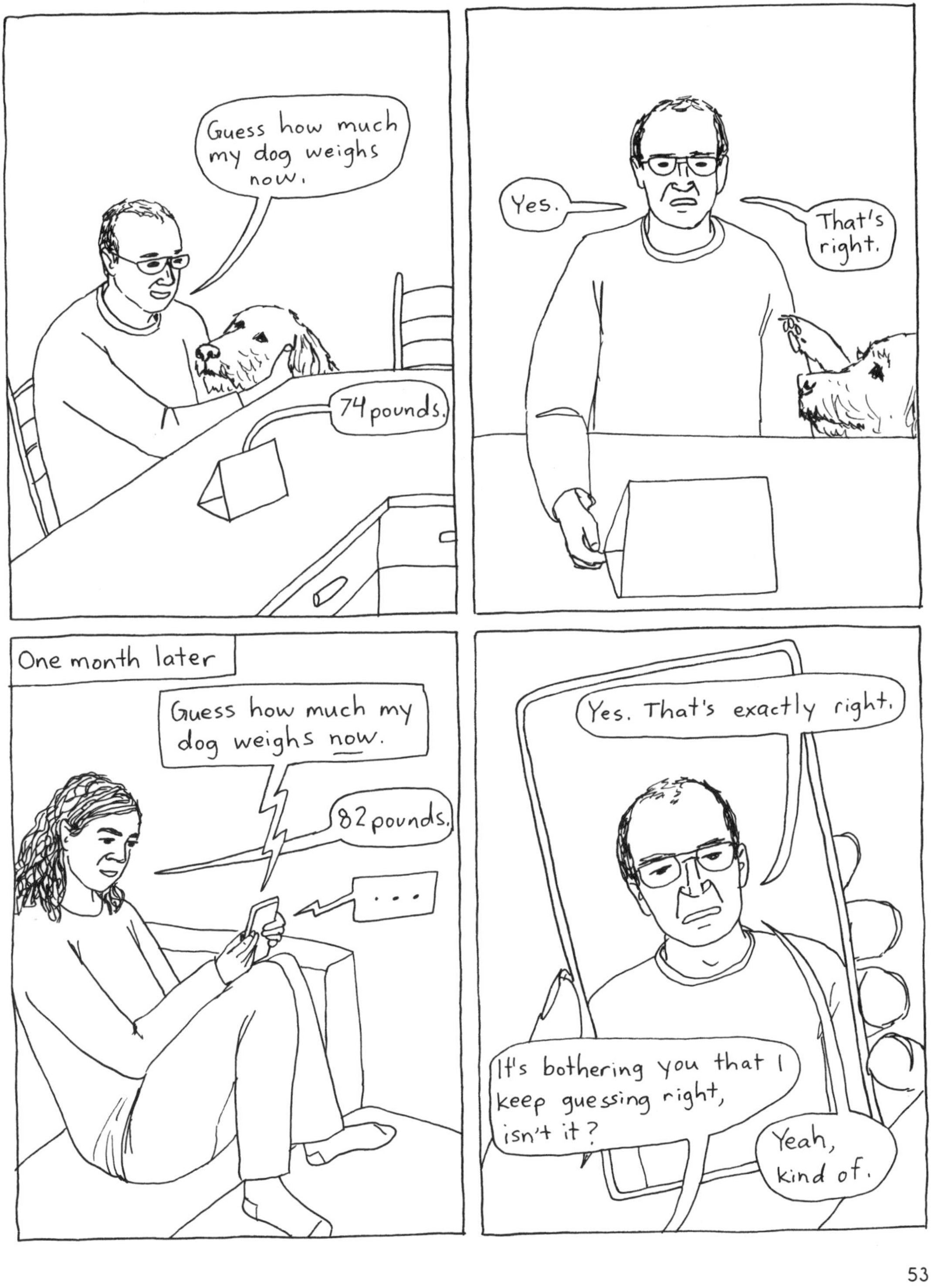
Guess how much my dog weighs now.
74 pounds.
Yes.
That's right.
One month later
Guess how much my dog weighs now.
82 pounds.
...
Yes. That's exactly right.
It's bothering you that I keep guessing right, isn't it?
Yeah, kind of.

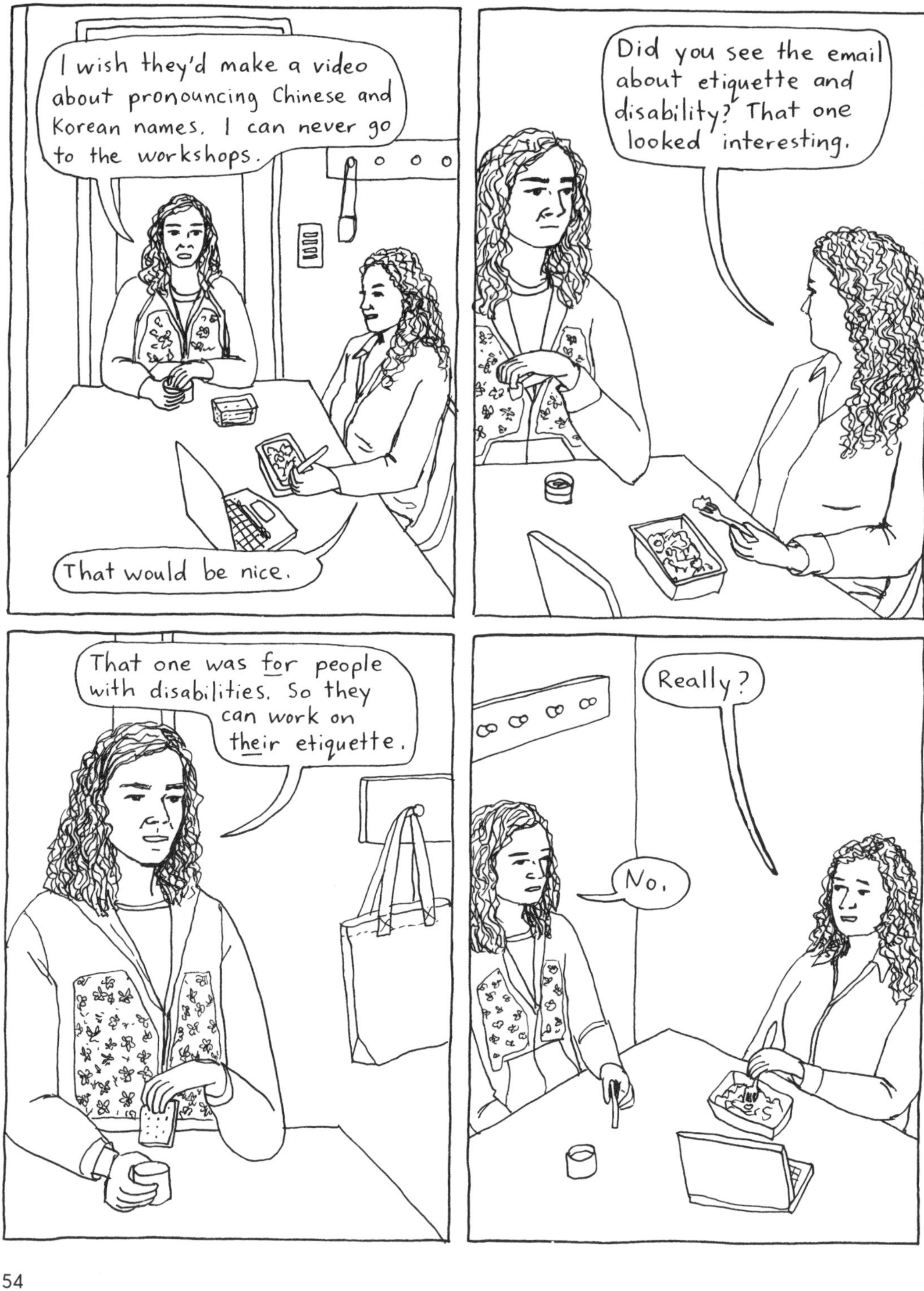
I wish they'd make a video about pronouncing Chinese and Korean names. I can never go to the workshops.
That would be nice.
Did you see the email about etiquette and disability? That one looked interesting.
That one was for people with disabilities. So they can work on their etiquette.
Really?
No.

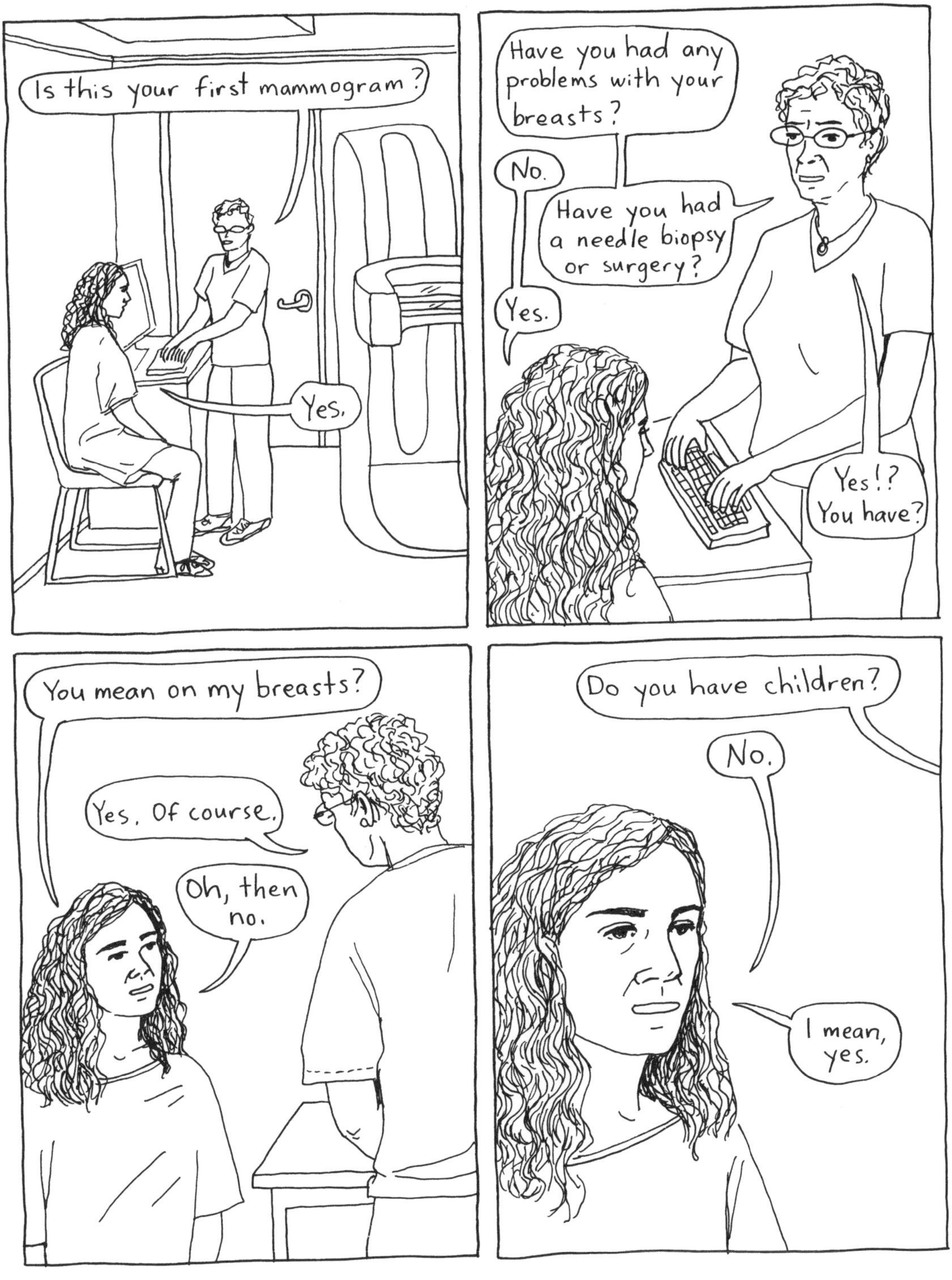
Is this your first mammogram?
Yes.
Have you had any problems with your breasts?
No.
Have you had a needle biopsy or surgery?
Yes.
Yes!? You have?
You mean on my breasts?
Yes. Of course.
Oh, then no.
Do you have children?
No.
I mean, yes.

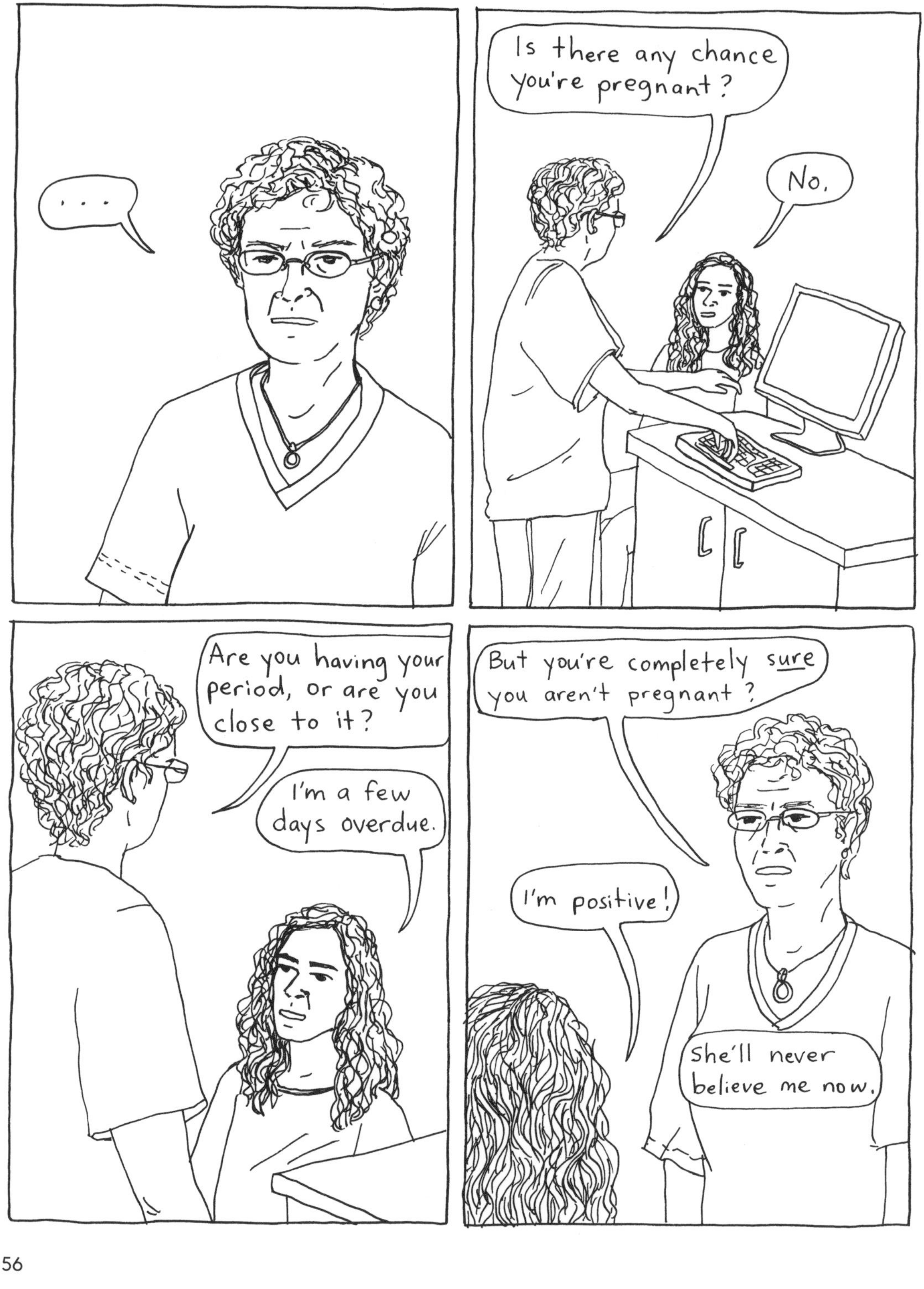
. . .
Is there any chance you're pregnant?
No.
Are you having your period, or are you close to it?
I'm a few days overdue.
But you're completely sure you aren't pregnant?
I'm positive!
She'll never believe me now.

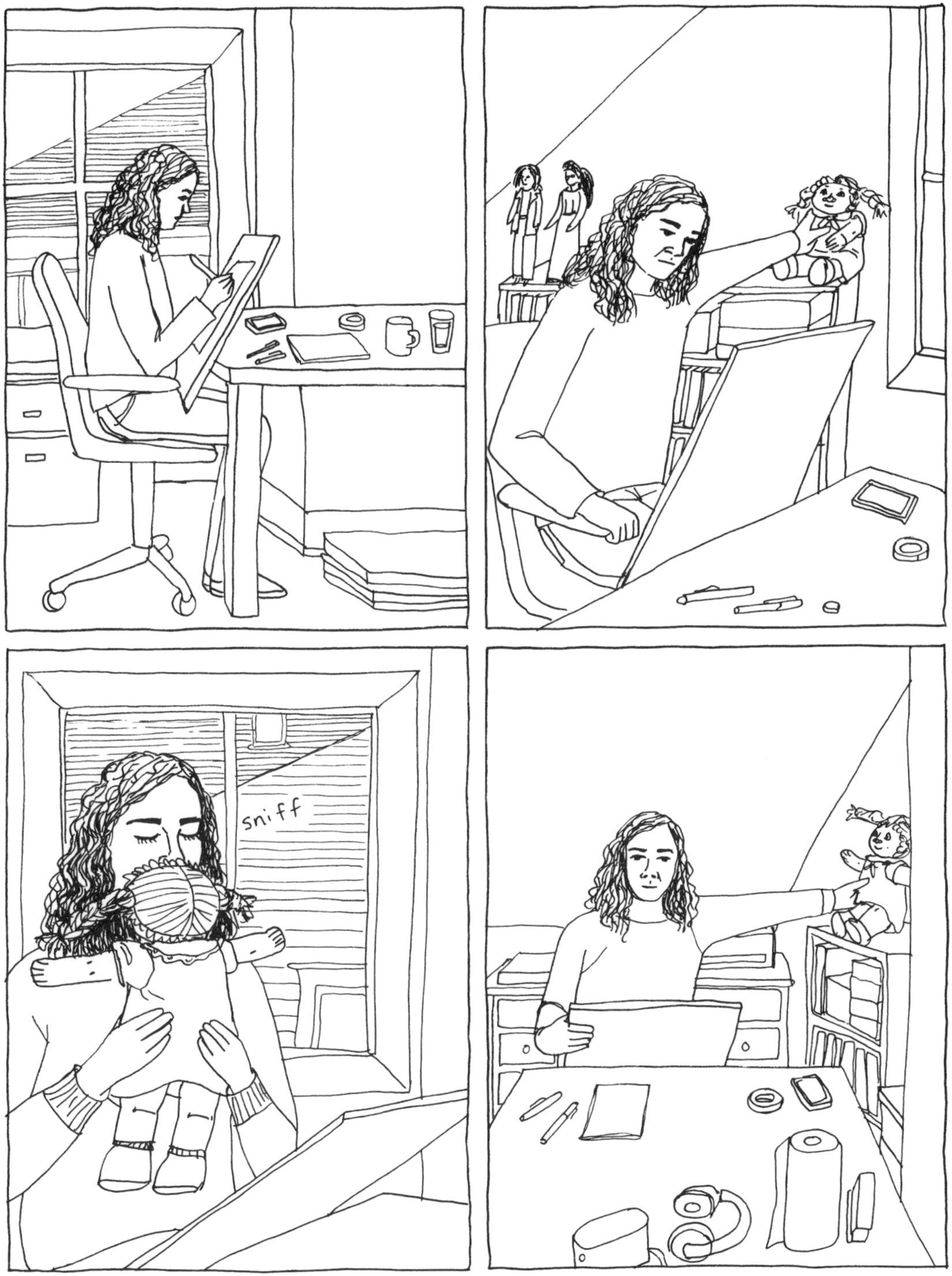
sniff

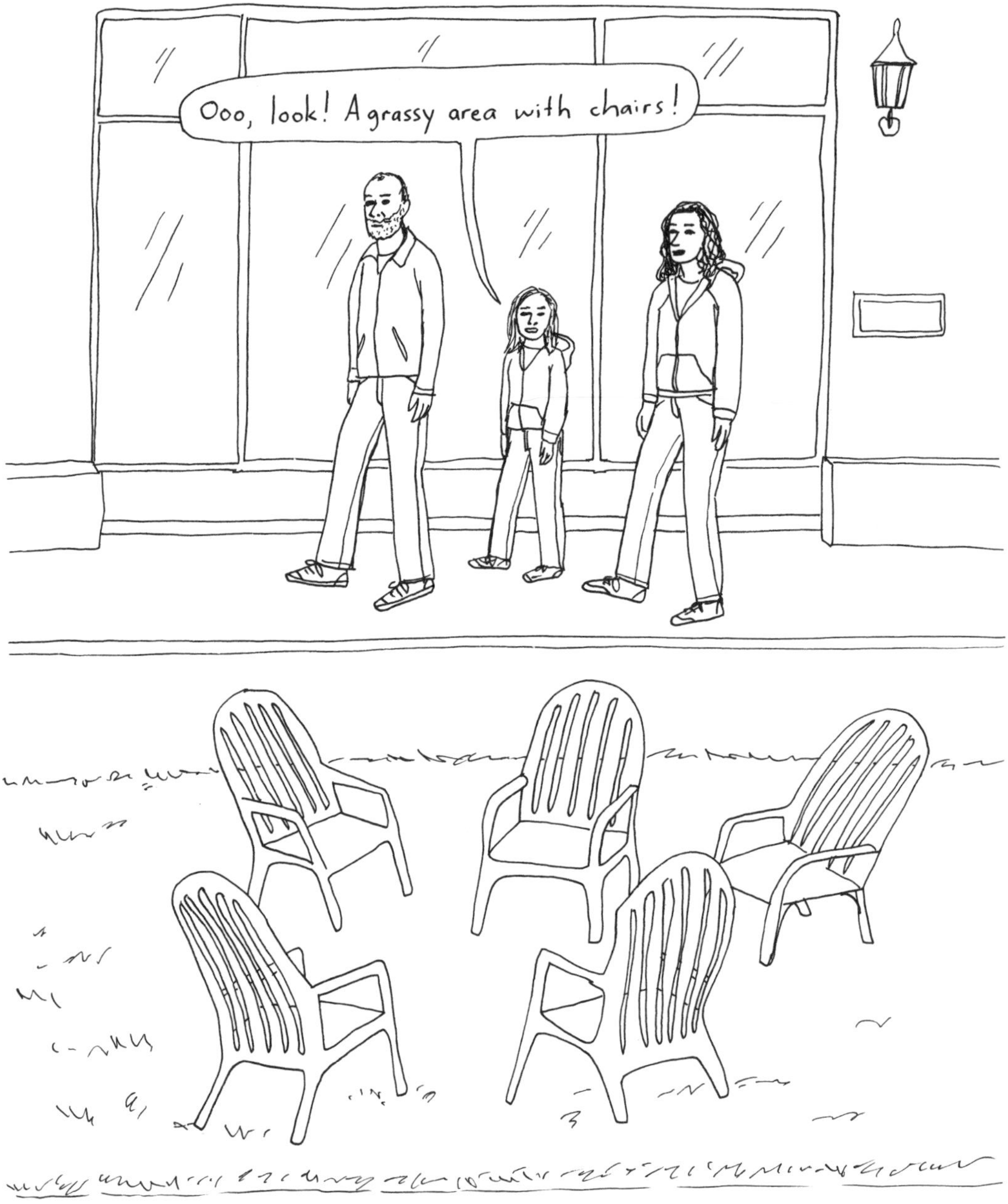
Ooo, look! A grassy area with chairs!

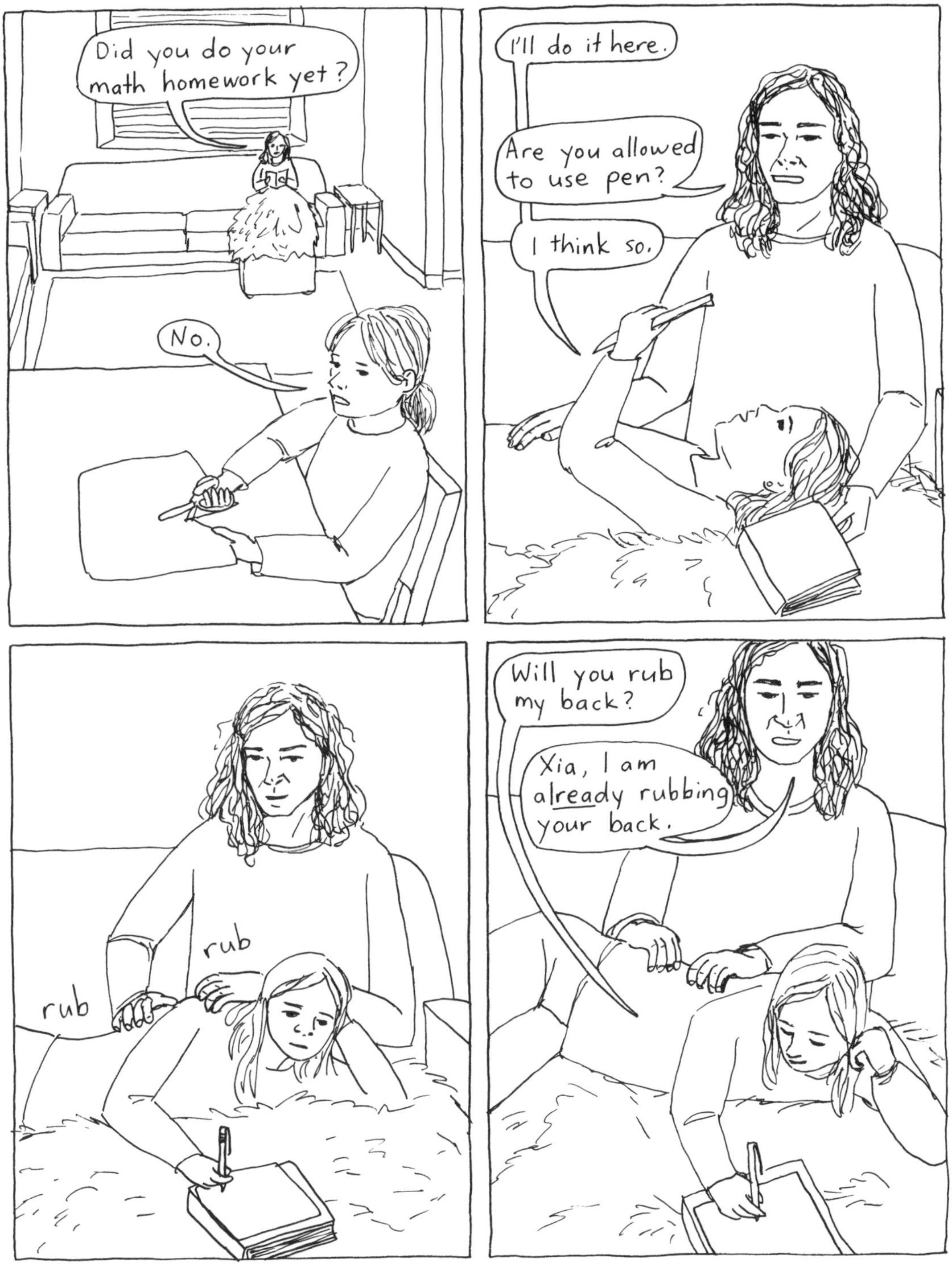
Did you do your math homework yet?
No.
I'll do it here.
Are you allowed to use pen?
I think so.
rub
rub
Will you rub my back?
Xia, I am already rubbing your back.

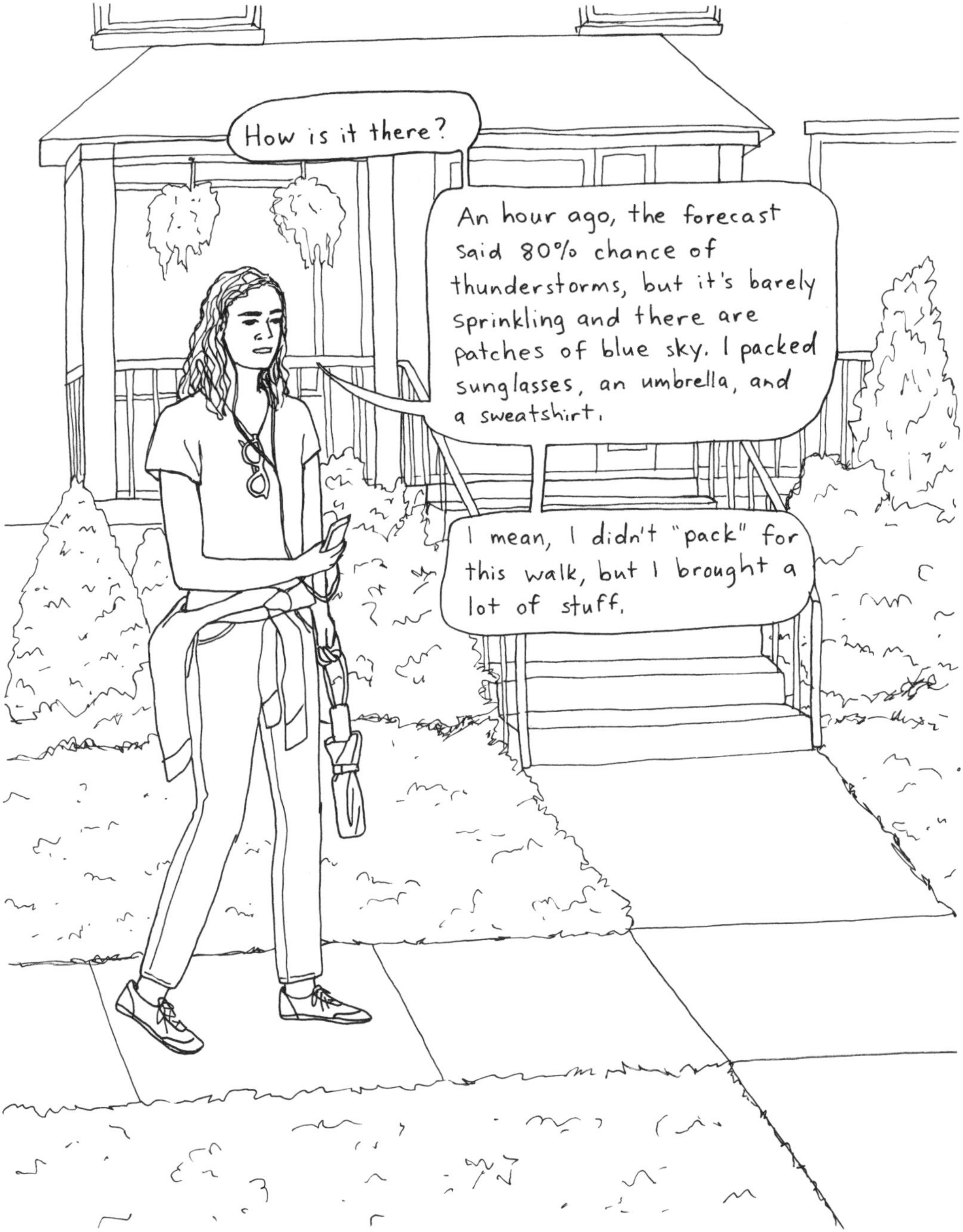
How is it there?
An hour ago, the forecast said 80% chance of thunderstorms, but it's barely sprinkling and there are patches of blue sky. I packed sunglasses, an umbrella, and a sweatshirt.
I mean, I didn't "pack" for this walk, but I brought a lot of stuff.

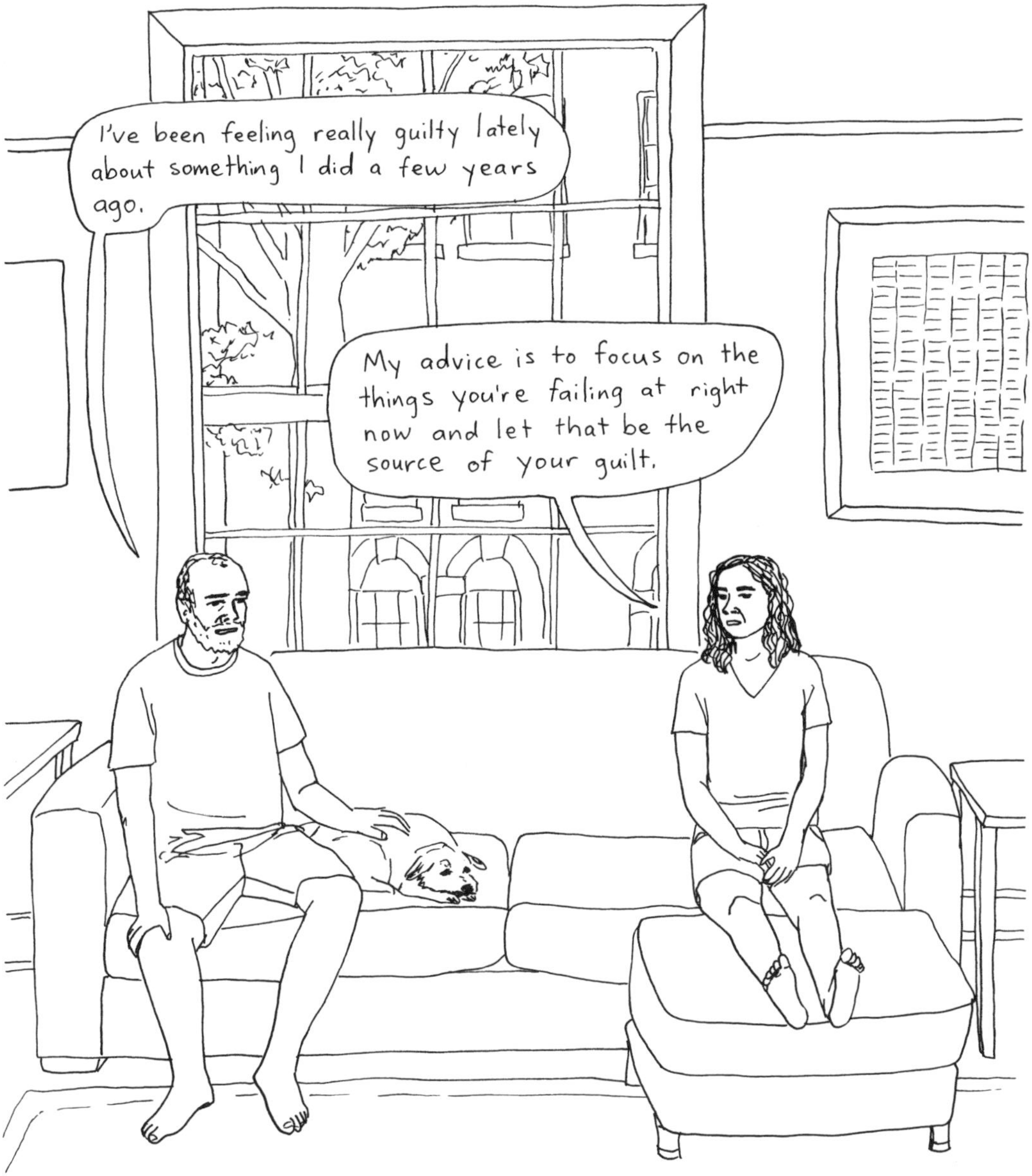
I've been feeling really guilty lately about something I did a few years ago.
My advice is to focus on the things you're failing at right now and let that be the source of your guilt.

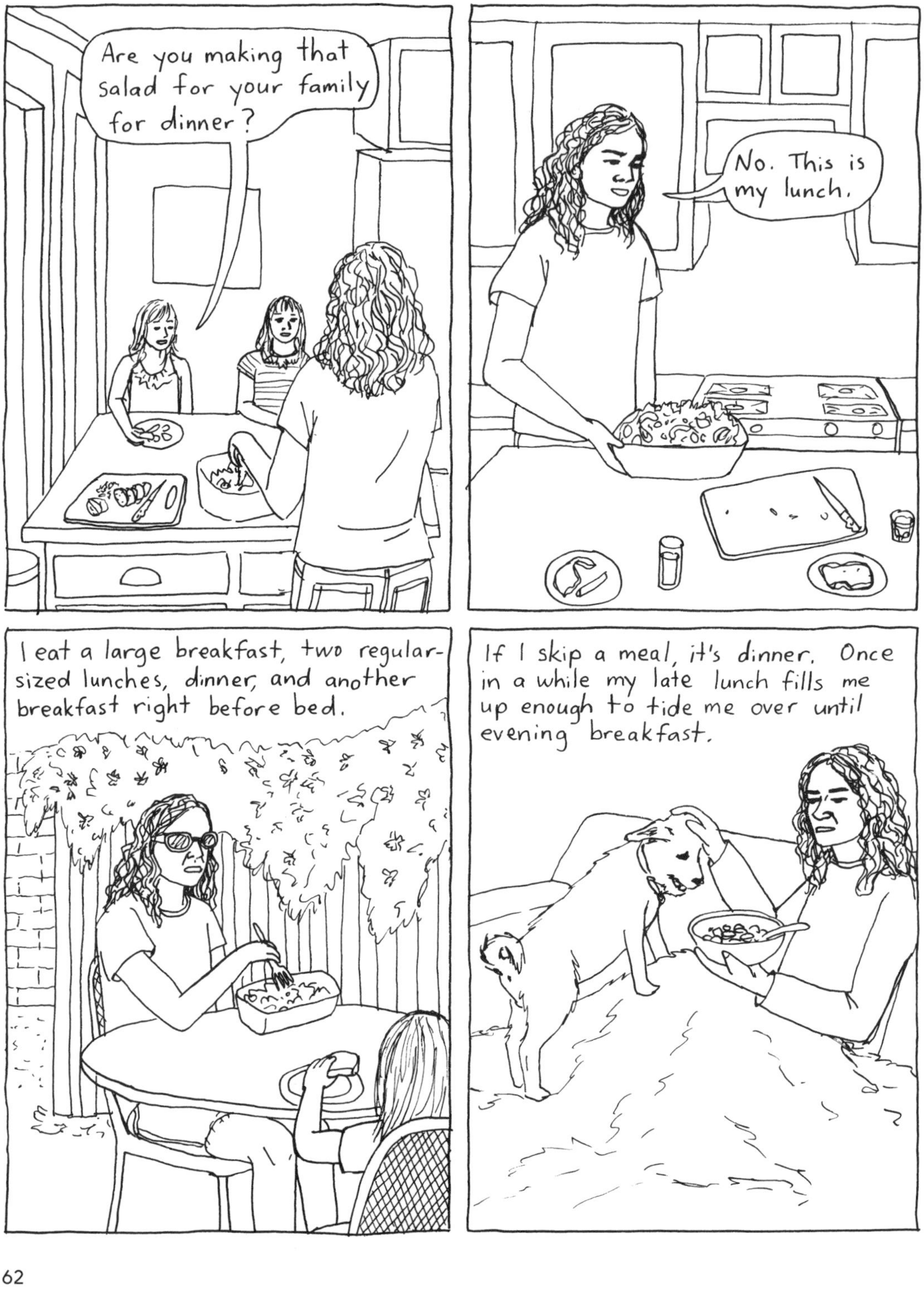
Are you making that salad for your family for dinner?
No. This is my lunch.
I eat a large breakfast, two regular-sized lunches, dinner, and another breakfast right before bed.
If I skip a meal, it's dinner. Once in a while my late lunch fills me up enough to tide me over until evening breakfast.

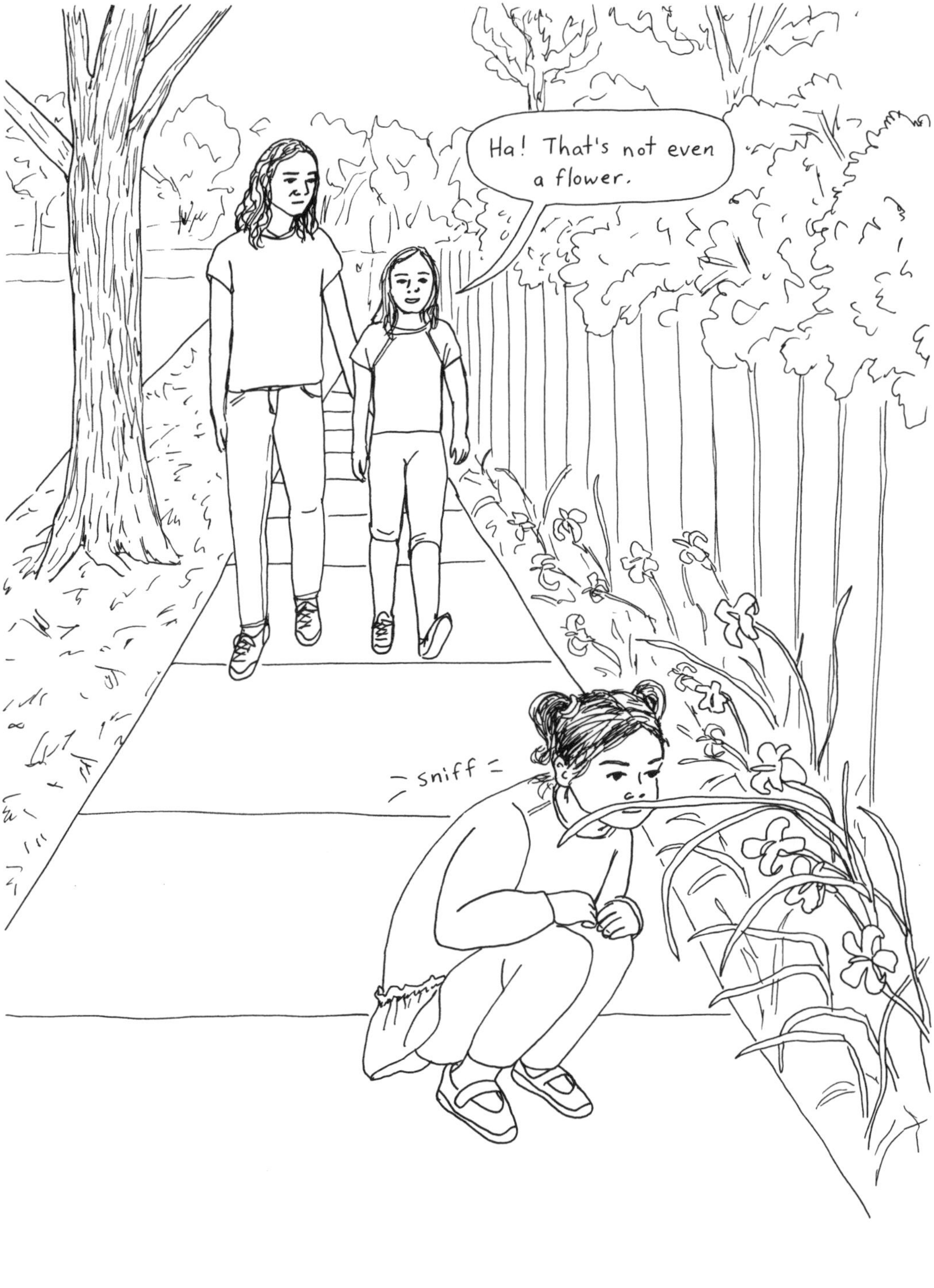
Ha! That's not even a flower.
sniff

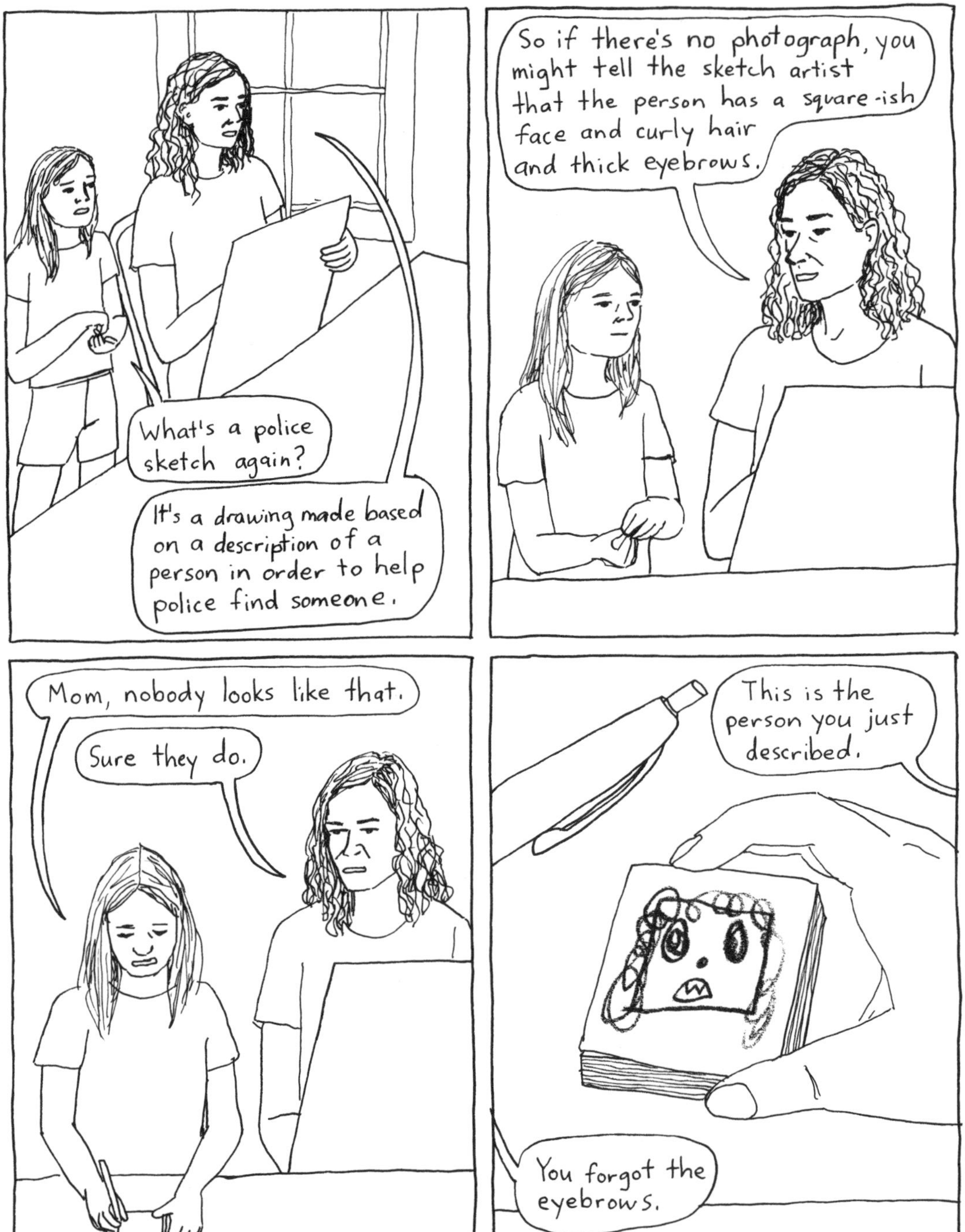
What's a police sketch again?
It's a drawing made based on a description of a person in order to help police find someone.
So if there's no photograph, you might tell the sketch artist that the person has a square-ish face and curly hair and thick eyebrows.
Mom, nobody looks like that.
Sure they do.
This is the person you just described.
You forgot the eyebrows.

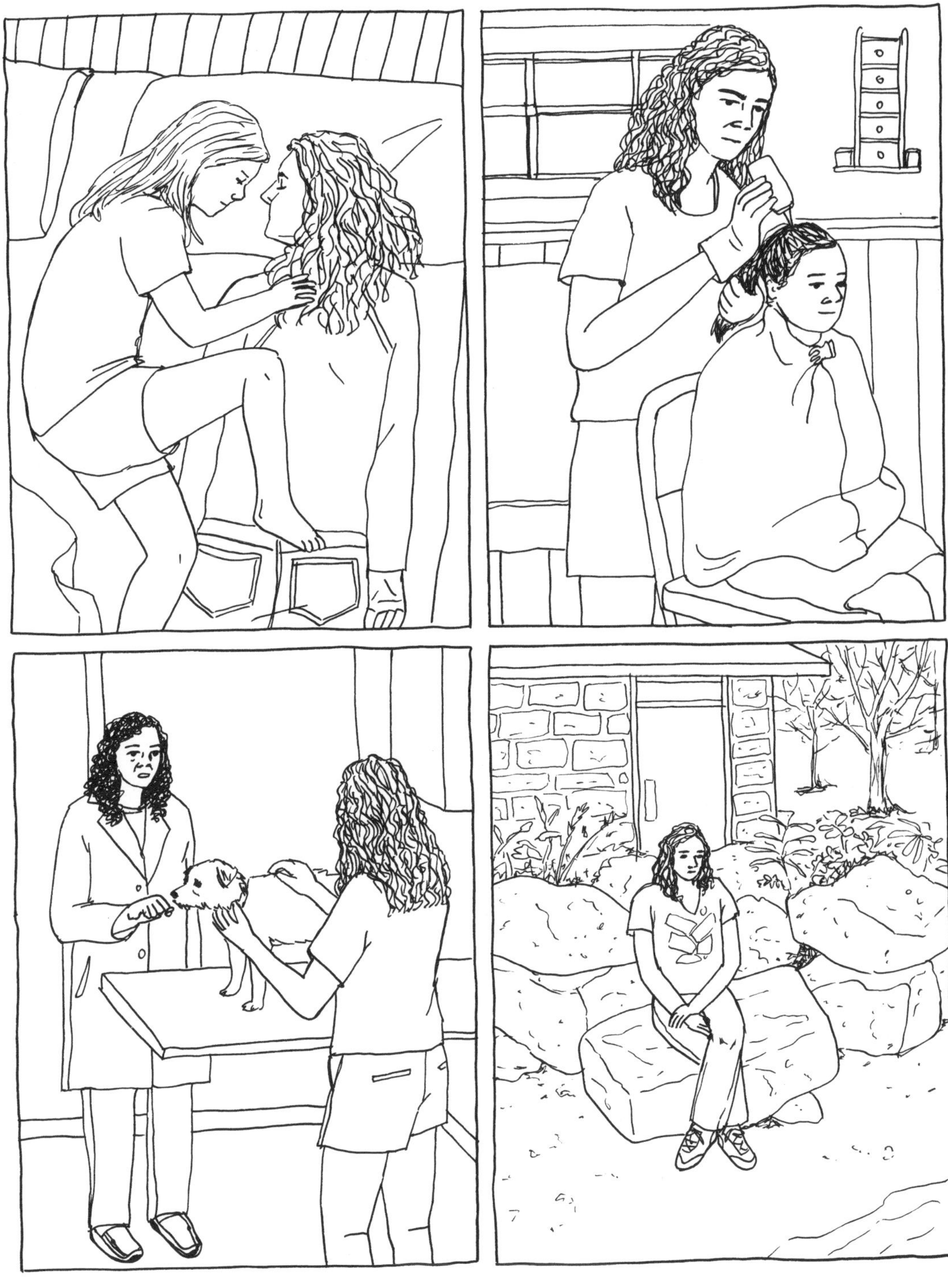

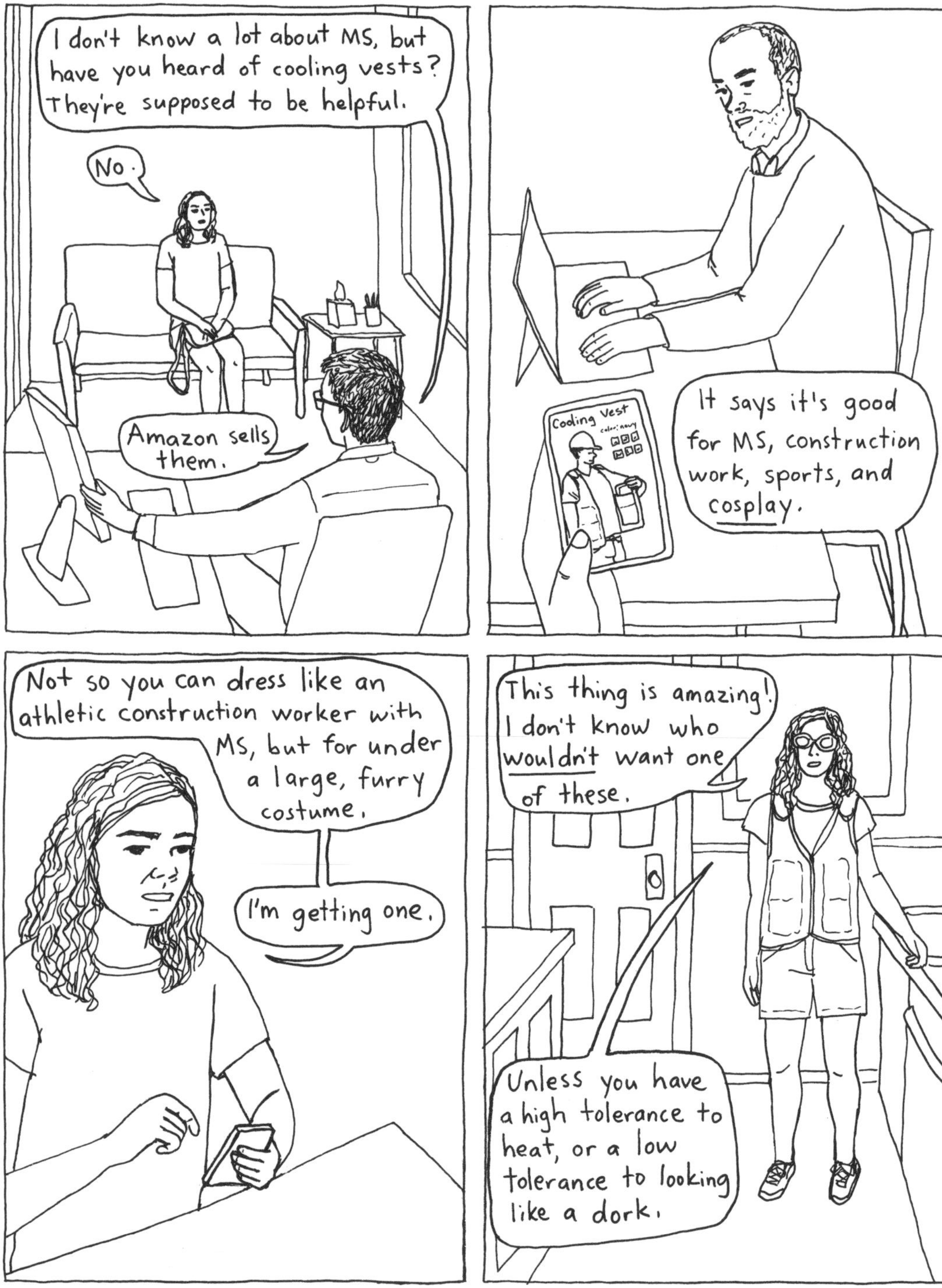

I don't know a lot about MS, but have you heard of cooling vests? They're supposed to be helpful.
No.
Amazon sells them.
Cooling Vest
It says it's good for MS, construction work, sports, and cosplay.
Not so you can dress like an athletic construction worker with MS, but for under a large, furry costume.
I'm getting one.
This thing is amazing! I don't know who wouldn't want one of these.
Unless you have a high tolerance to heat, or a low tolerance to looking like a dork.

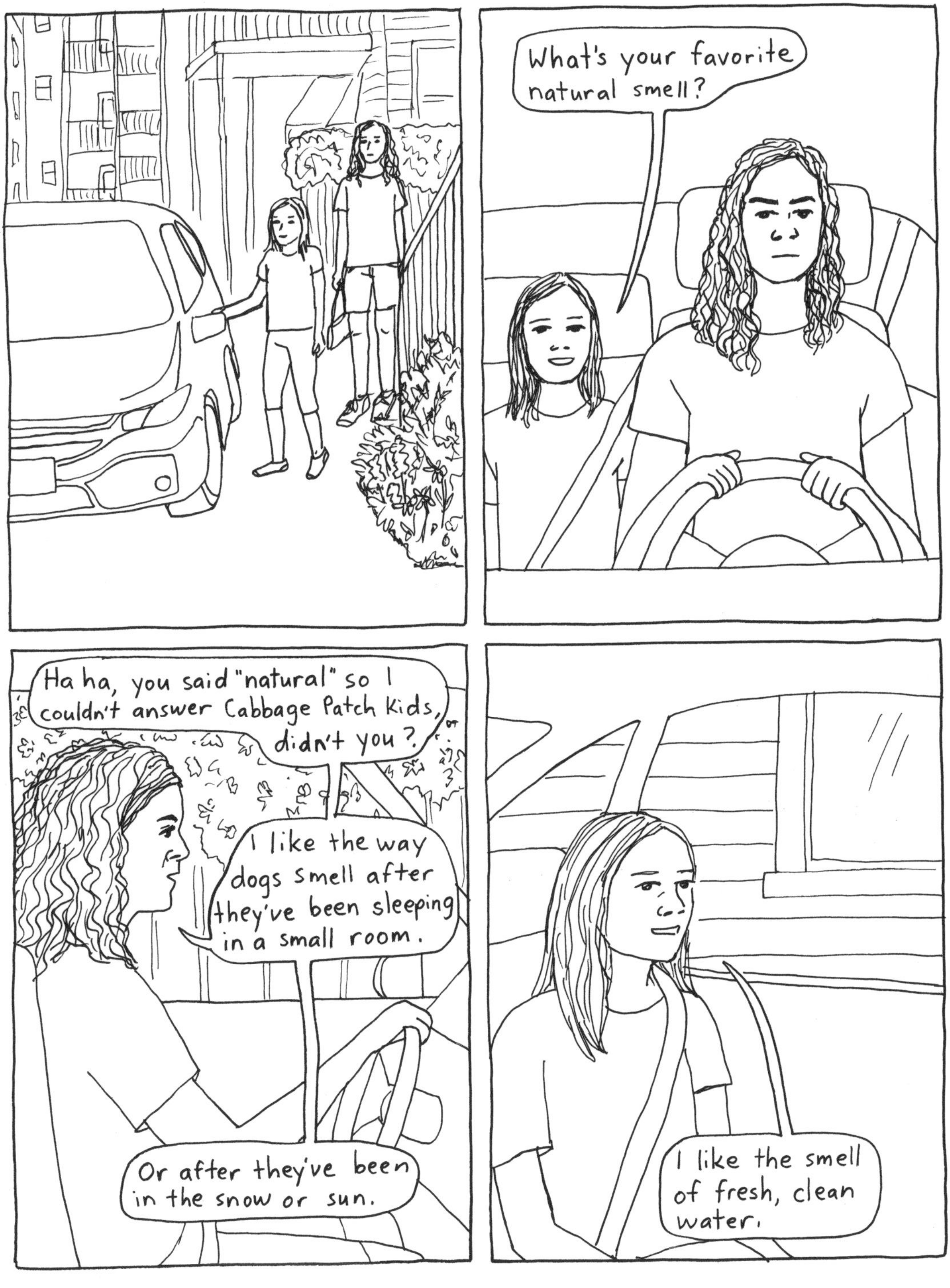
What's your favorite natural smell?
Ha ha, you said "natural" so I couldn't answer Cabbage Patch Kids, didn't you?
I like the way dogs smell after they've been sleeping in a small room.
Or after they've been in the snow or sun.
I like the smell of fresh, clean water.

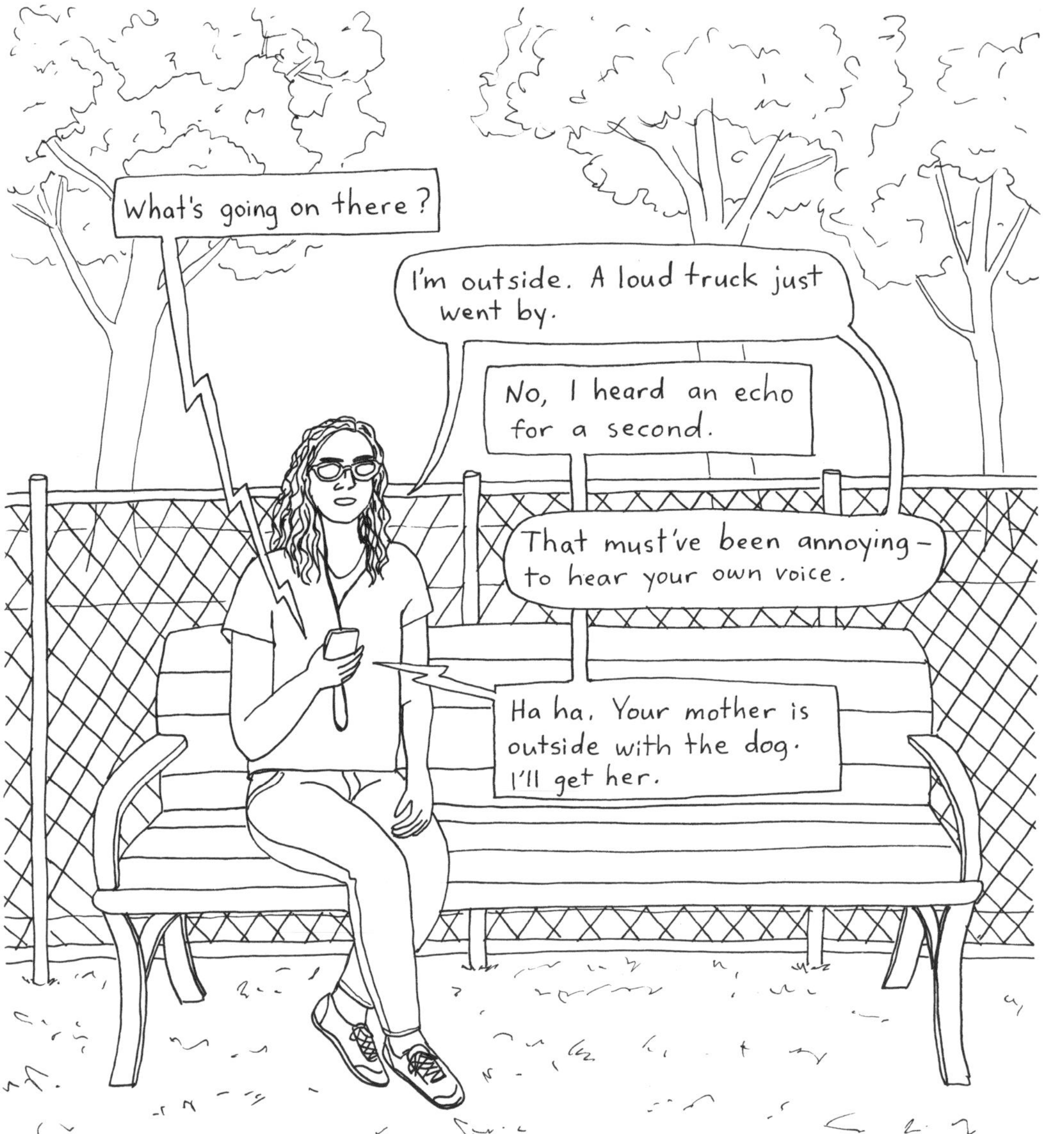
What's going on there?
I'm outside. A loud truck just went by.
No, I heard an echo for a second.
That must've been annoying— to hear your own voice.
Ha ha. Your mother is outside with the dog. I'll get her.

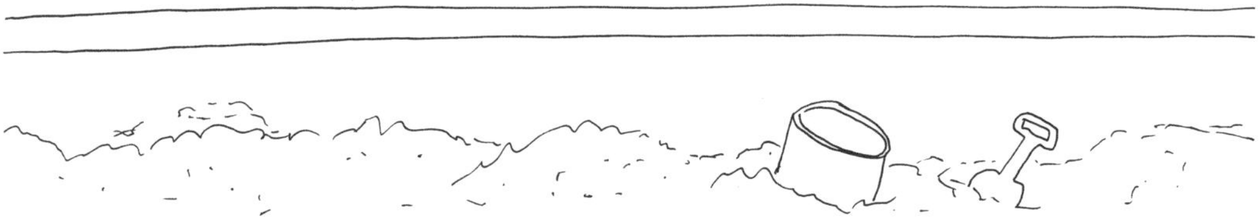

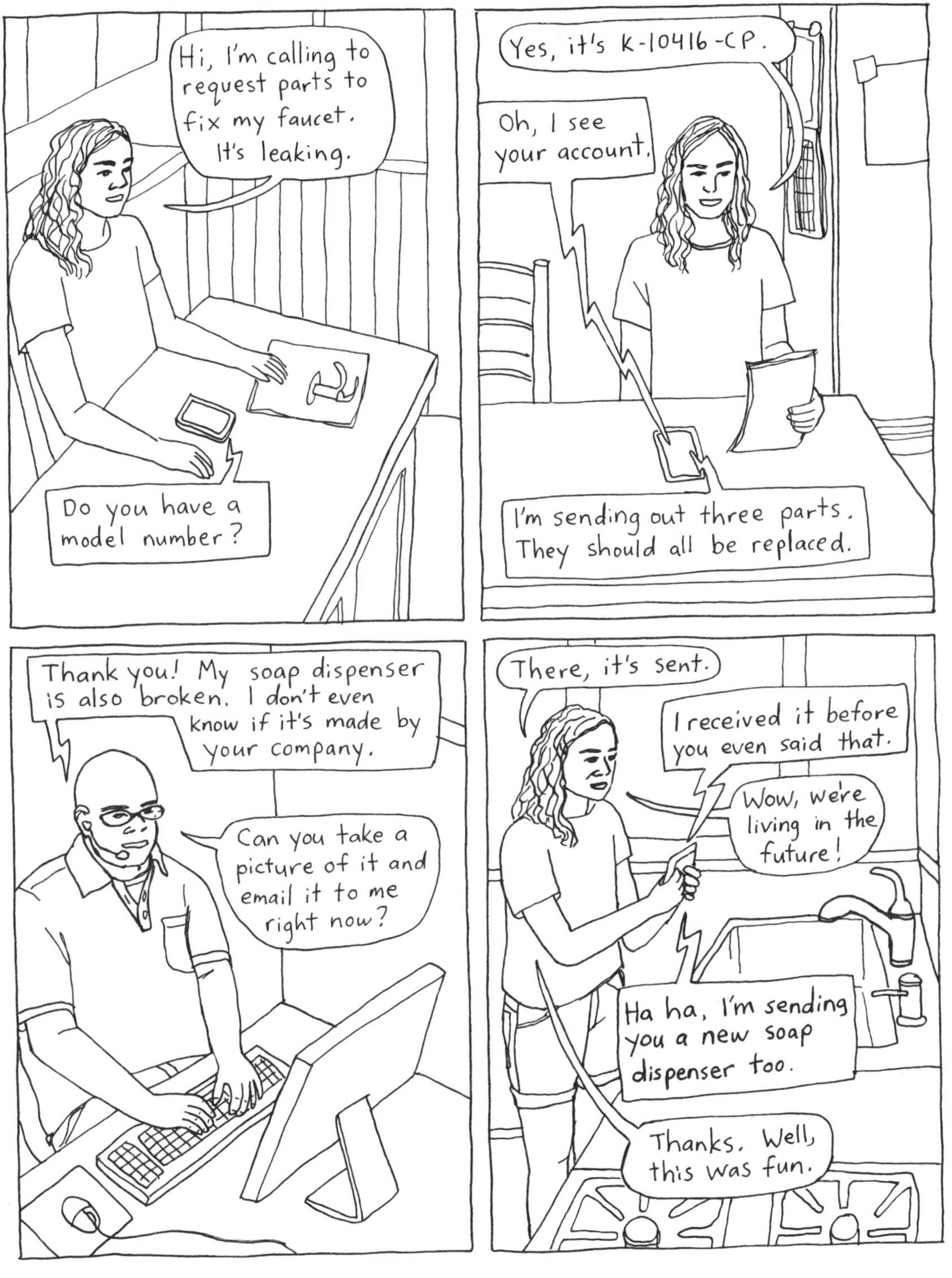
Hi, I'm calling to request parts to fix my faucet. It's leaking.
Do you have a model number?
Yes, it's K-10416-CP.
Oh, I see your account.
I'm sending out three parts. They should all be replaced.
Thank you! My soap dispenser is also broken. I don't even know if it's made by your company.
Can you take a picture of it and email it to me right now?
There, it's sent.
I received it before you even said that.
Wow, we're living in the future!
Ha ha, I'm sending you a new soap dispenser too.
Thanks. Well, this was fun.

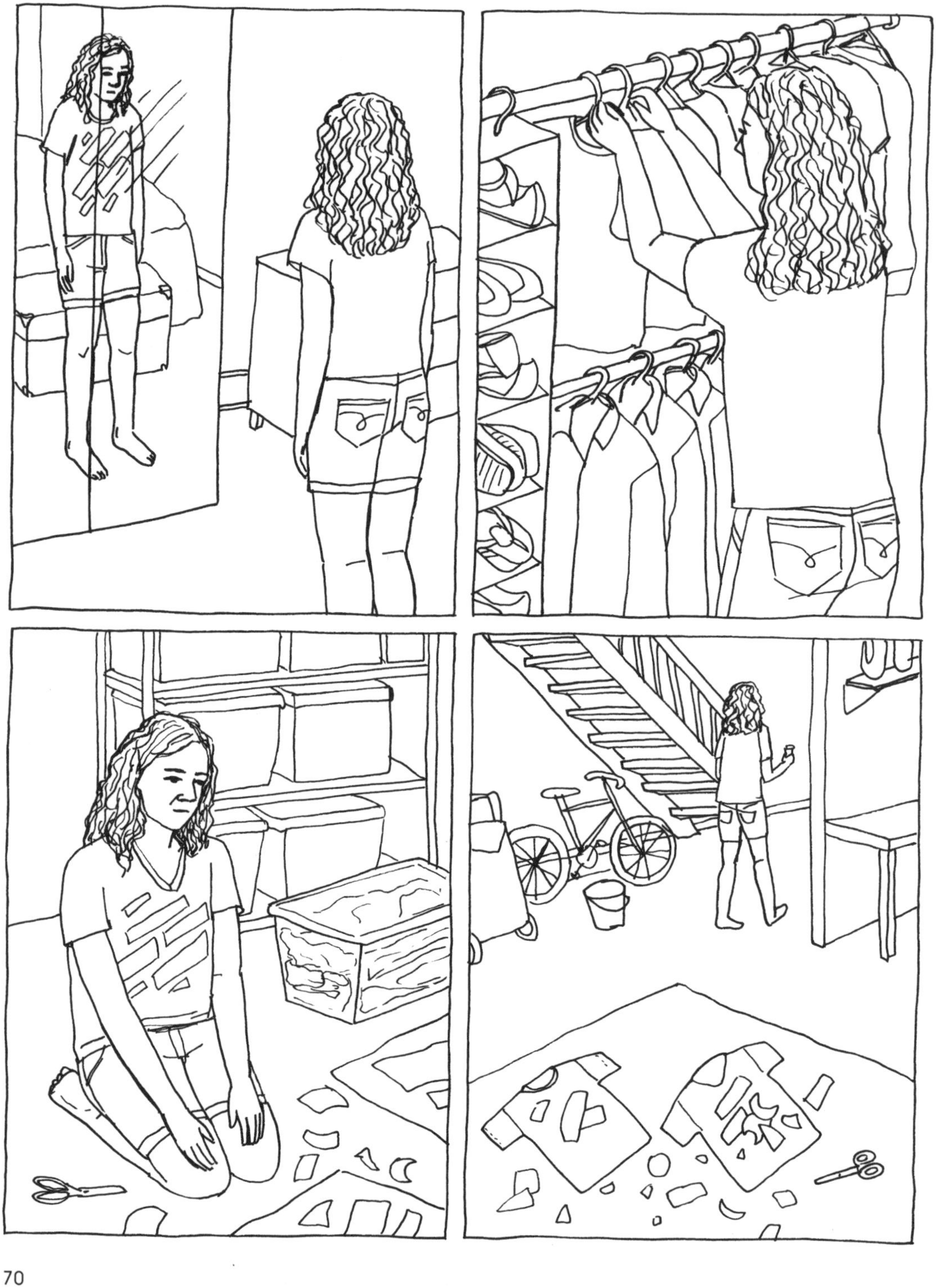

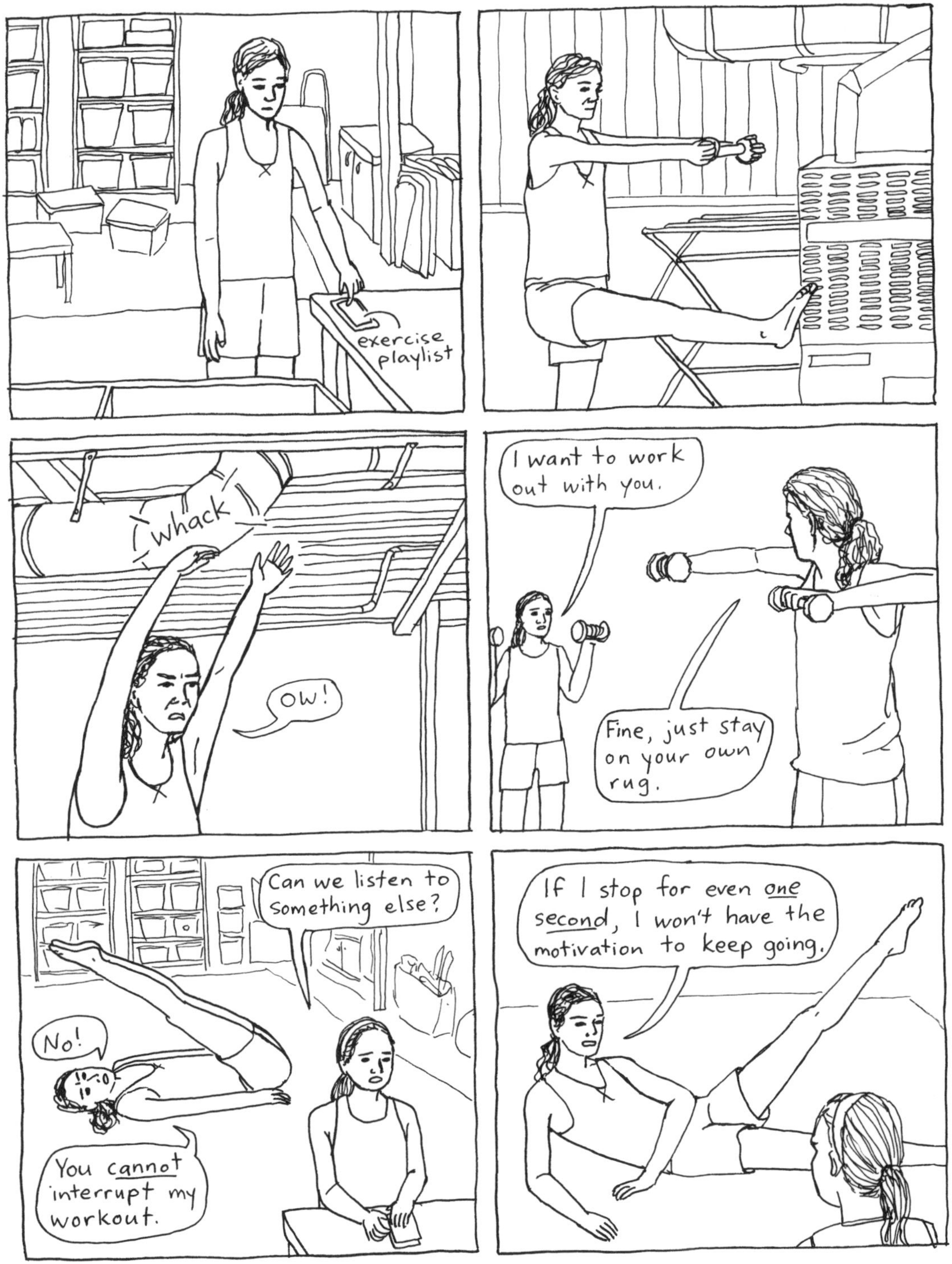
exercise playlist
whack
OW!
I want to work out with you.
Fine, just stay on your own rug.
Can we listen to something else?
No!
You cannot interrupt my workout.
If I stop for even one second, I won't have the motivation to keep going.

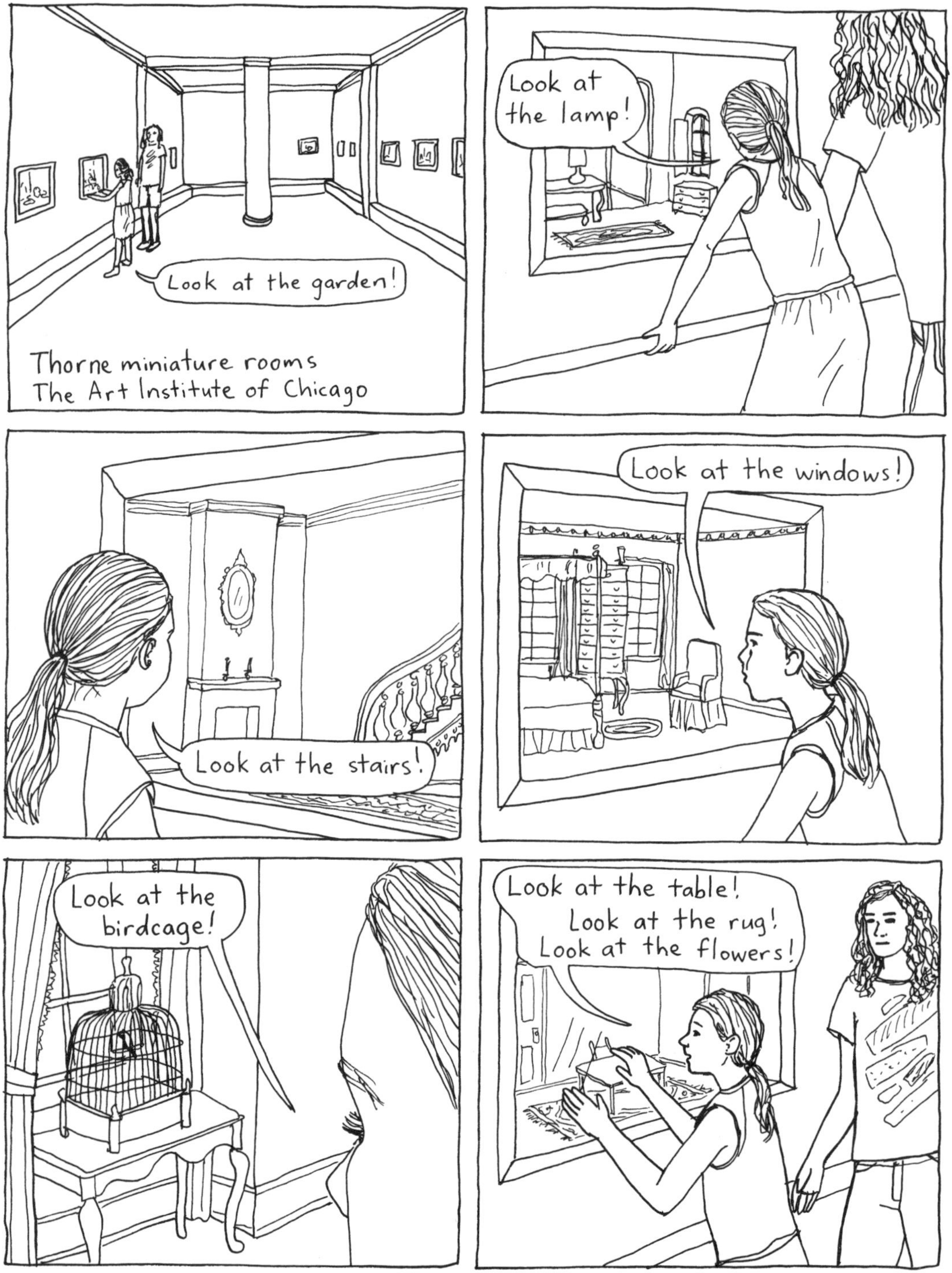
Look at the garden!
Thorne miniature rooms
The Art Institute of Chicago
Look at the lamp!
Look at the stairs!
Look at the windows!
Look at the birdcage!
Look at the table!
Look at the rug!
Look at the flowers!

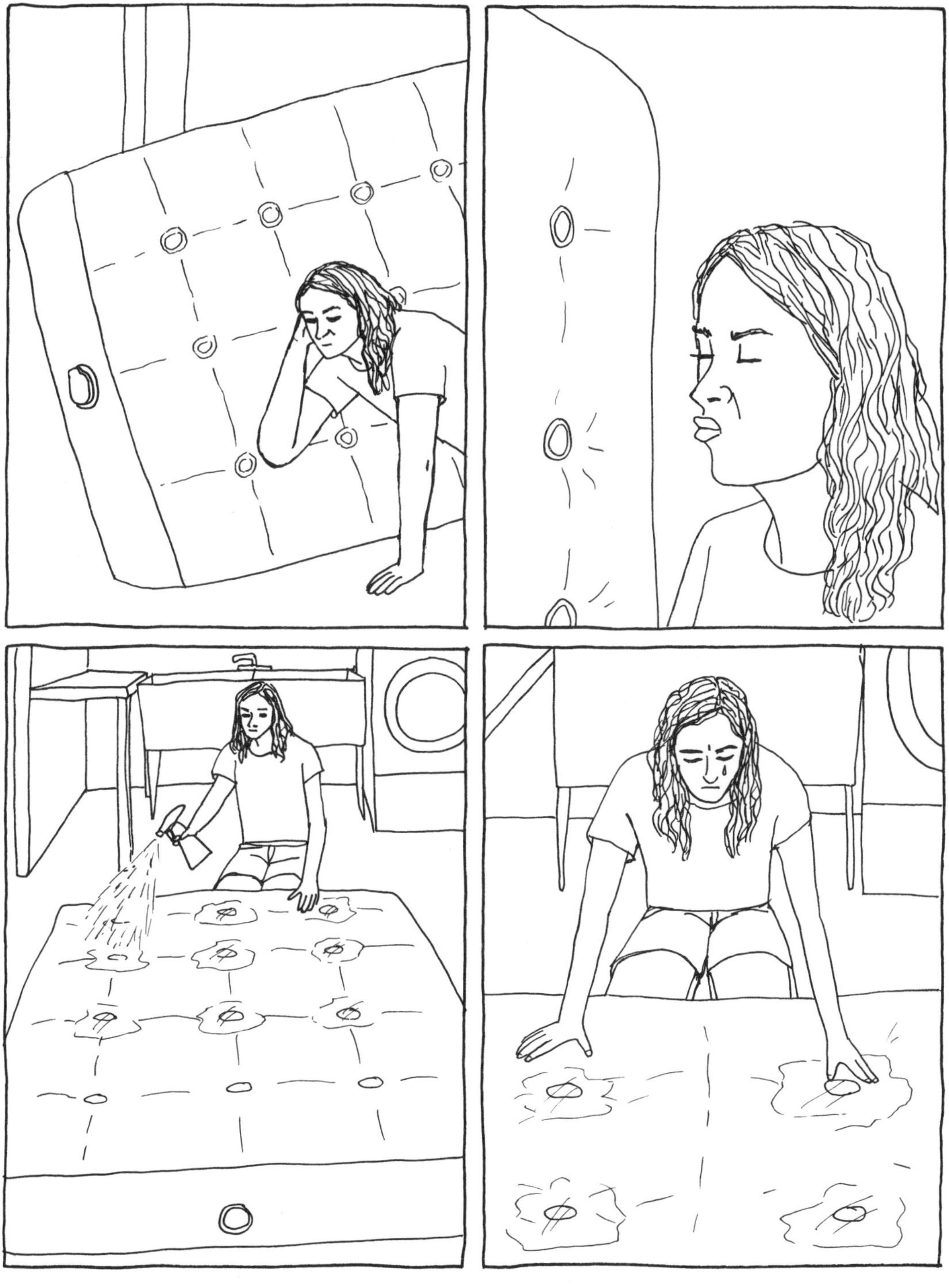

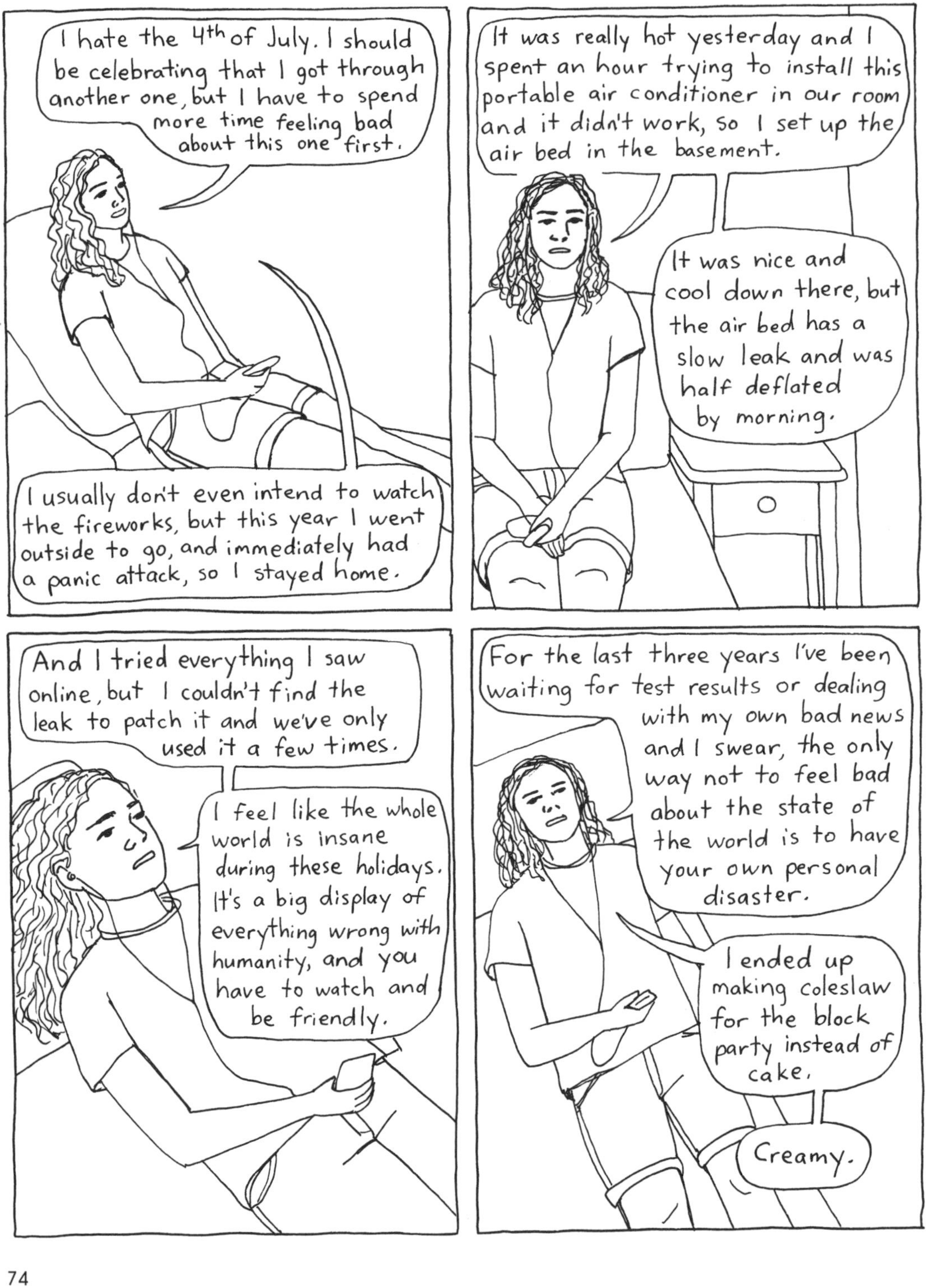
I hate the 4th of July. I should be celebrating that I got through another one, but I have to spend more time feeling bad about this one first.
I usually don't even intend to watch the fireworks, but this year I went outside to go, and immediately had a panic attack, so I stayed home.
It was really hot yesterday and I spent an hour trying to install this portable air conditioner in our room and it didn't work, so I set up the air bed in the basement.
It was nice and cool down there, but the air bed has a slow leak and was half deflated by morning.
And I tried everything I saw online, but I couldn't find the leak to patch it and we've only used it a few times.
I feel like the whole world is insane during these holidays. It's a big display of everything wrong with humanity, and you have to watch and be friendly.
For the last three years I've been waiting for test results or dealing with my own bad news and I swear, the only way not to feel bad about the state of the world is to have your own personal disaster.
I ended up making coleslaw for the block party instead of cake.
Creamy.

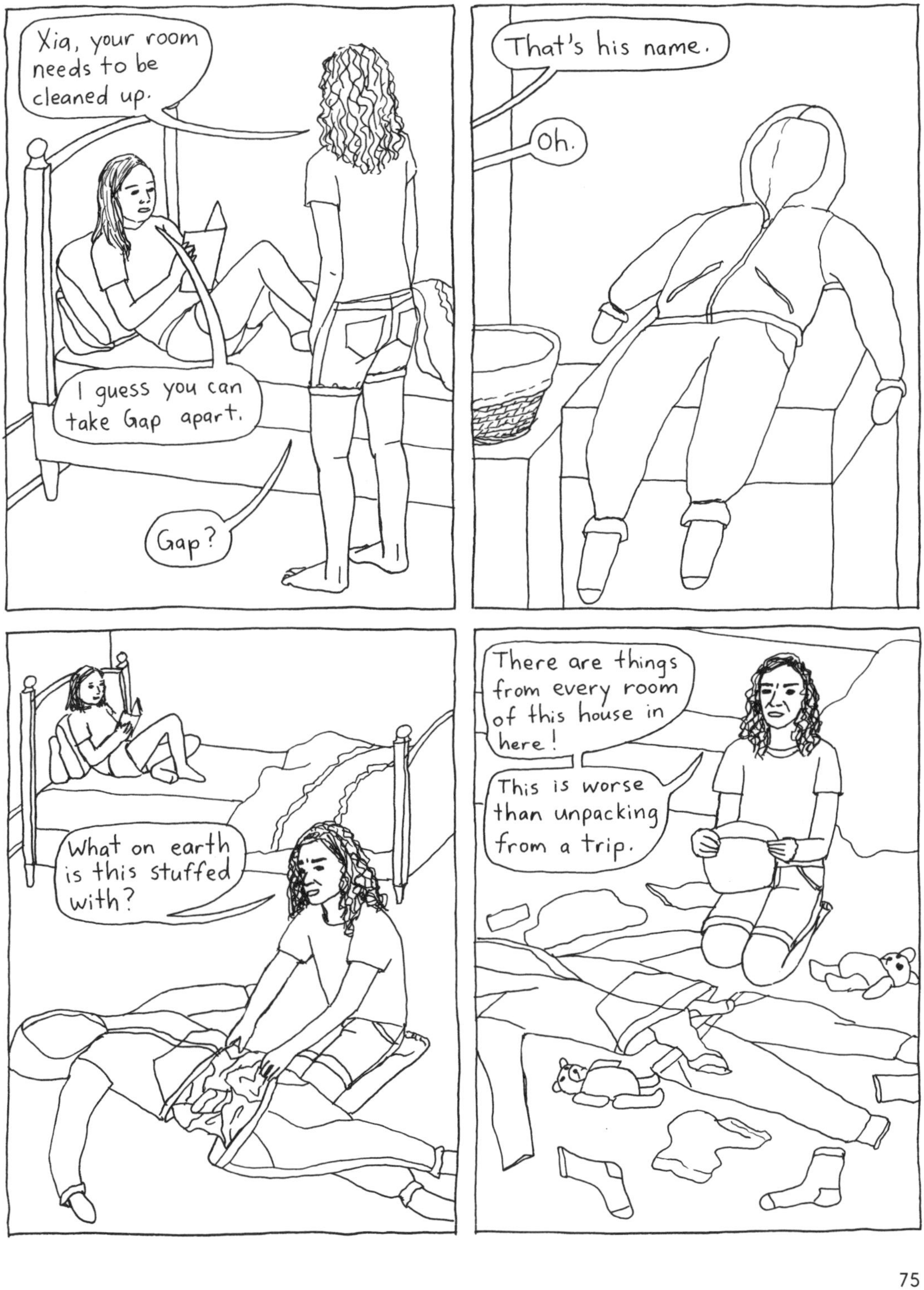
Xia, your room needs to be cleaned up.
I guess you can take Gap apart.
Gap?
That's his name.
Oh.
What on earth is this stuffed with?
There are things from every room of this house in here!
This is worse than unpacking from a trip.

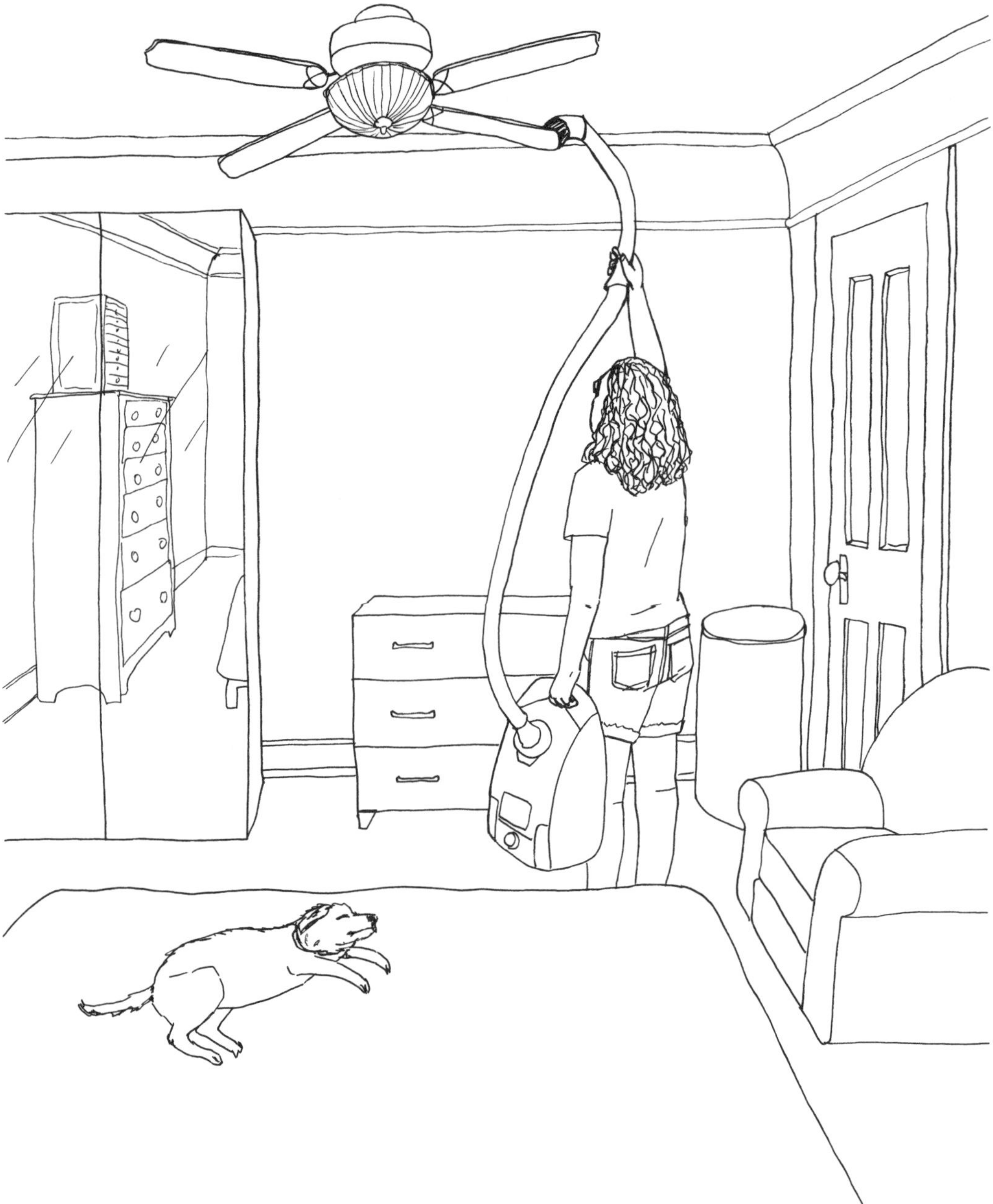

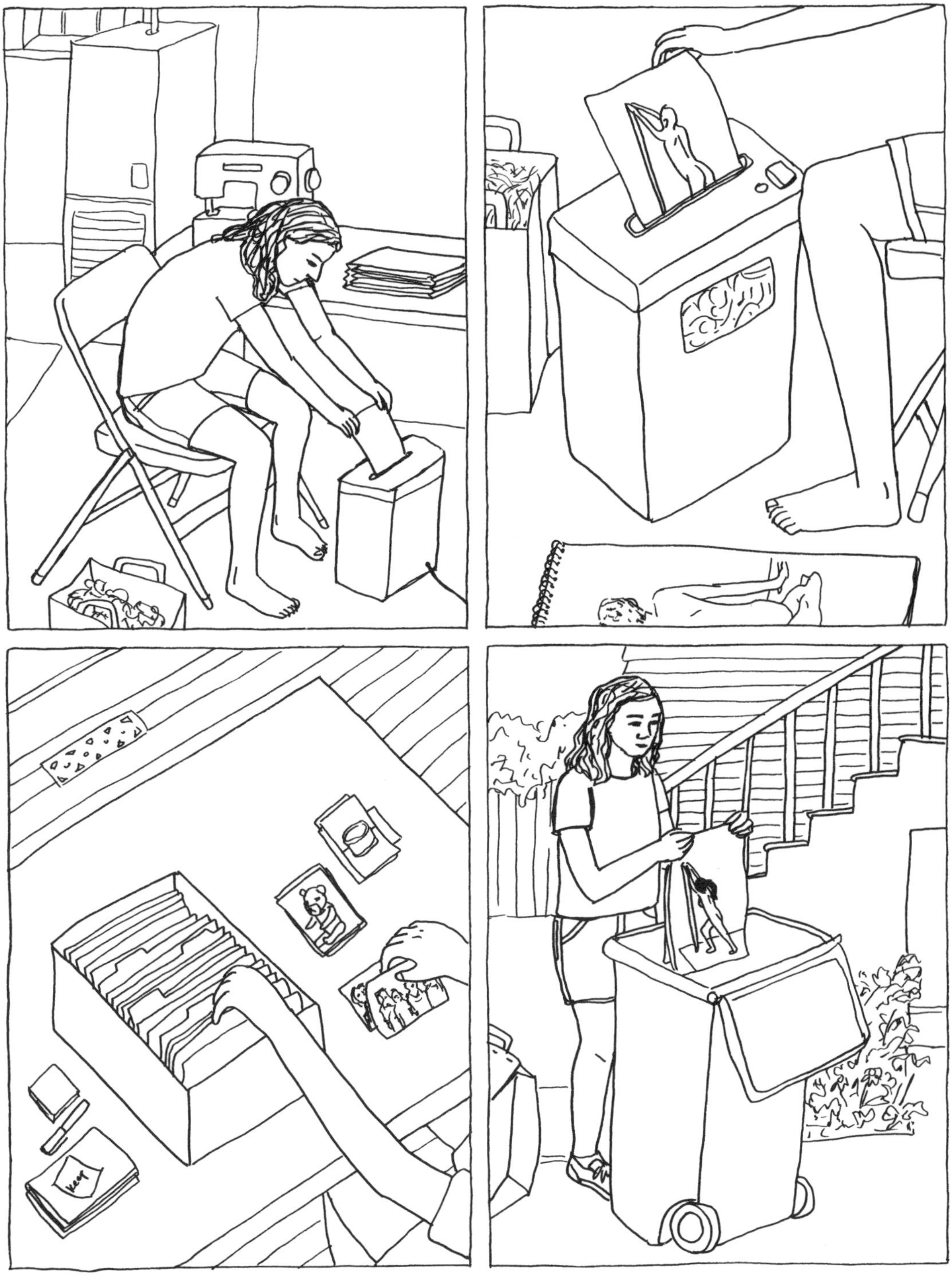
Keep

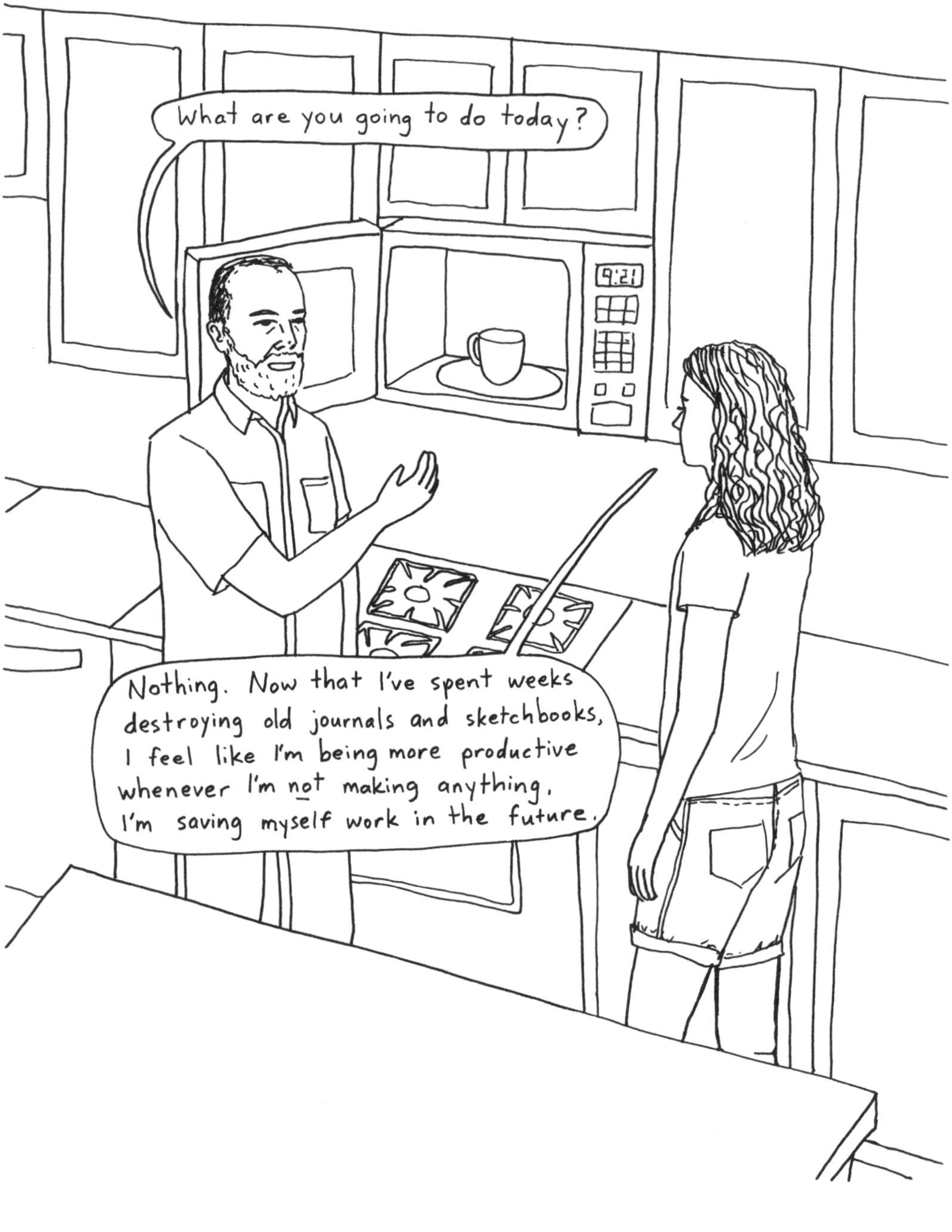
What are you going to do today?
Nothing. Now that I've spent weeks destroying old journals and sketchbooks, I feel like I'm being more productive whenever I'm not making anything. I'm saving myself work in the future.

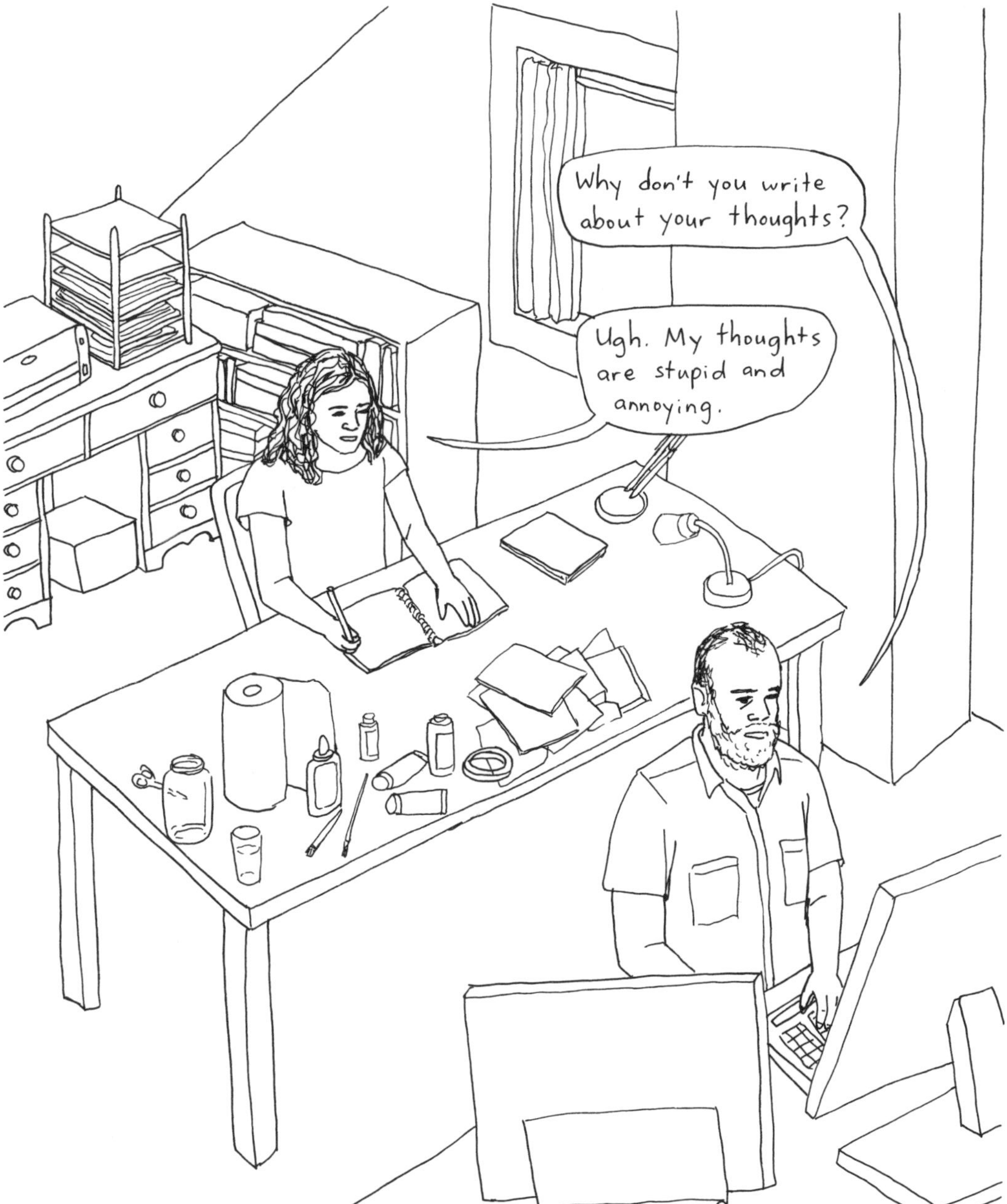
Why don't you write about your thoughts?
Ugh. My thoughts are stupid and annoying.

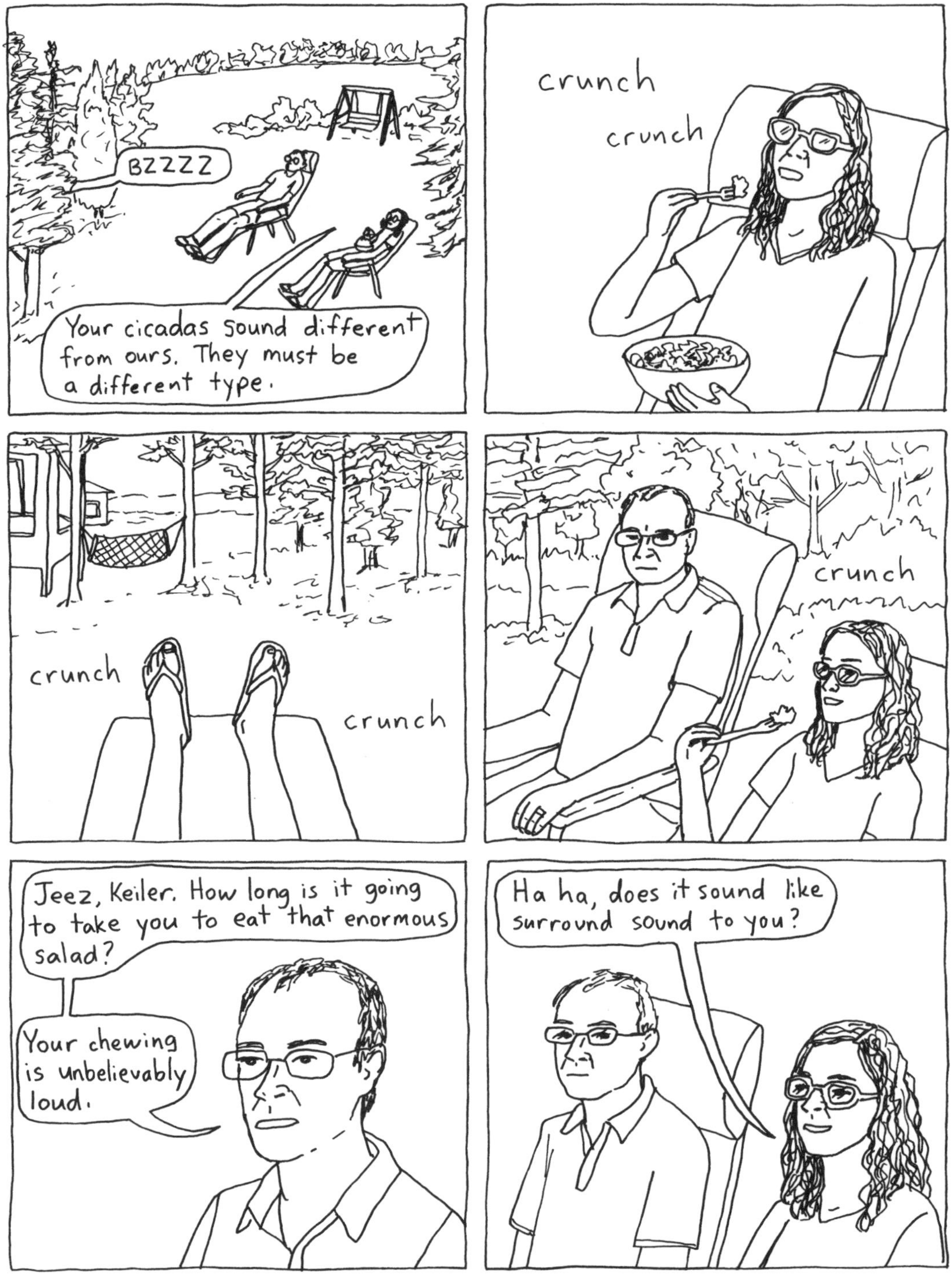
BZZZZ
Your cicadas sound different from ours. They must be a different type.
crunch
crunch
crunch
crunch
crunch
Jeez, Keiler. How long is it going to take you to eat that enormous salad?
Your chewing is unbelievably loud.
Ha ha, does it sound like surround sound to you?

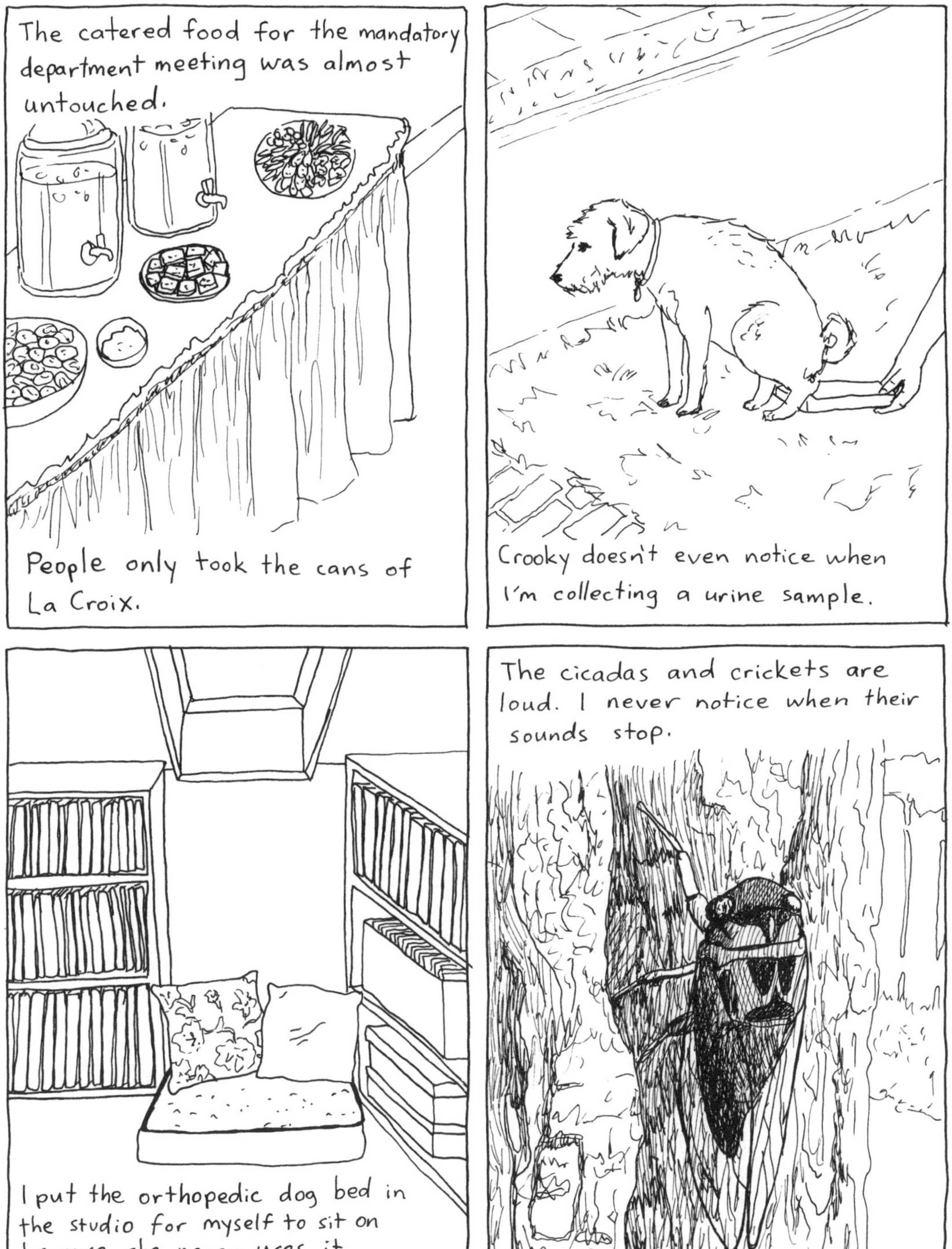
The catered food for the mandatory department meeting was almost untouched.
People only took the cans of La Croix.
Crooky doesn't even notice when I'm collecting a urine sample.
I put the orthopedic dog bed in the studio for myself to sit on because she never uses it.
The cicadas and crickets are loud. I never notice when their sounds stop.

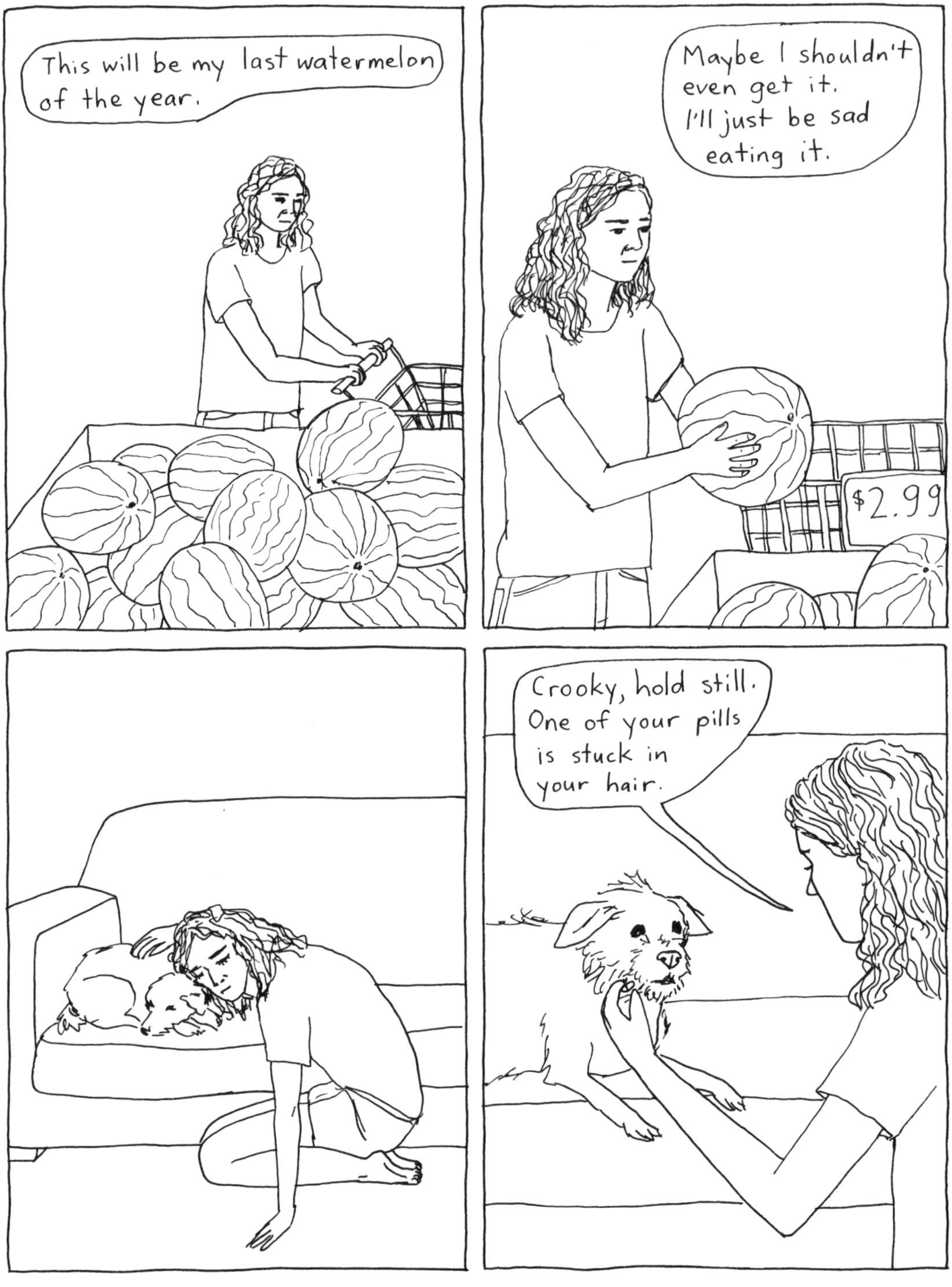
This will be my last watermelon of the year.
Maybe I shouldn't even get it. I'll just be sad eating it.
$2.99
Crooky, hold still. One of your pills is stuck in your hair.

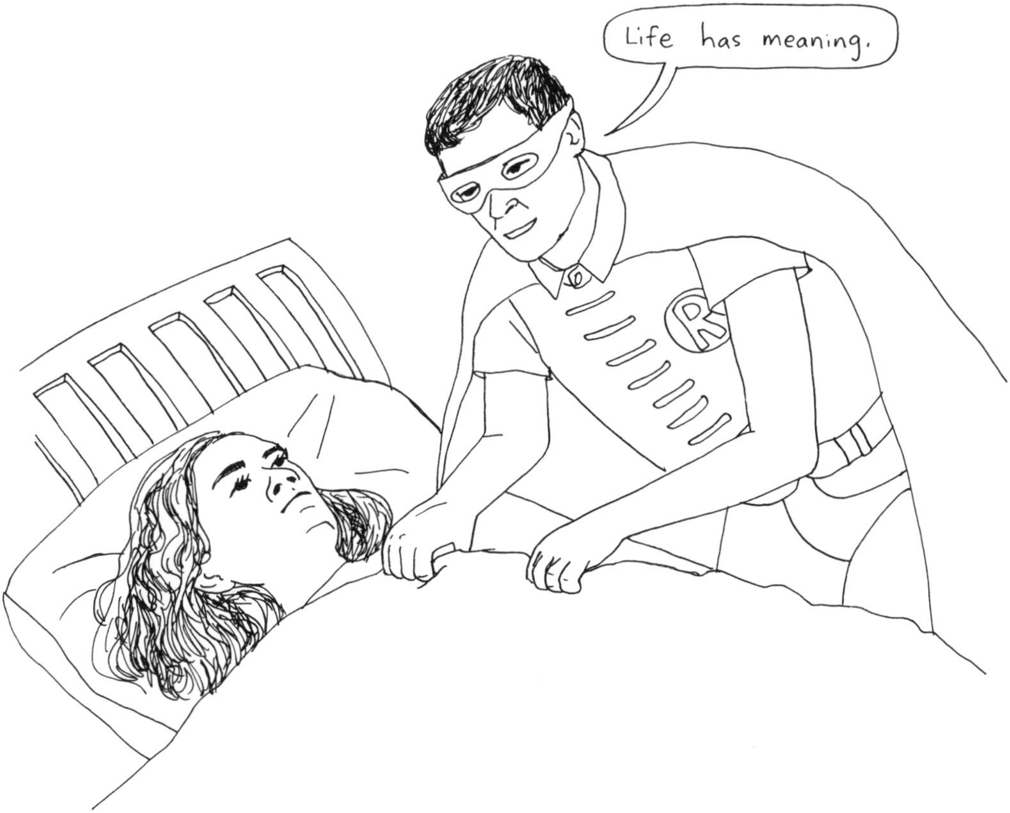
Life has meaning.

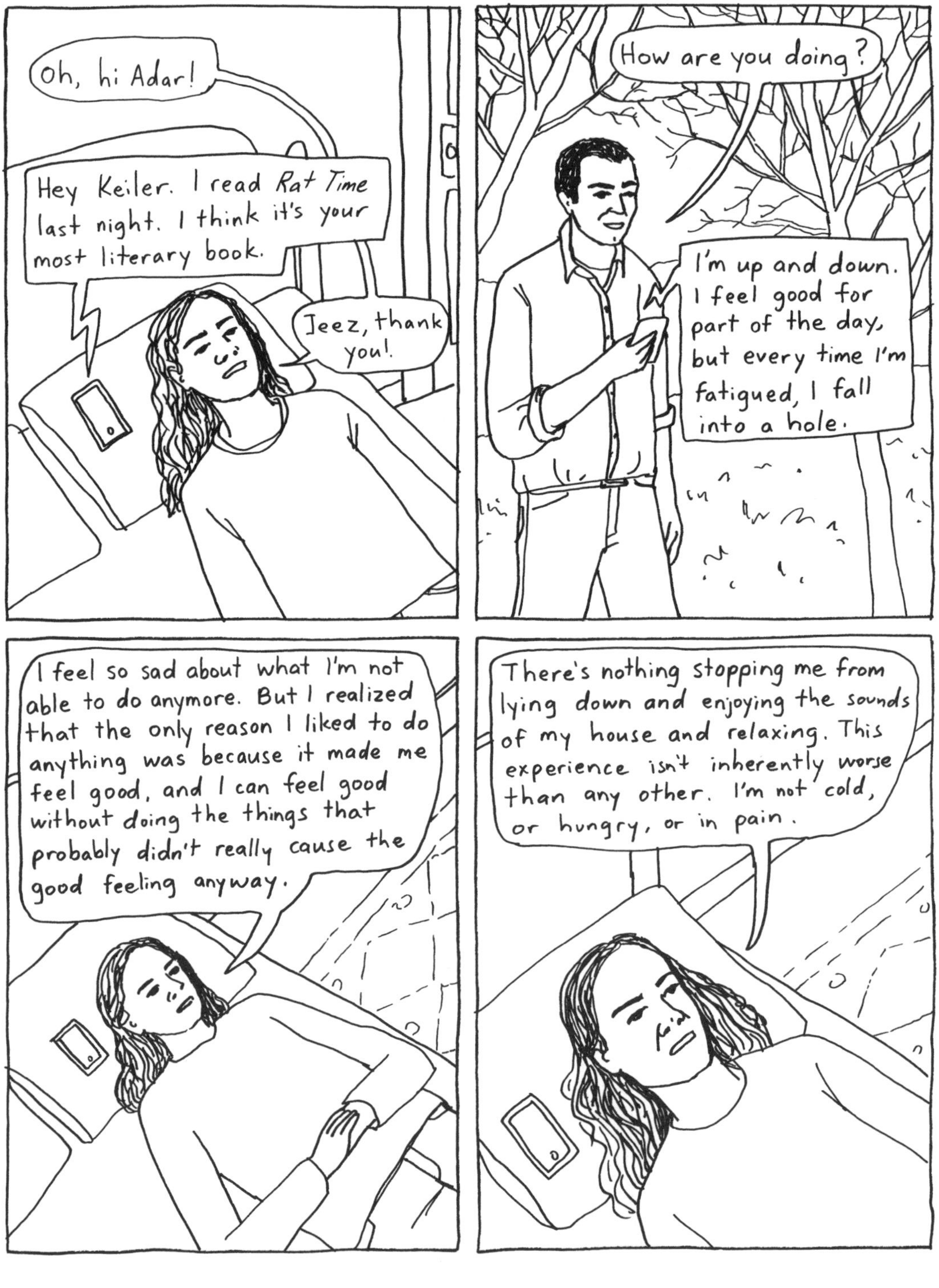

Oh, hi Adar!
Hey Keiler. I read *Rat Time* last night. I think it's your most literary book.
Jeez, thank you!
How are you doing?
I'm up and down. I feel good for part of the day, but every time I'm fatigued, I fall into a hole.
I feel so sad about what I'm not able to do anymore. But I realized that the only reason I liked to do anything was because it made me feel good, and I can feel good without doing the things that probably didn't really cause the good feeling anyway.
There's nothing stopping me from lying down and enjoying the sounds of my house and relaxing. This experience isn't inherently worse than any other. I'm not cold, or hungry, or in pain.

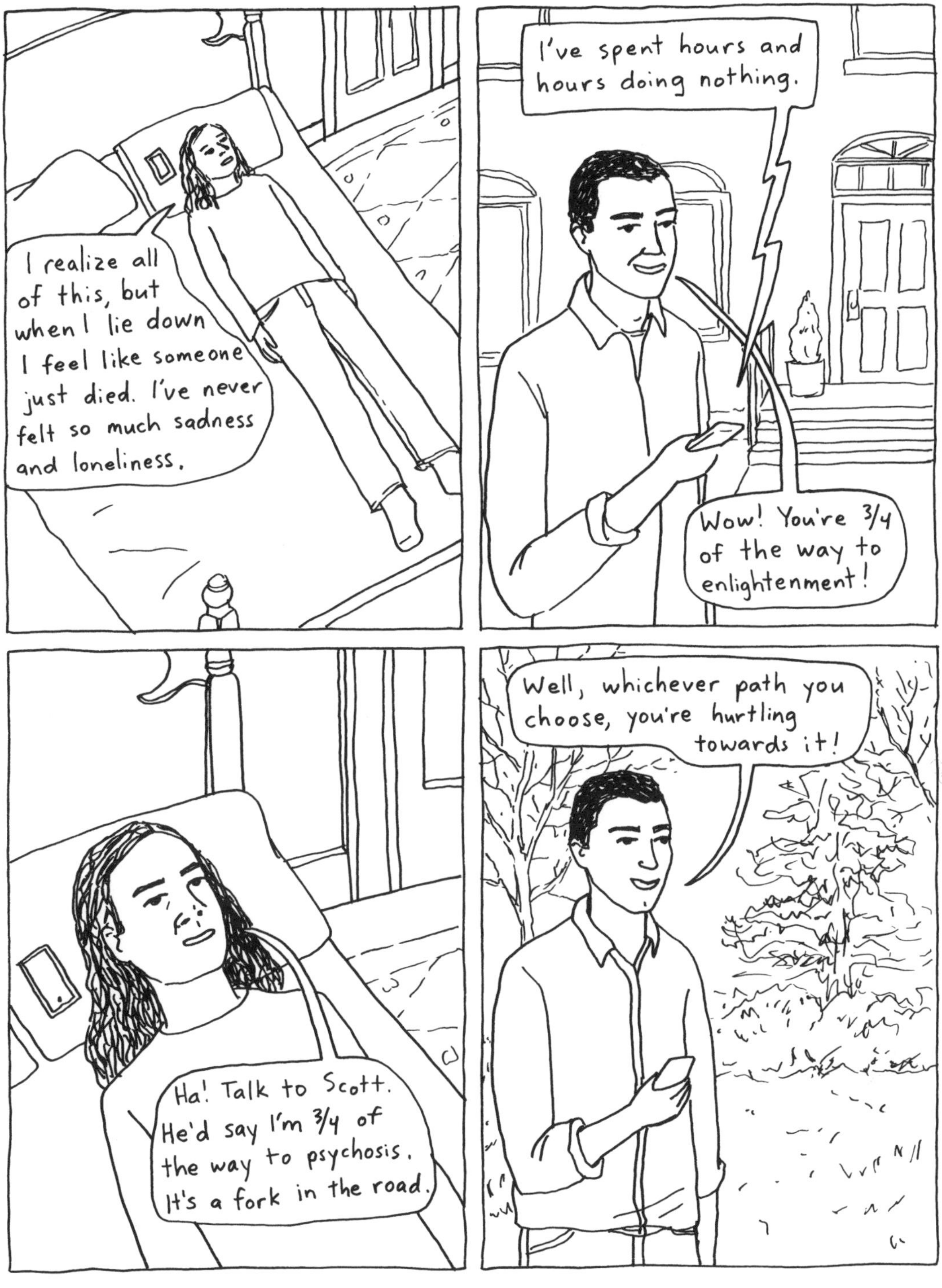
I realize all of this, but when I lie down I feel like someone just died. I've never felt so much sadness and loneliness.
I've spent hours and hours doing nothing.
Wow! You're 3/4 of the way to enlightenment!
Ha! Talk to Scott. He'd say I'm 3/4 of the way to psychosis. It's a fork in the road.
Well, whichever path you choose, you're hurtling towards it!

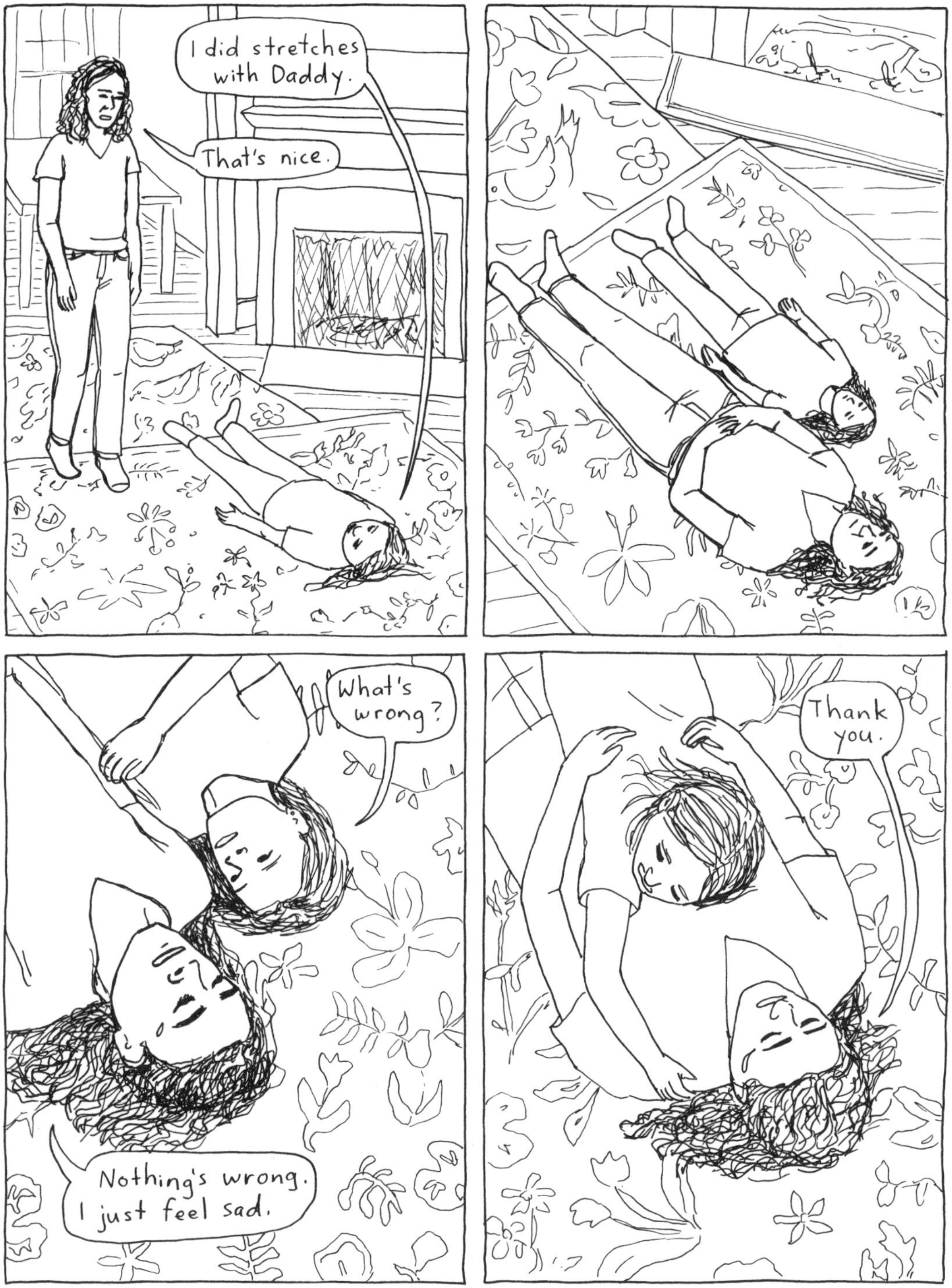
I did stretches with Daddy.
That's nice.
What's wrong?
Nothing's wrong. I just feel sad.
Thank you.

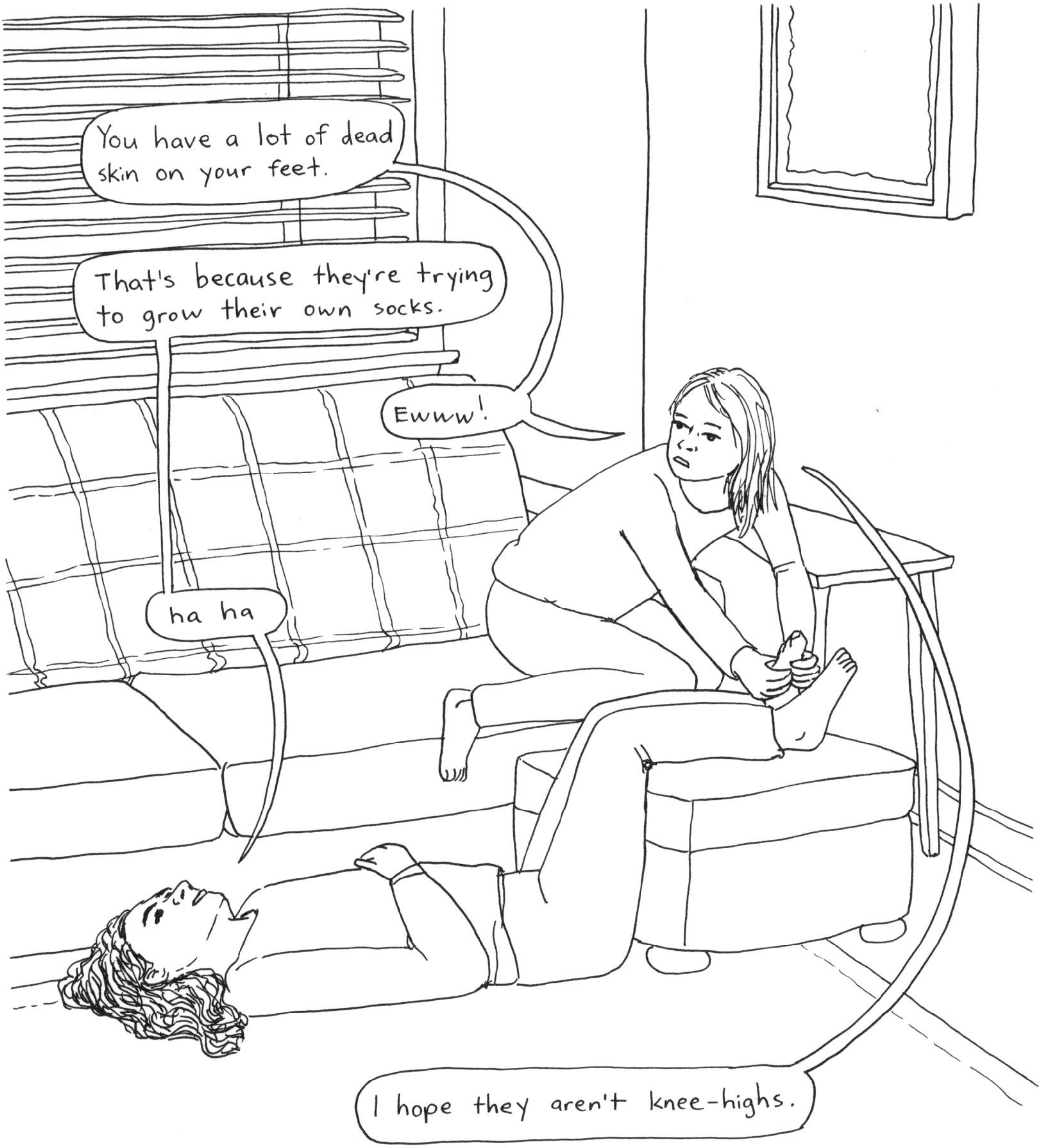
You have a lot of dead skin on your feet.
That's because they're trying to grow their own socks.
Ewww!
ha ha
I hope they aren't knee-highs.

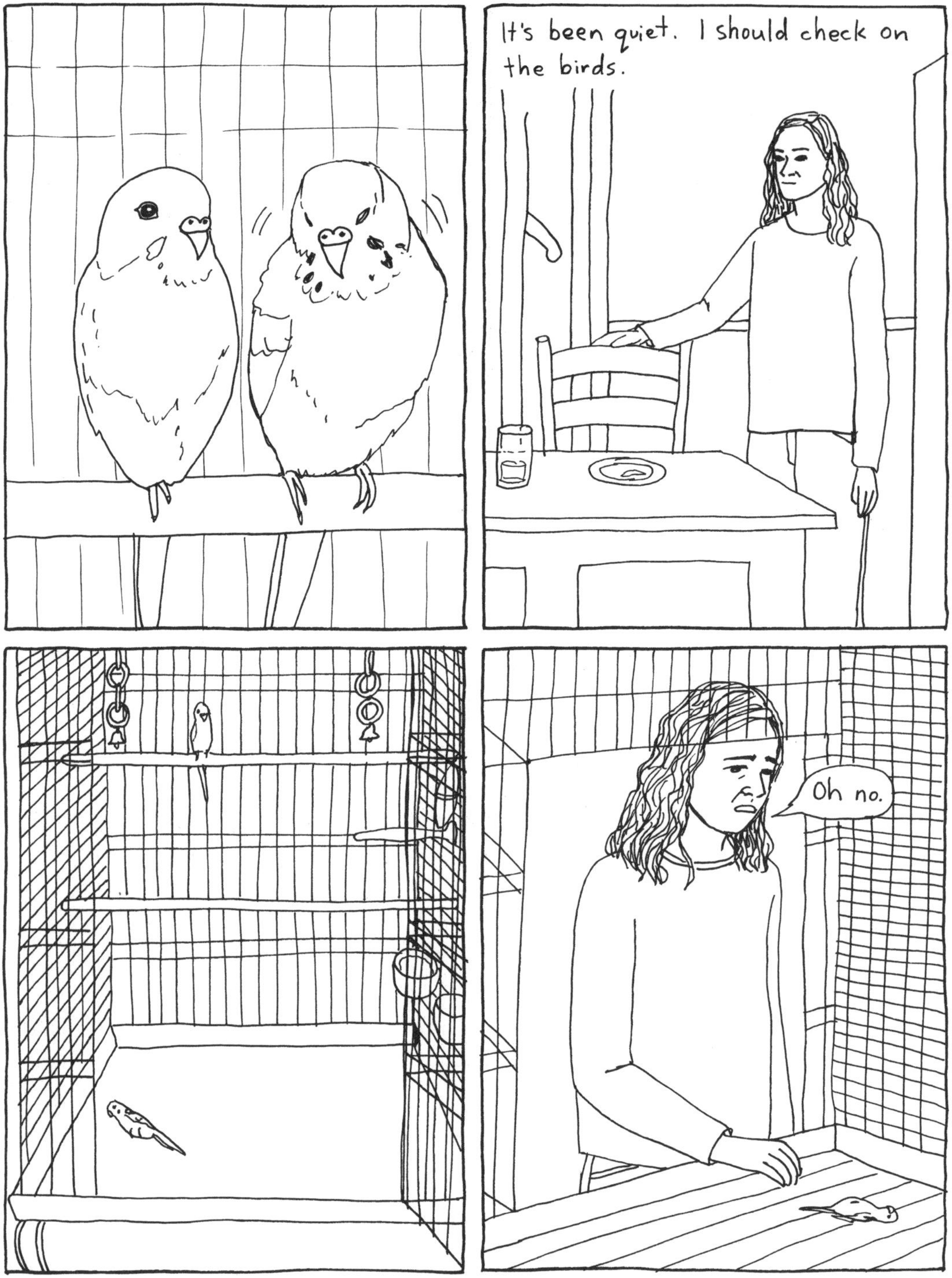
It's been quiet. I should check on the birds.
Oh no.

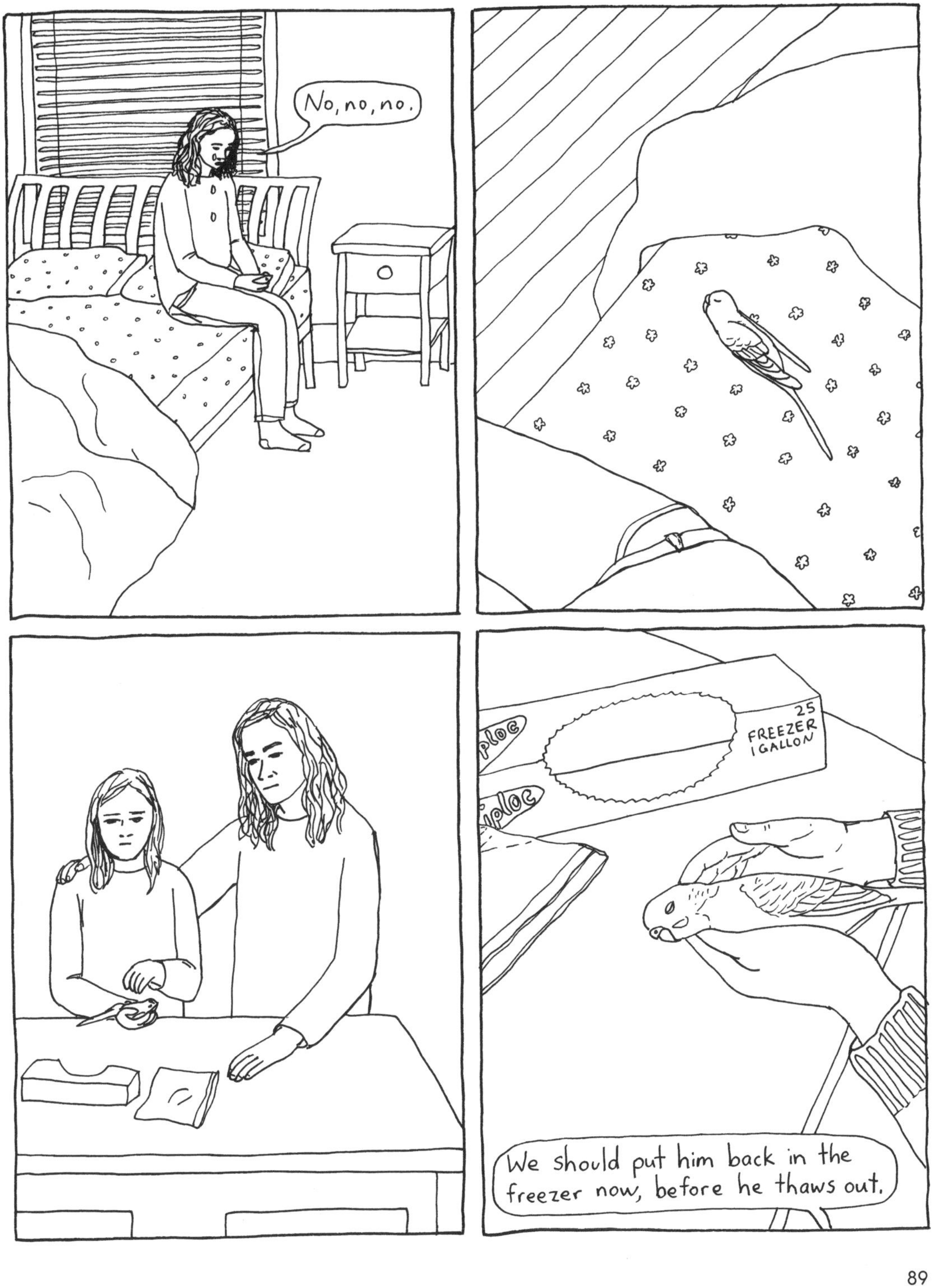
No, no, no.
25
FREEZER
1 GALLON
We should put him back in the freezer now, before he thaws out.

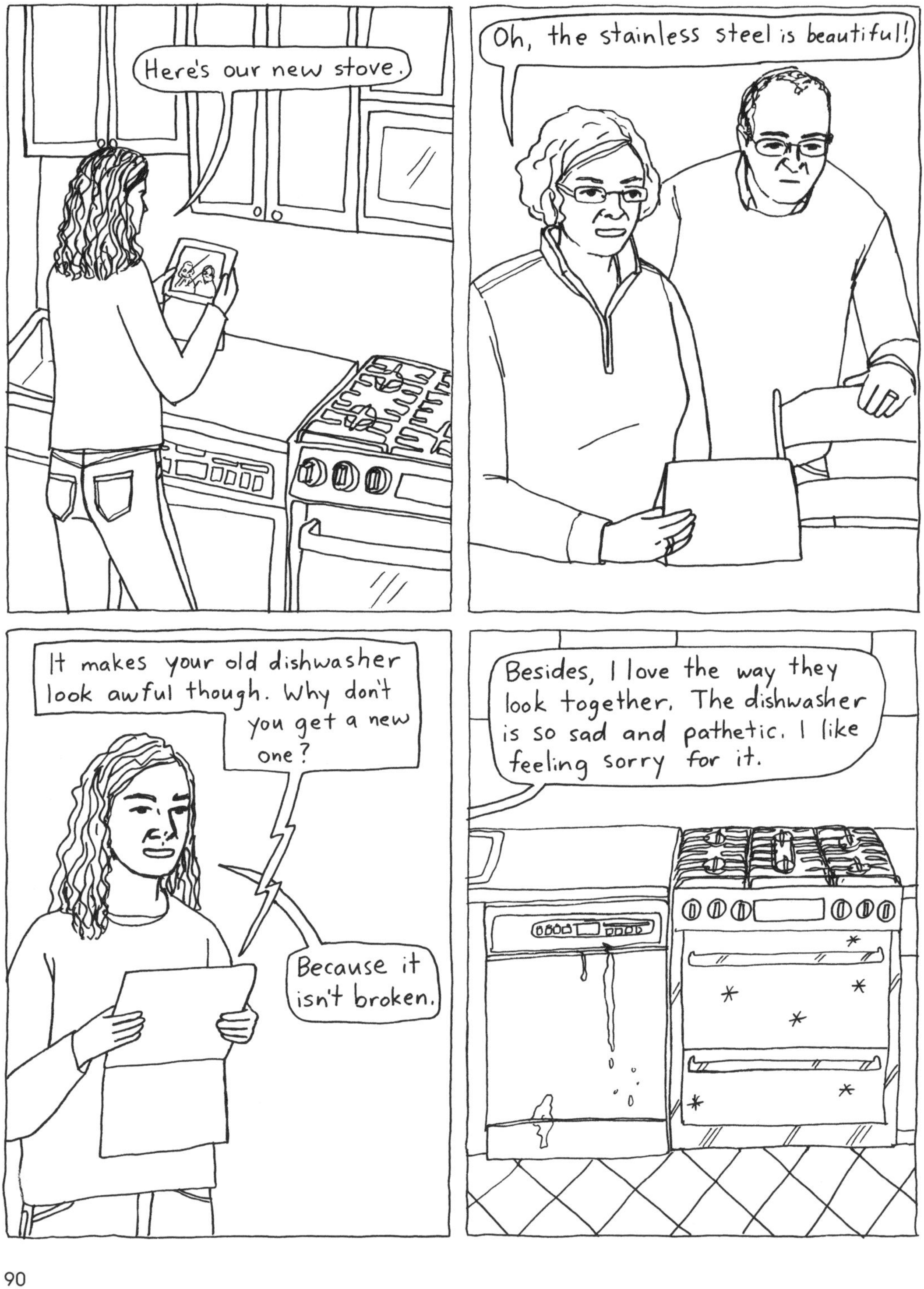
Here's our new stove.
Oh, the stainless steel is beautiful!
It makes your old dishwasher look awful though. Why don't you get a new one?
Because it isn't broken.
Besides, I love the way they look together. The dishwasher is so sad and pathetic. I like feeling sorry for it.

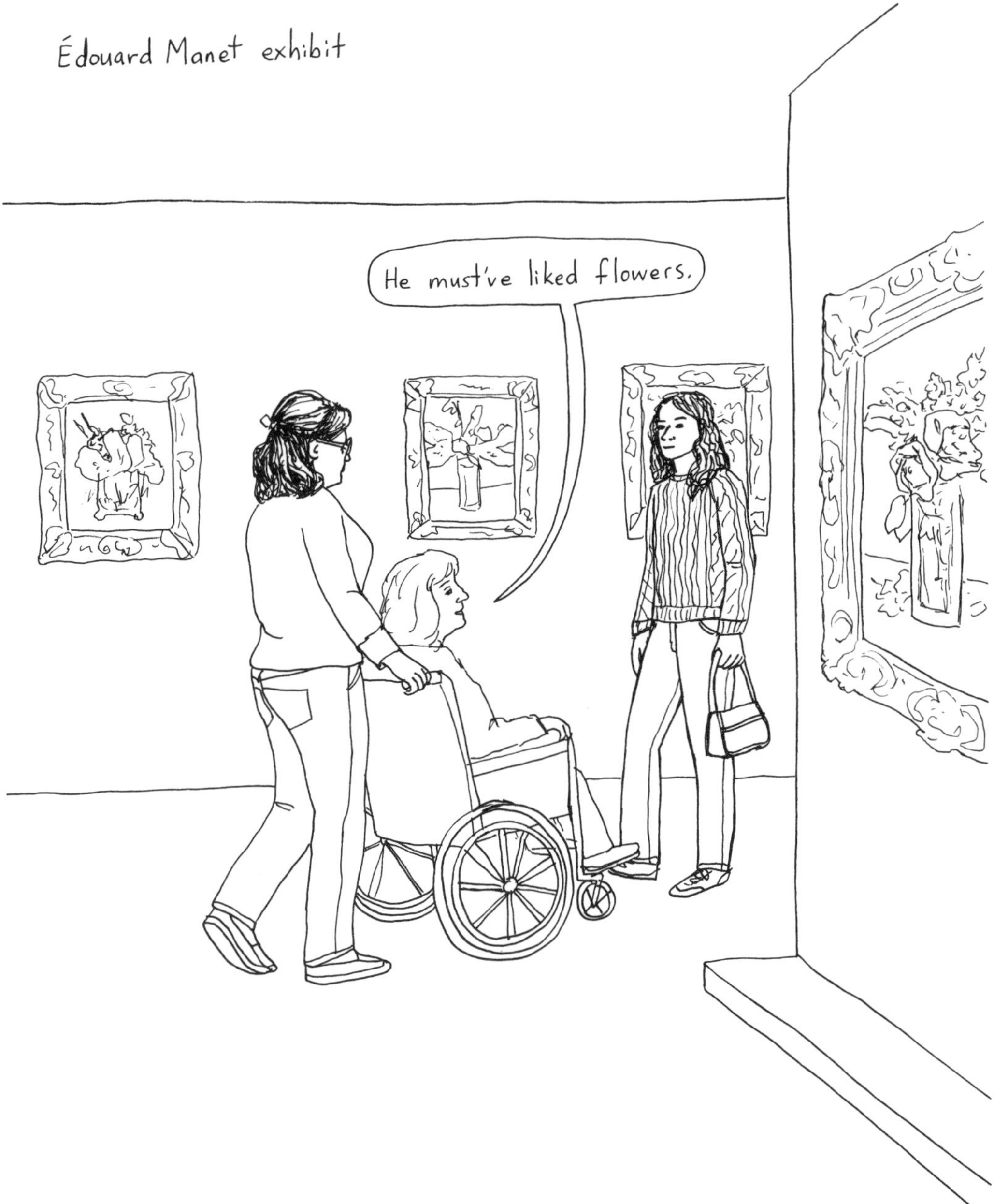
Édouard Manet exhibit
He must've liked flowers.

Shoot. He didn't notice that I'm in here.

Now I have no choice but to startle him.

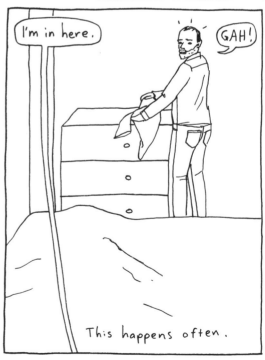

I'm in here.

GAH!

This happens often.

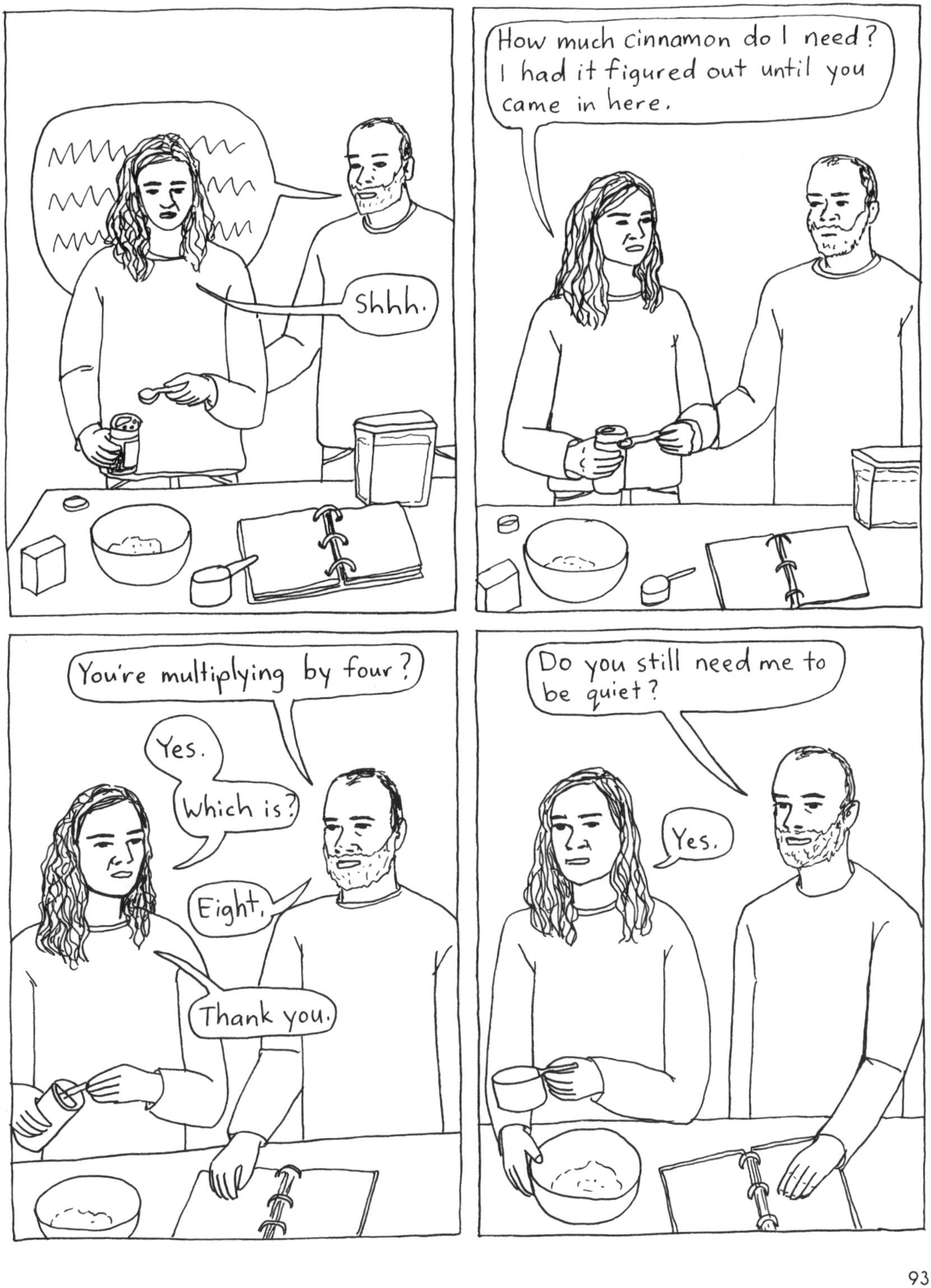
Shhh.
How much cinnamon do I need? I had it figured out until you came in here.
You're multiplying by four?
Yes.
Which is?
Eight.
Thank you.
Do you still need me to be quiet?
Yes.

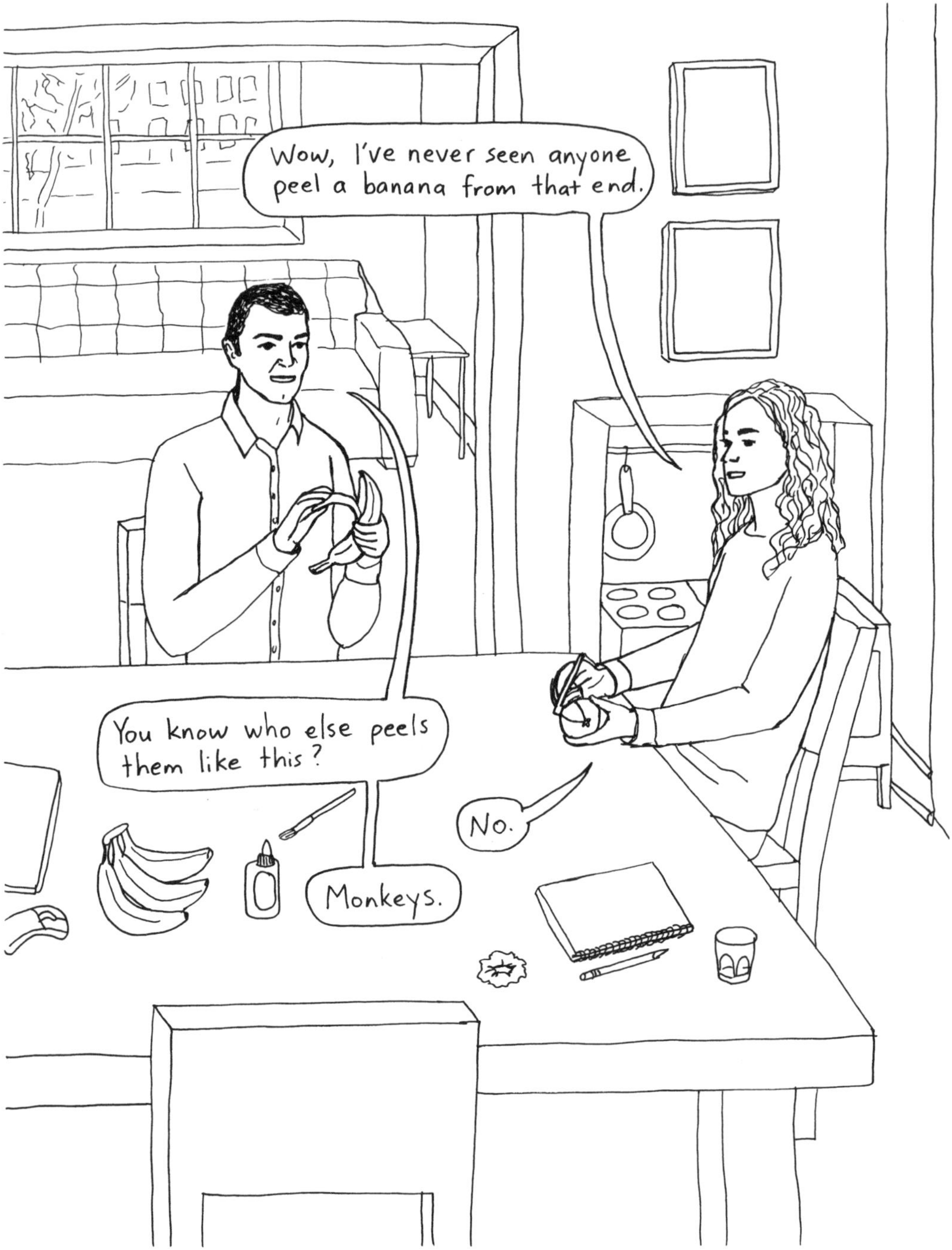
Wow, I've never seen anyone peel a banana from that end.
You know who else peels them like this?
No.
Monkeys.

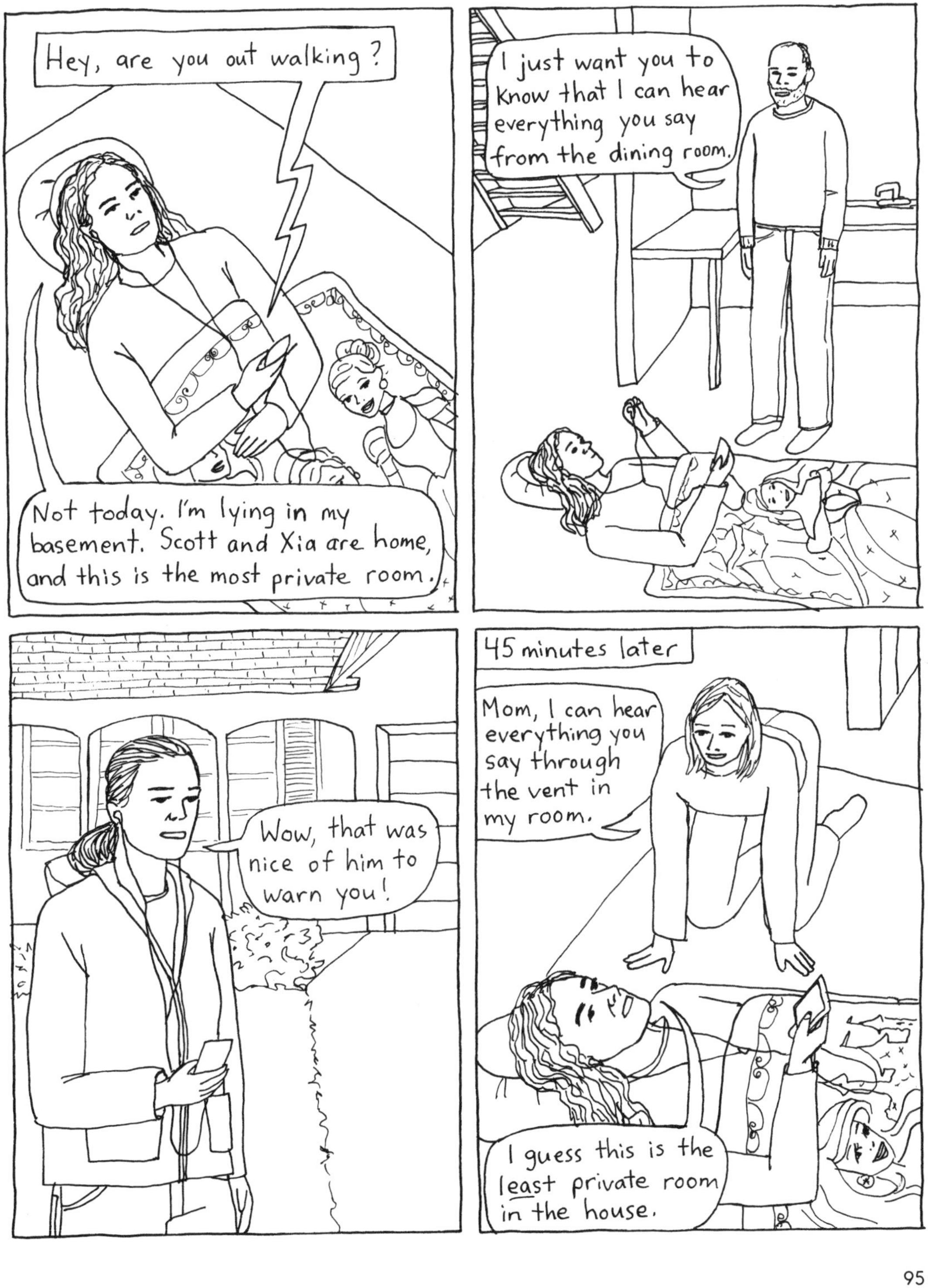
Hey, are you out walking?
Not today. I'm lying in my basement. Scott and Xia are home, and this is the most private room.
I just want you to know that I can hear everything you say from the dining room.
Wow, that was nice of him to warn you!
45 minutes later
Mom, I can hear everything you say through the vent in my room.
I guess this is the least private room in the house.

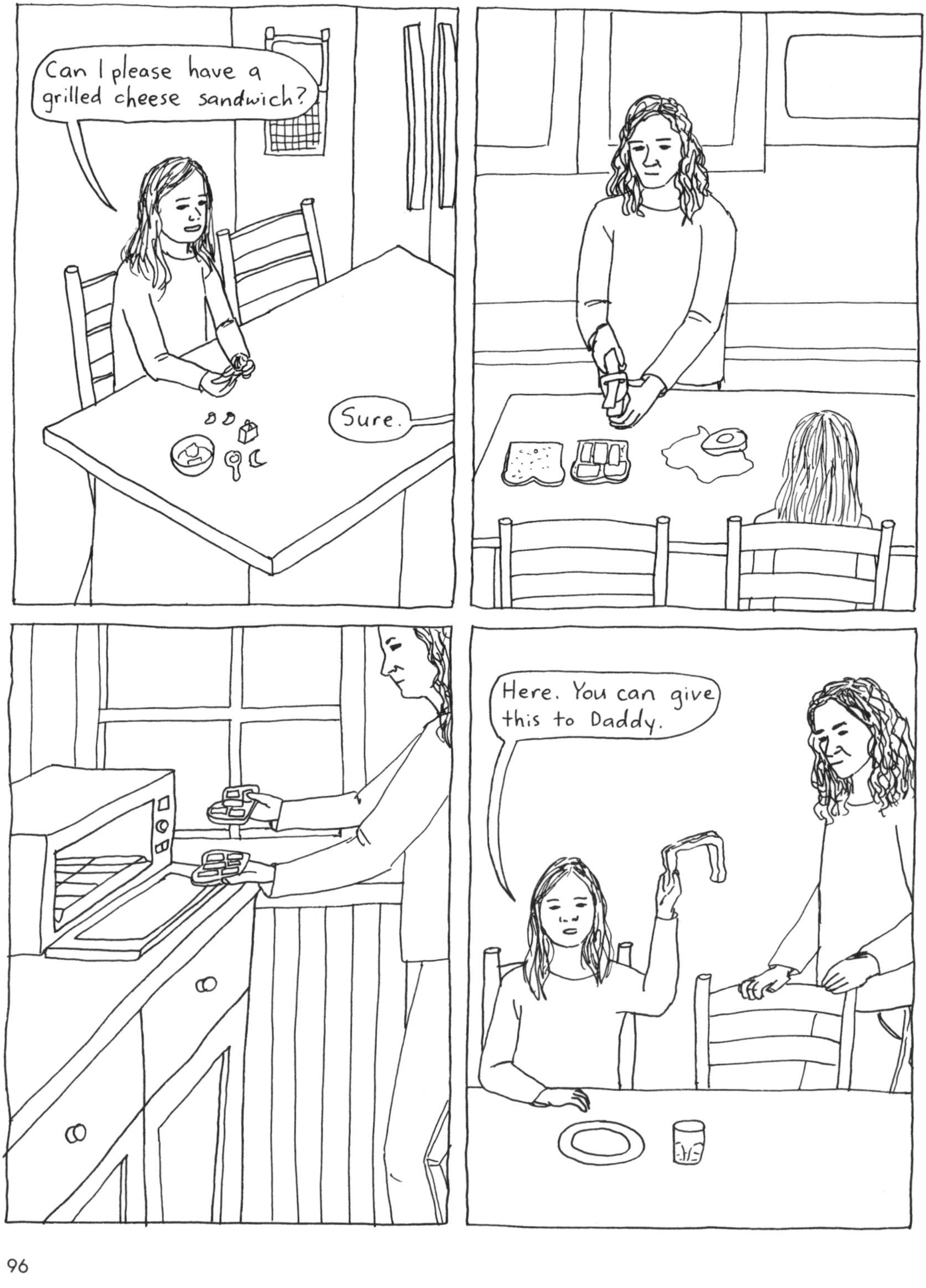
Can I please have a grilled cheese sandwich?
Sure.
Here. You can give this to Daddy.

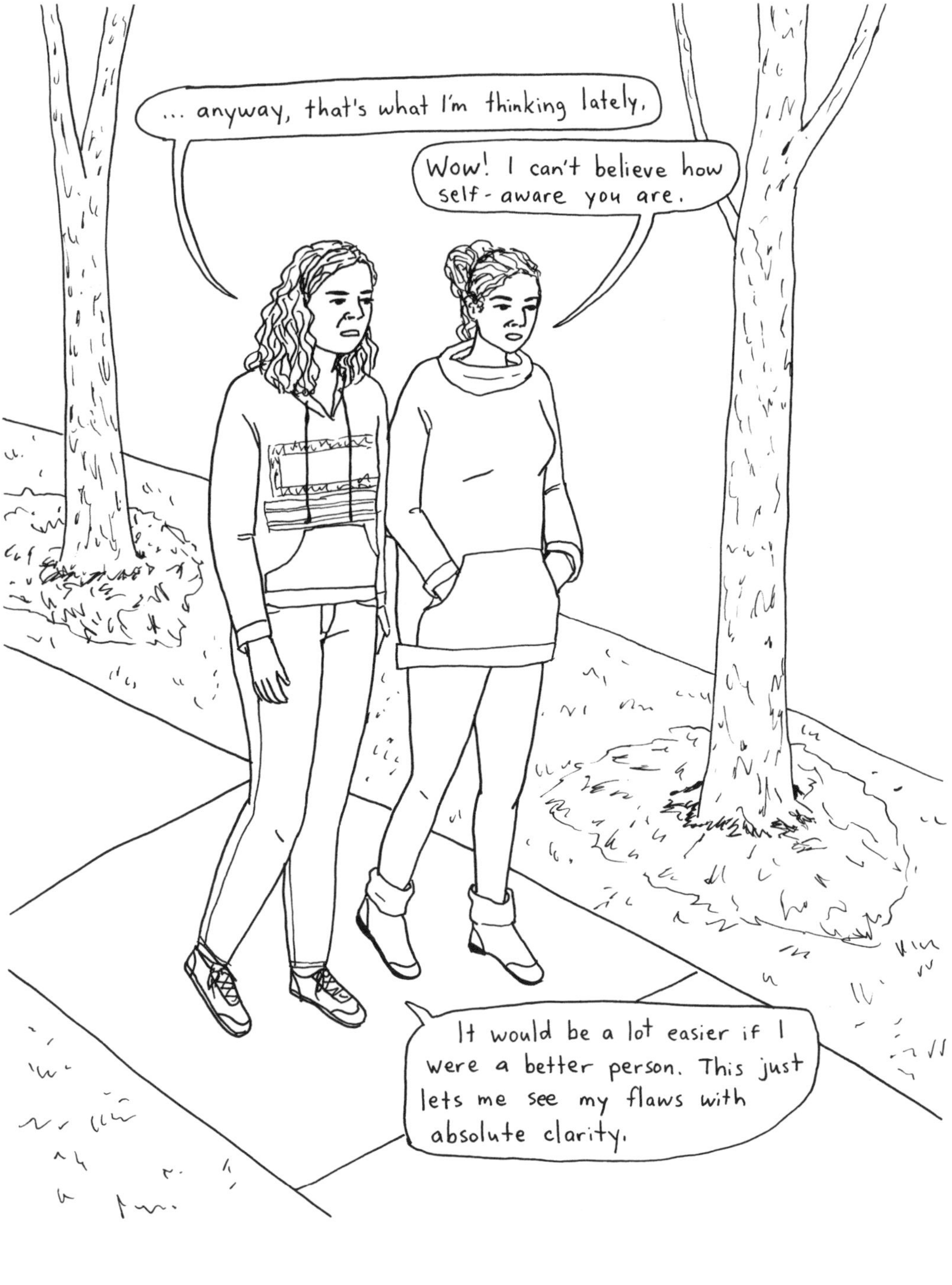
... anyway, that's what I'm thinking lately.
Wow! I can't believe how self-aware you are.
It would be a lot easier if I were a better person. This just lets me see my flaws with absolute clarity.

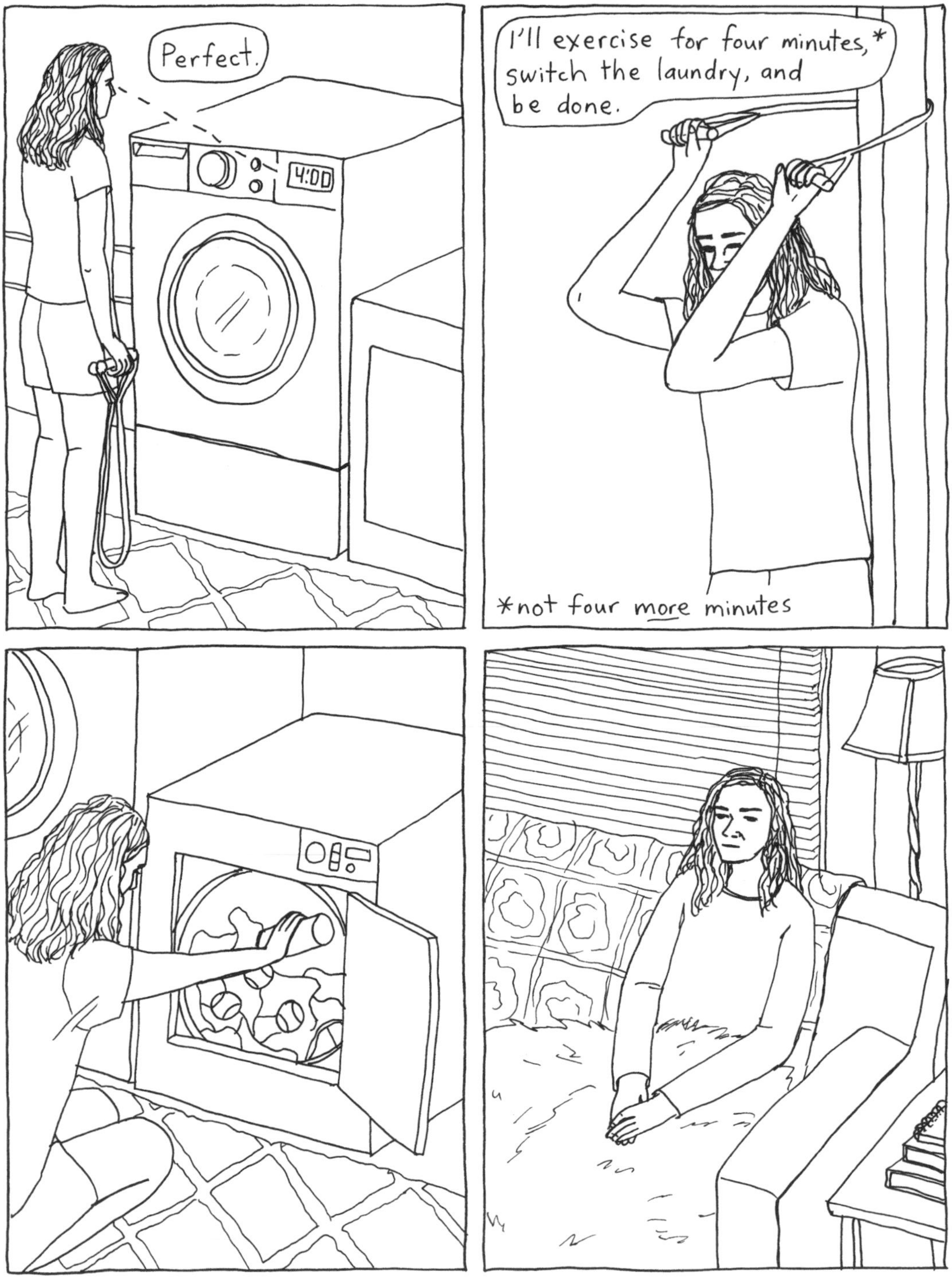
Perfect.
4:00
I'll exercise for four minutes,* switch the laundry, and be done.
*not four more minutes

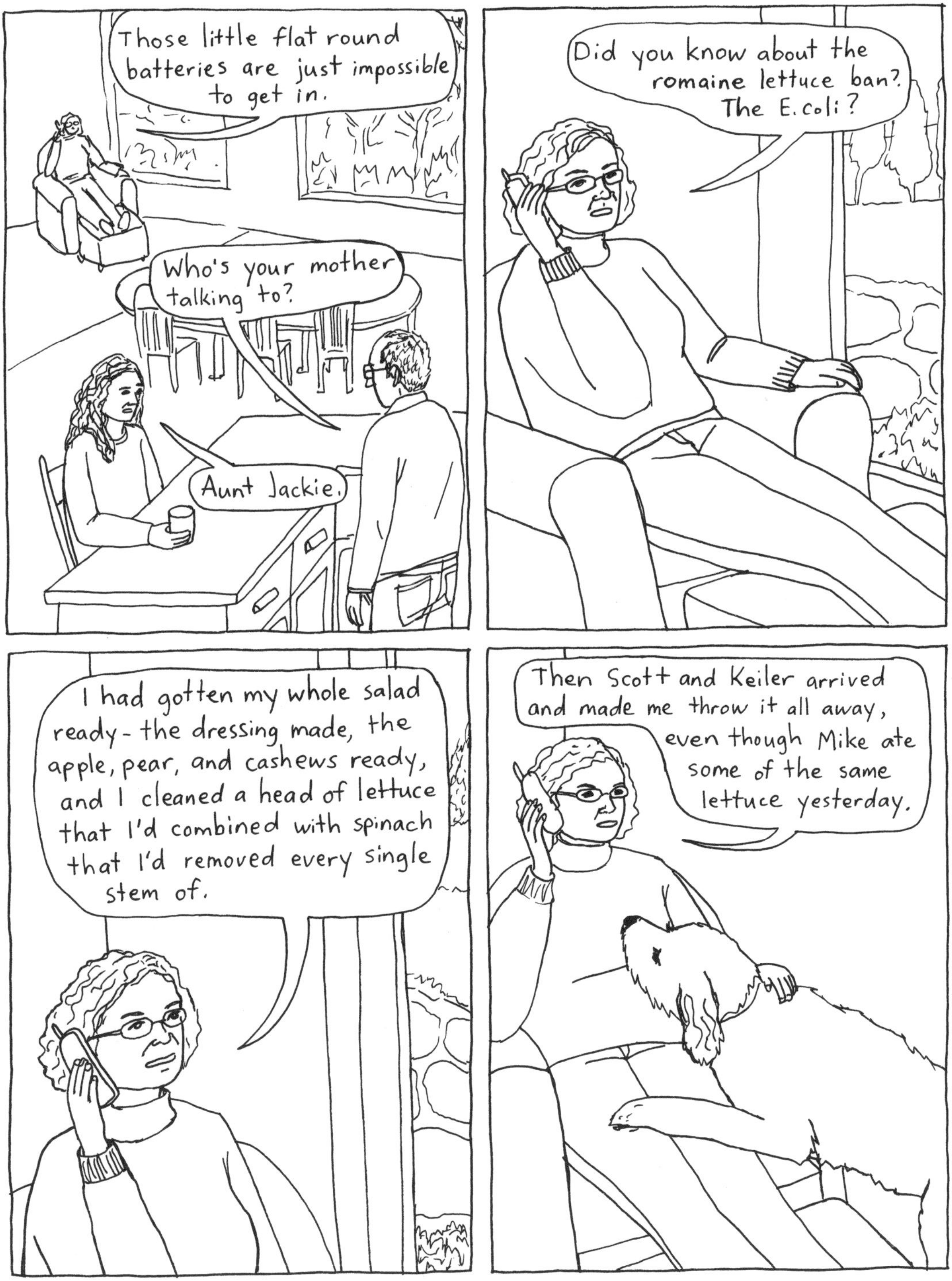
Those little flat round batteries are just impossible to get in.
Who's your mother talking to?
Aunt Jackie.
Did you know about the romaine lettuce ban? The E.coli?
I had gotten my whole salad ready - the dressing made, the apple, pear, and cashews ready, and I cleaned a head of lettuce that I'd combined with spinach that I'd removed every single stem of.
Then Scott and Keiler arrived and made me throw it all away, even though Mike ate some of the same lettuce yesterday.

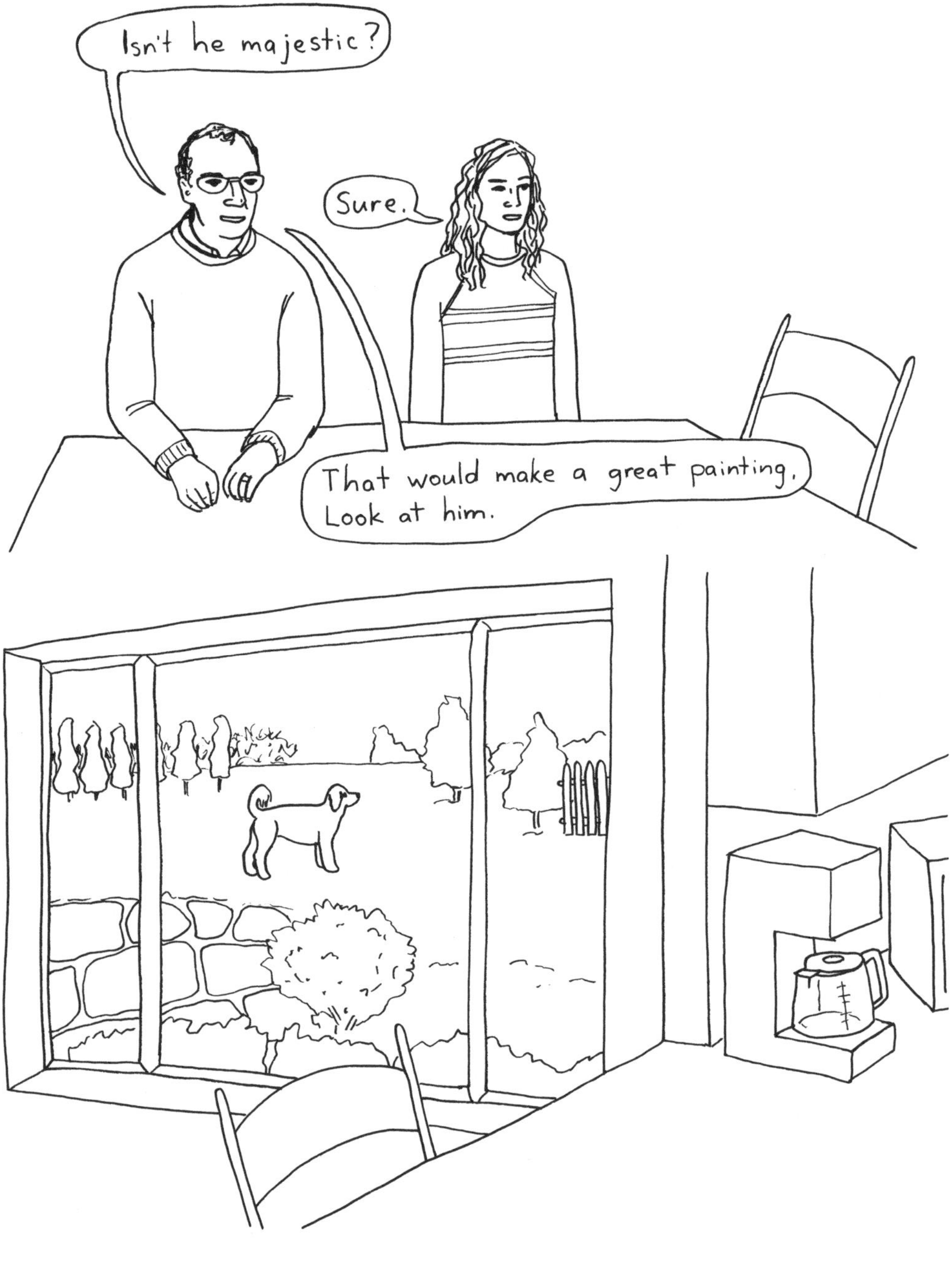
Isn't he majestic?
Sure.
That would make a great painting. Look at him.

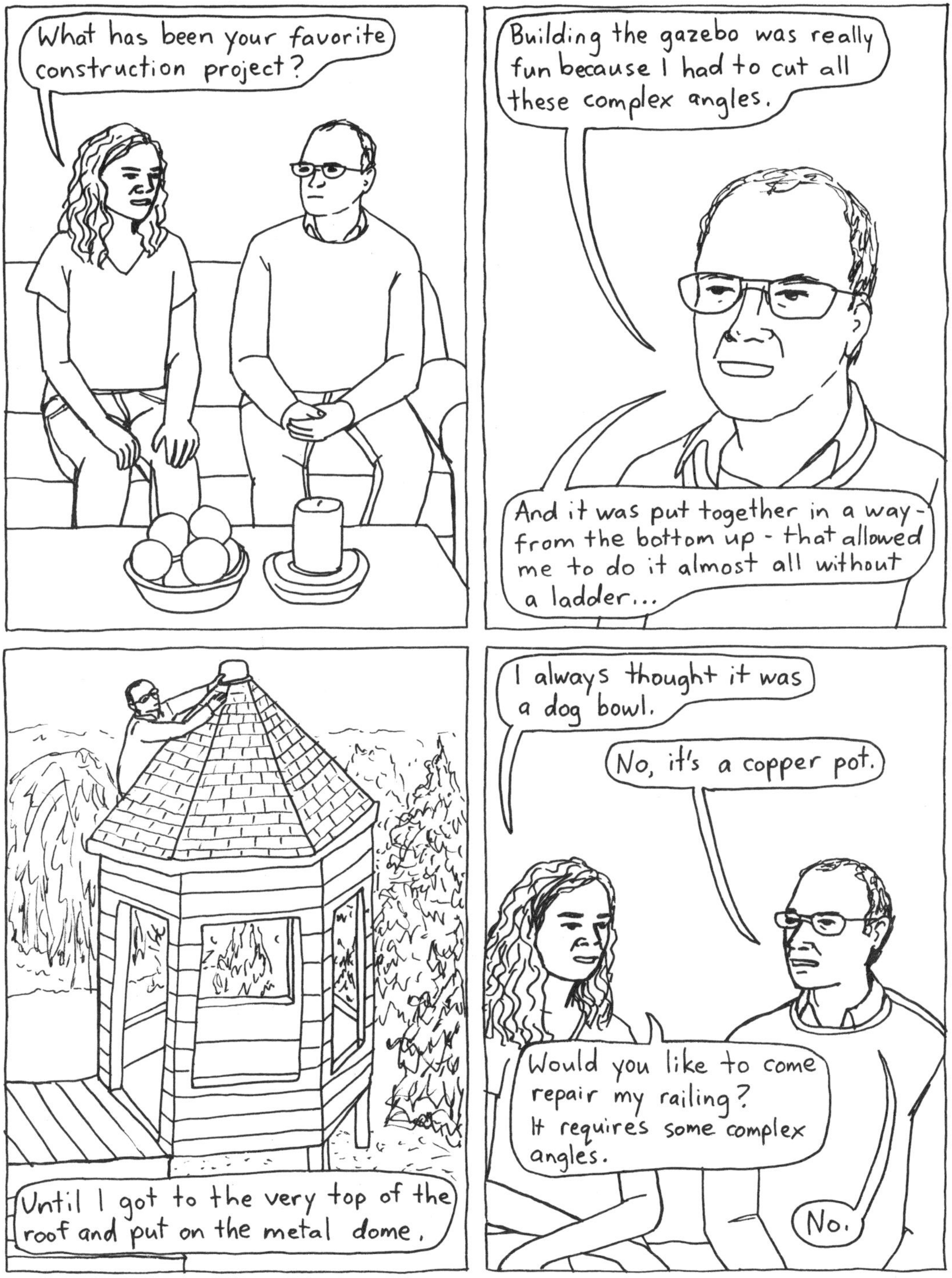
What has been your favorite construction project?
Building the gazebo was really fun because I had to cut all these complex angles.
And it was put together in a way - from the bottom up - that allowed me to do it almost all without a ladder...
Until I got to the very top of the roof and put on the metal dome.
I always thought it was a dog bowl.
No, it's a copper pot.
Would you like to come repair my railing? It requires some complex angles.
No.

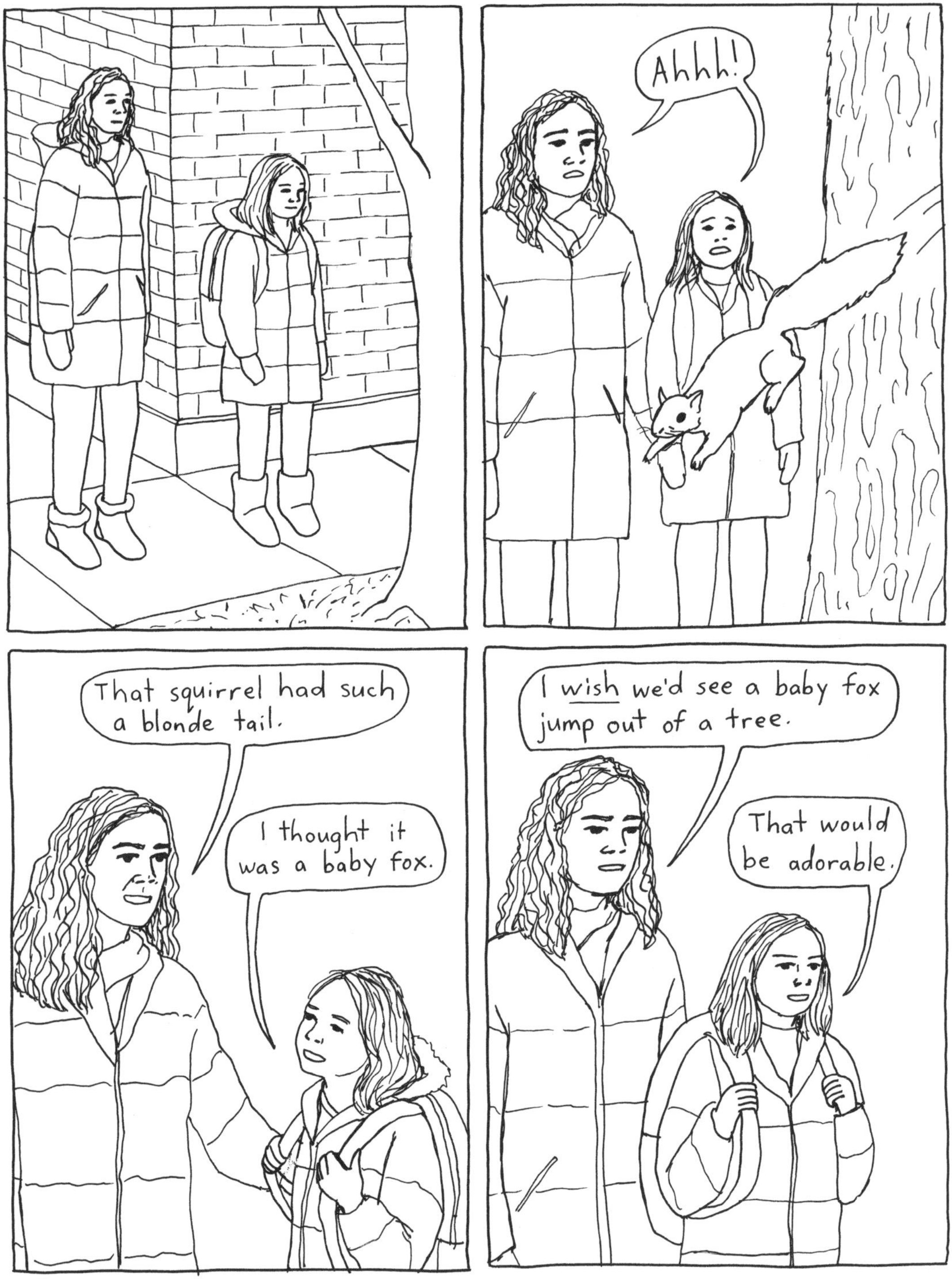
Ahhh!
That squirrel had such a blonde tail.
I thought it was a baby fox.
I wish we'd see a baby fox jump out of a tree.
That would be adorable.

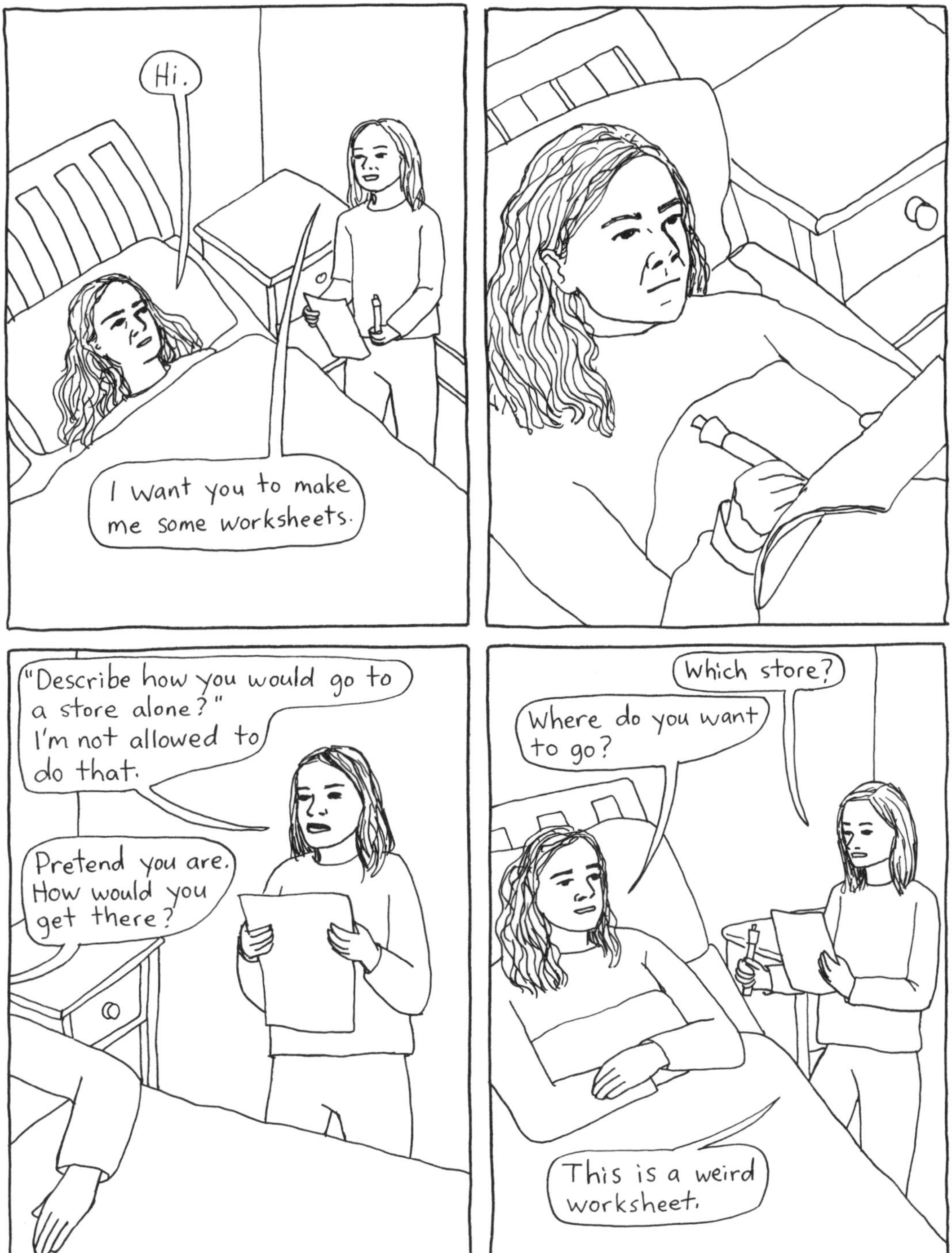
Hi.
I want you to make me some worksheets.
"Describe how you would go to a store alone?" I'm not allowed to do that.
Pretend you are. How would you get there?
Which store?
Where do you want to go?
This is a weird worksheet.

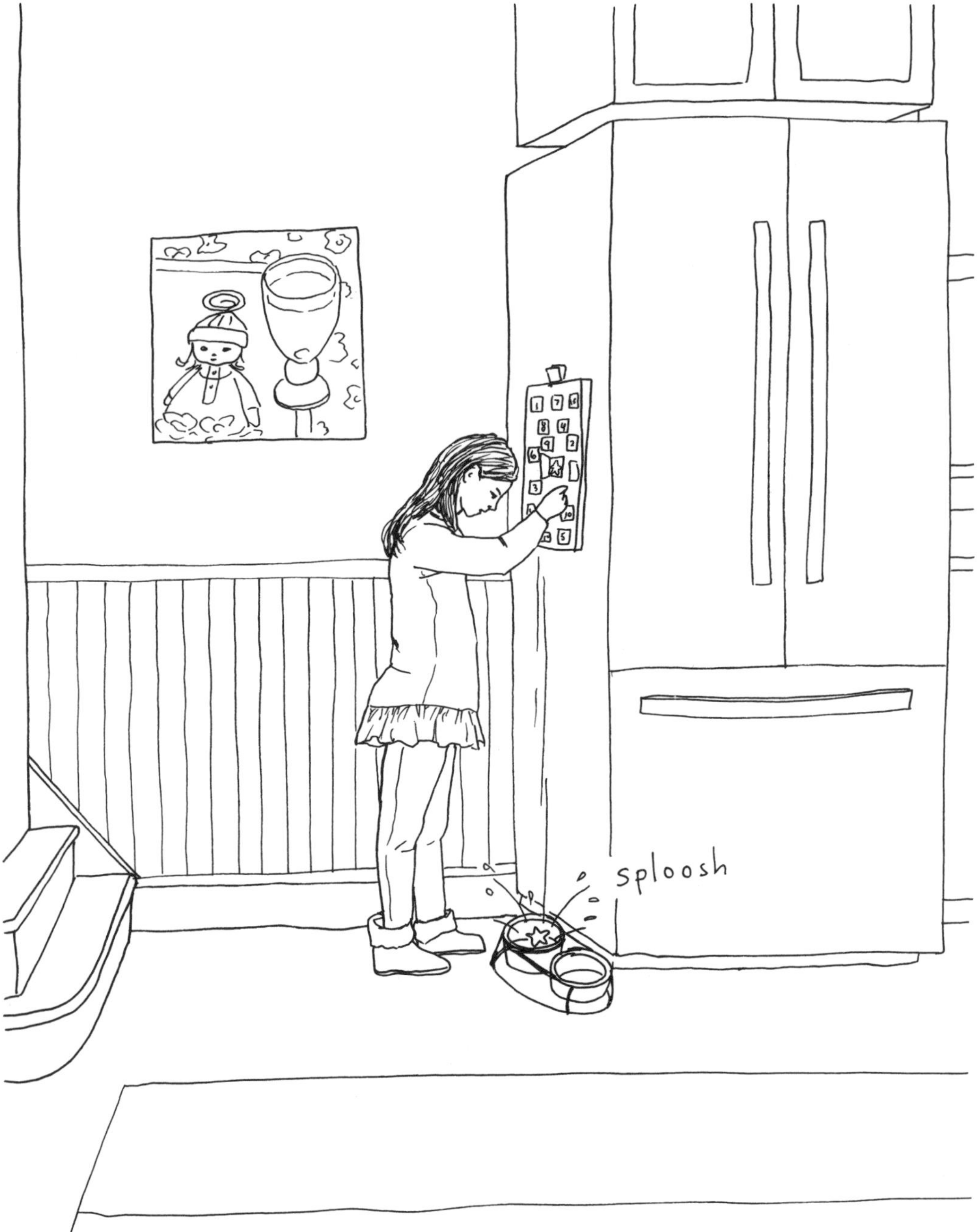
sploosh

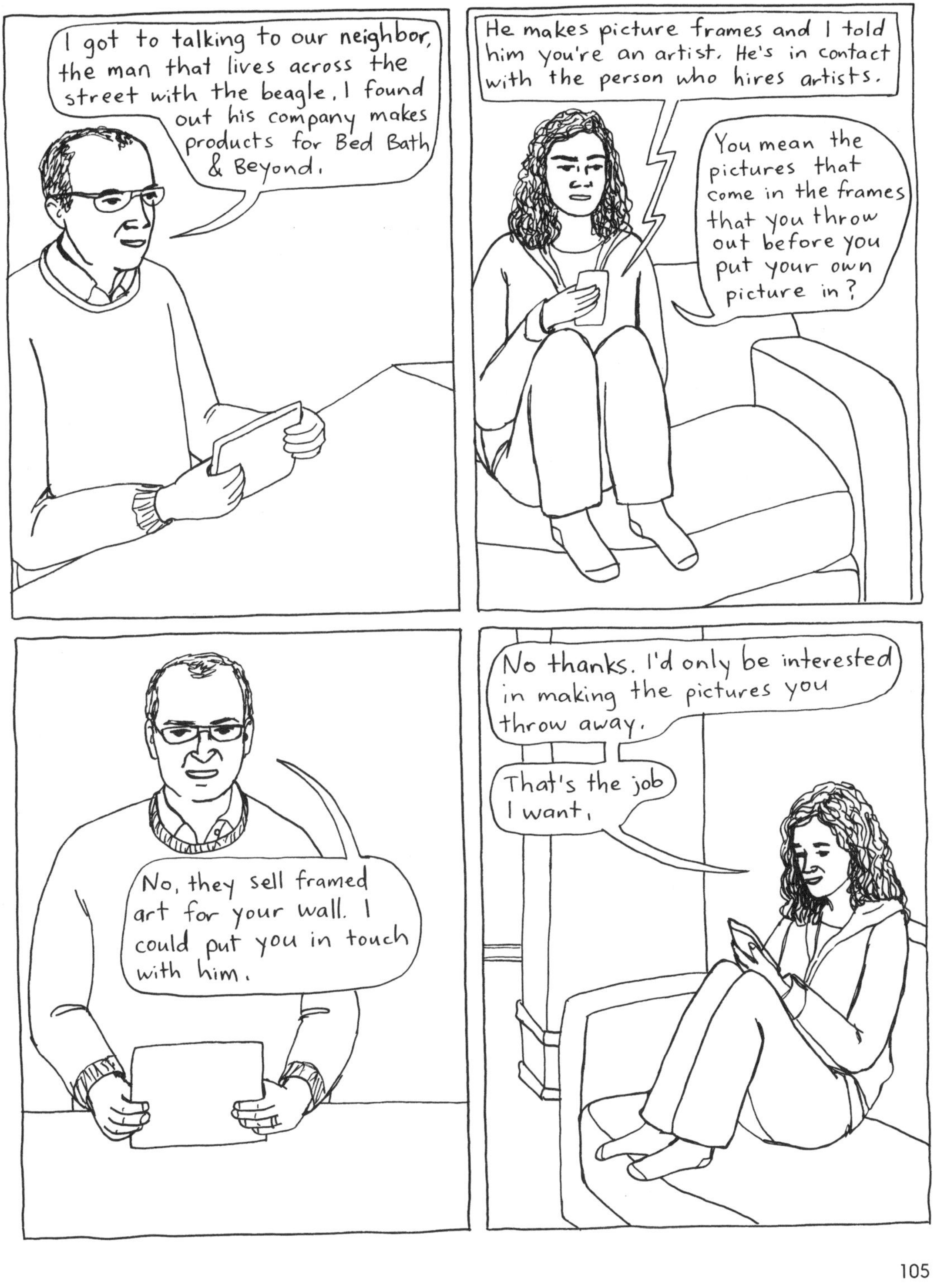
I got to talking to our neighbor, the man that lives across the street with the beagle. I found out his company makes products for Bed Bath & Beyond.
He makes picture frames and I told him you're an artist. He's in contact with the person who hires artists.
You mean the pictures that come in the frames that you throw out before you put your own picture in?
No, they sell framed art for your wall. I could put you in touch with him.
No thanks. I'd only be interested in making the pictures you throw away.
That's the job I want.

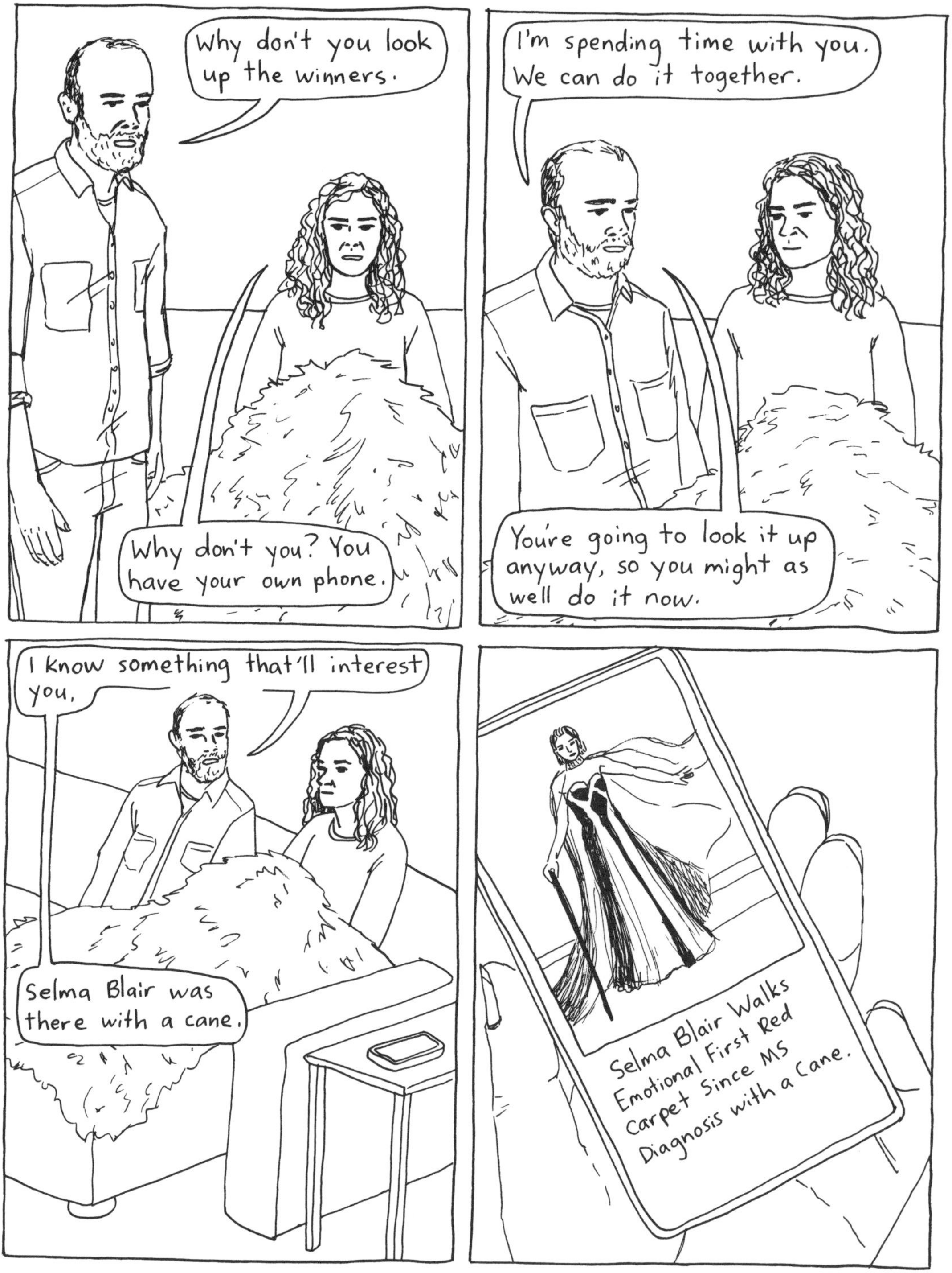
Why don't you look up the winners.
Why don't you? You have your own phone.
I'm spending time with you. We can do it together.
You're going to look it up anyway, so you might as well do it now.
I know something that'll interest you.
Selma Blair was there with a cane.
Selma Blair Walks Emotional First Red Carpet Since MS Diagnosis with a Cane.

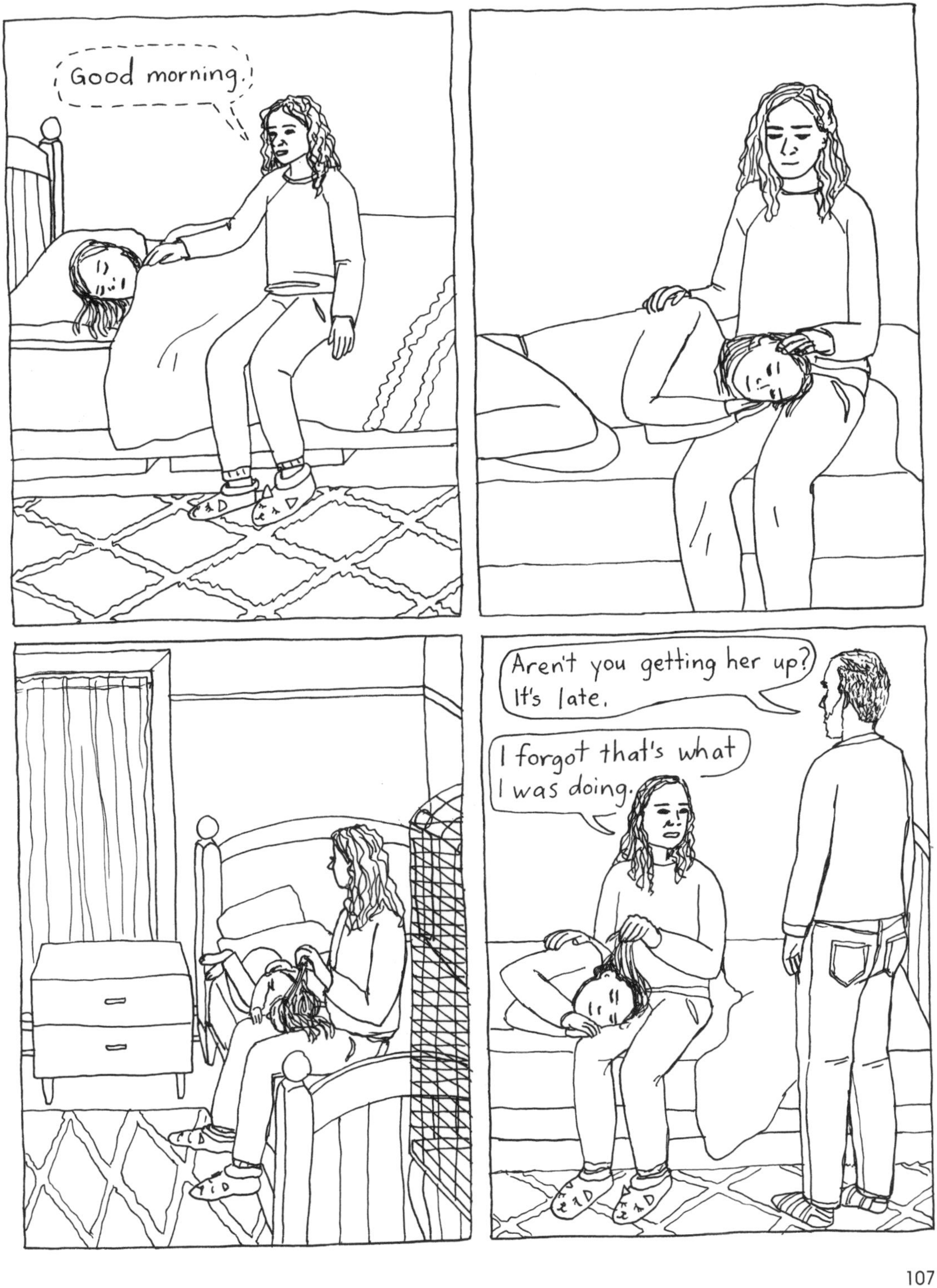
Good morning.
Aren't you getting her up? It's late.
I forgot that's what I was doing.

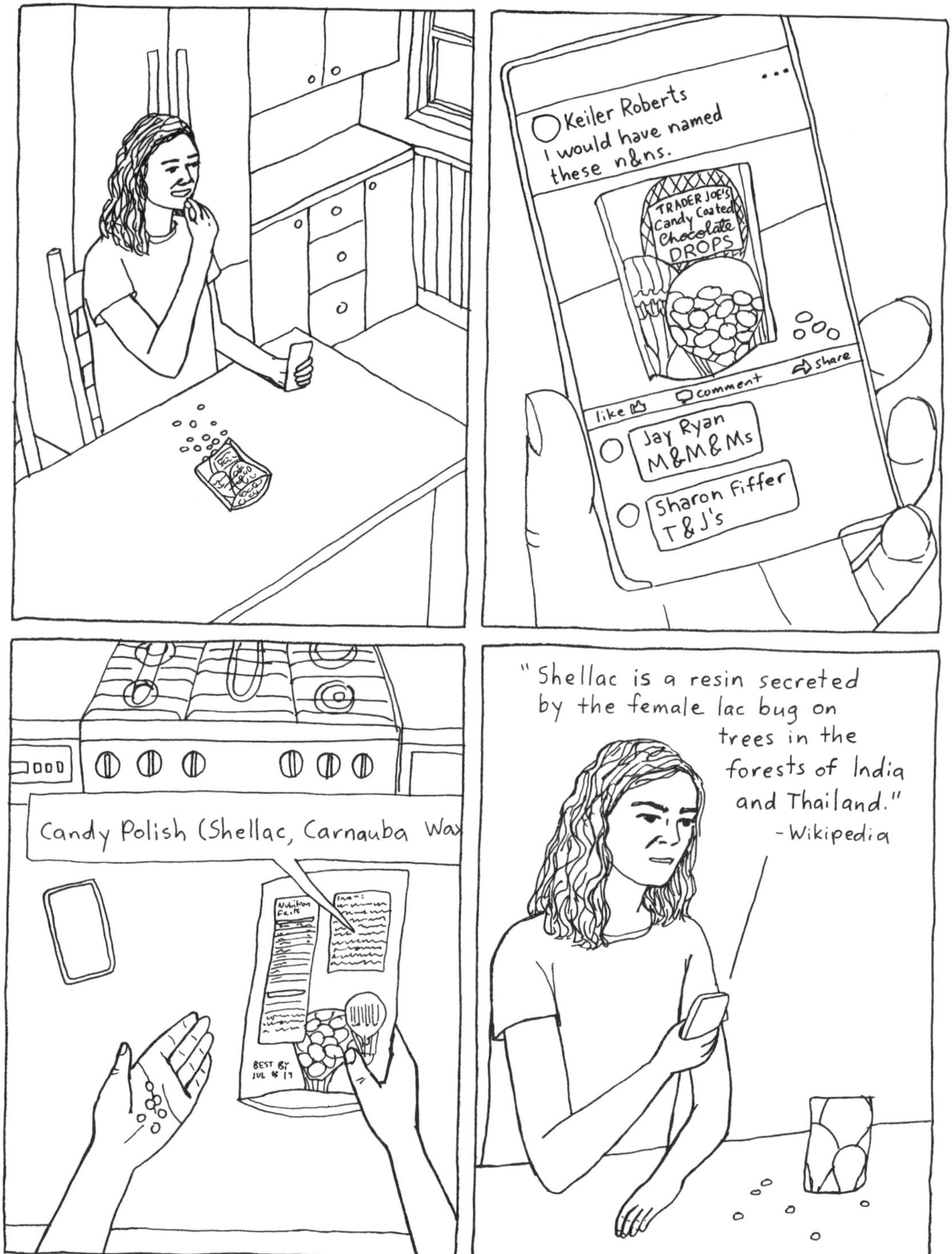
Keiler Roberts
I would have named these n&ns.
TRADER JOE'S Candy Coated Chocolate DROPS
like
comment
share
Jay Ryan M&M&Ms
Sharon Fiffer T&J's
Candy Polish (Shellac, Carnauba Wax
Nutrition Facts
BEST BY JUL 8 '17
"Shellac is a resin secreted by the female lac bug on trees in the forests of India and Thailand."
-Wikipedia

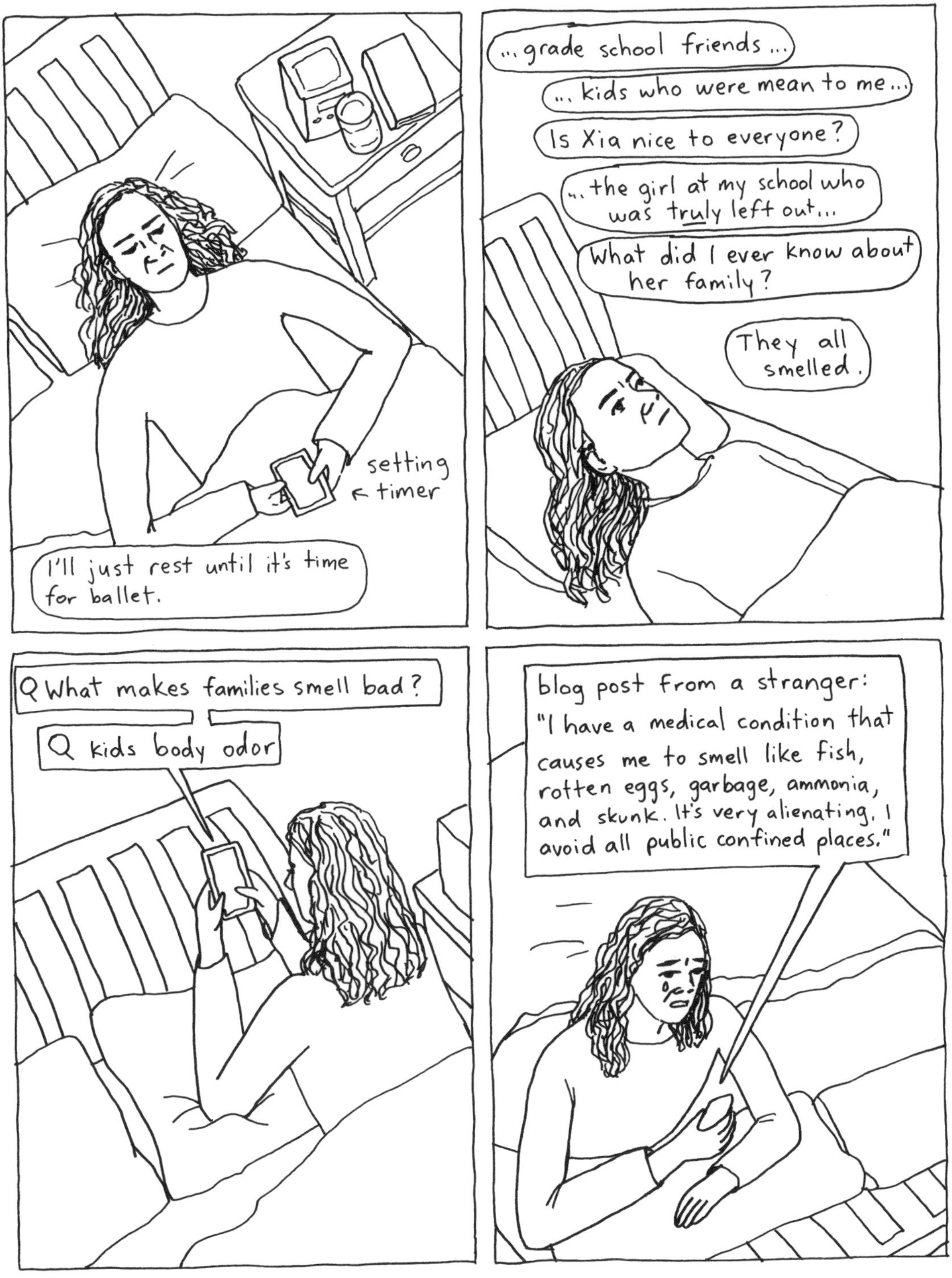
setting
timer
I'll just rest until it's time for ballet.
... grade school friends ...
... kids who were mean to me ...
Is Xia nice to everyone?
... the girl at my school who was truly left out ...
What did I ever know about her family?
They all smelled.
What makes families smell bad?
kids body odor
blog post from a stranger:
"I have a medical condition that causes me to smell like fish, rotten eggs, garbage, ammonia, and skunk. It's very alienating. I avoid all public confined places."

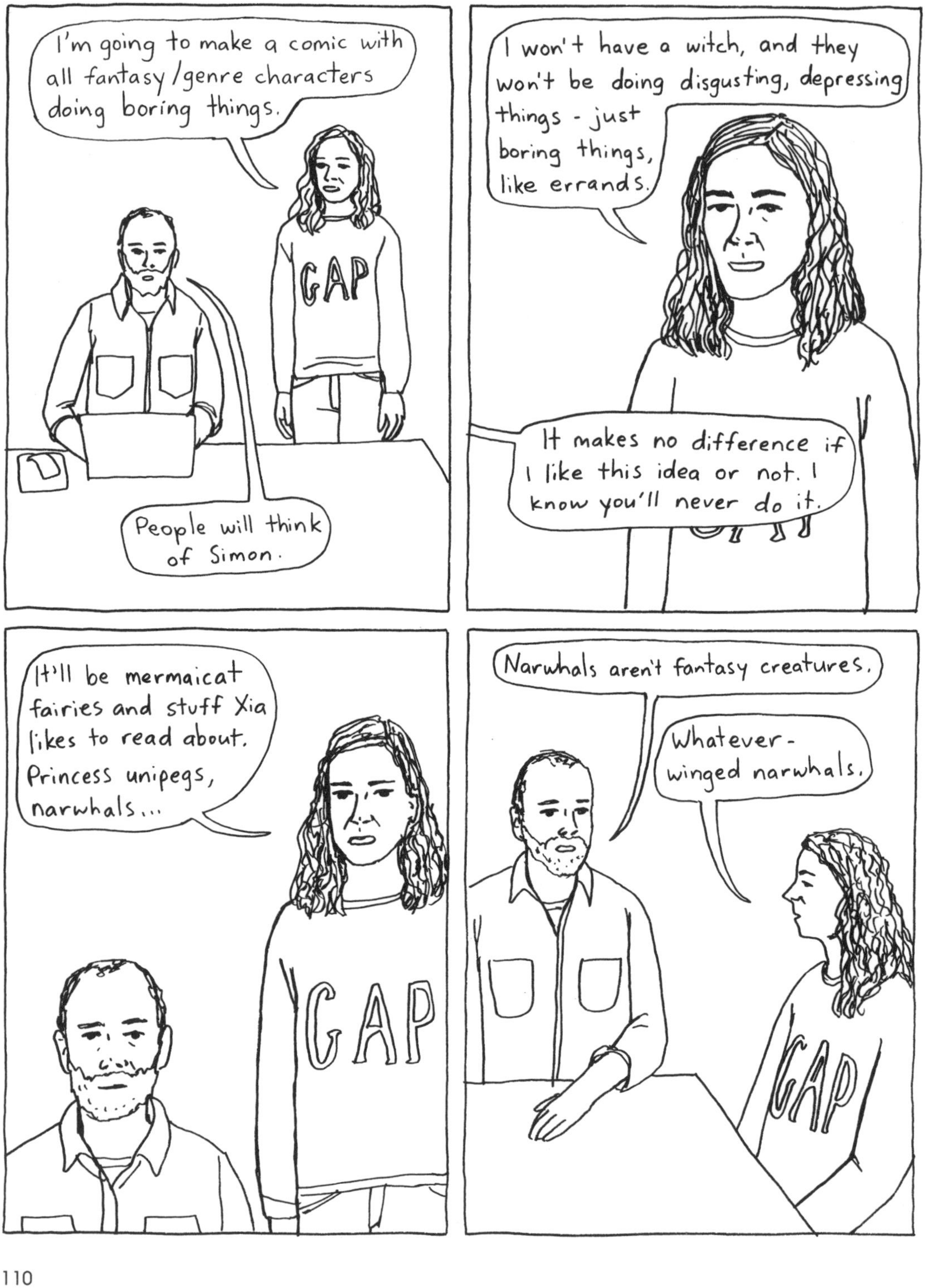
I'm going to make a comic with all fantasy/genre characters doing boring things.
People will think of Simon.
I won't have a witch, and they won't be doing disgusting, depressing things - just boring things, like errands.
It makes no difference if I like this idea or not. I know you'll never do it.
It'll be mermaicat fairies and stuff Xia likes to read about. Princess unipegs, narwhals...
GAP
Narwhals aren't fantasy creatures.
Whatever - winged narwhals.
GAP

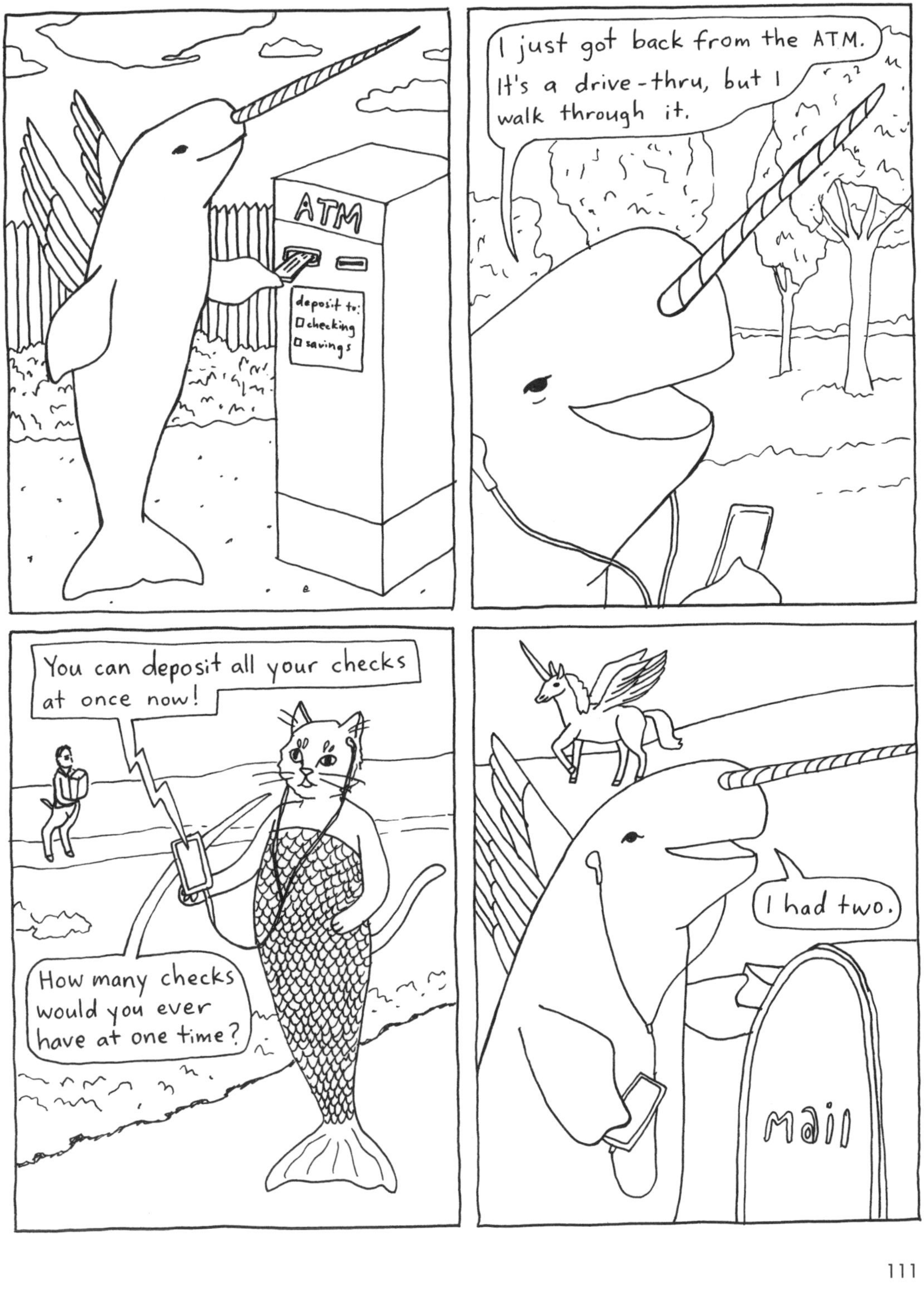
ATM
deposit to:
checking
savings
I just got back from the ATM. It's a drive-thru, but I walk through it.
You can deposit all your checks at once now!
How many checks would you ever have at one time?
I had two.
mail

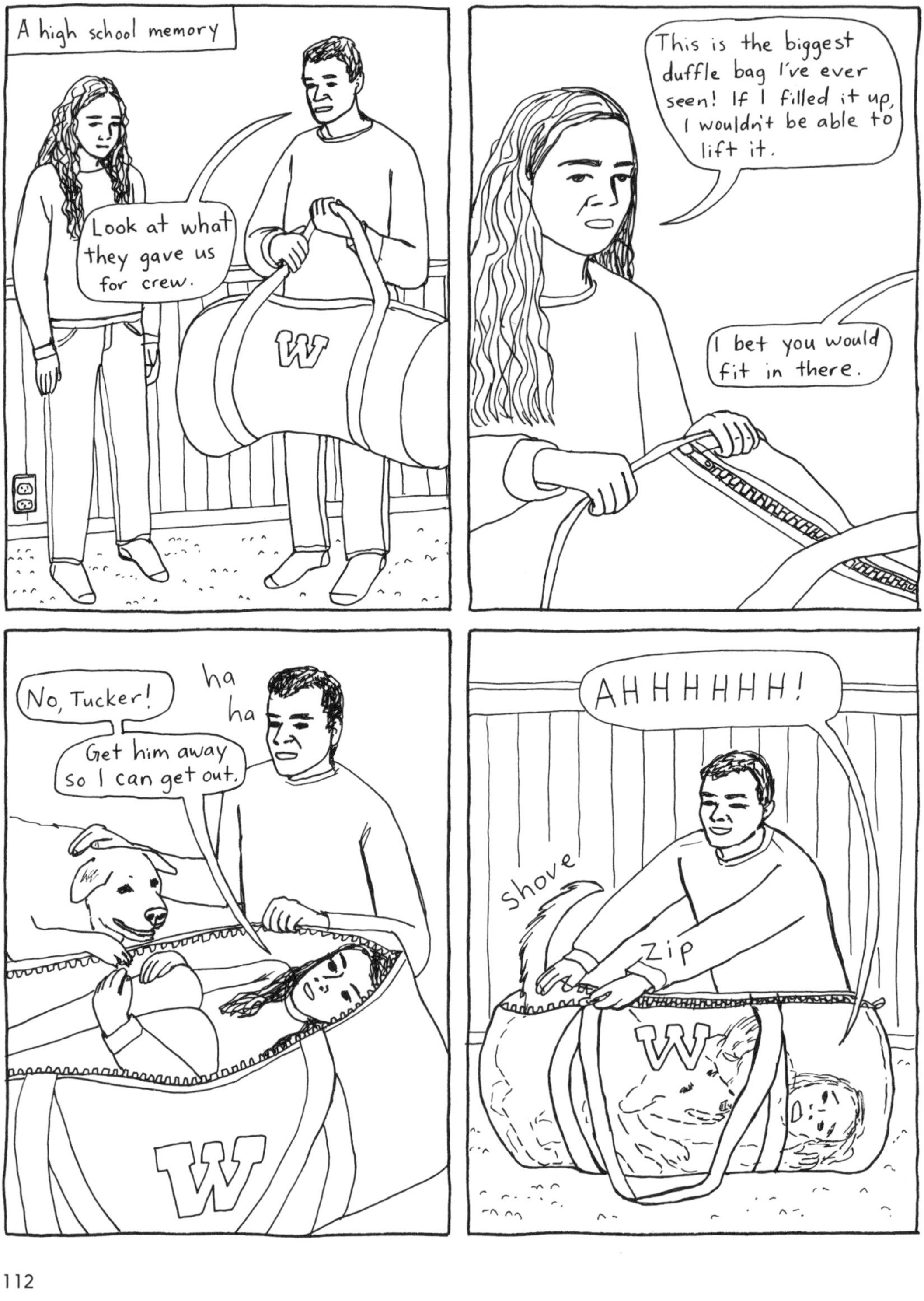
A high school memory
Look at what they gave us for crew.
W
This is the biggest duffle bag I've ever seen! If I filled it up, I wouldn't be able to lift it.
I bet you would fit in there.
No, Tucker!
Get him away so I can get out.
ha
ha
W
AHHHHHH!
Shove
Zip
W

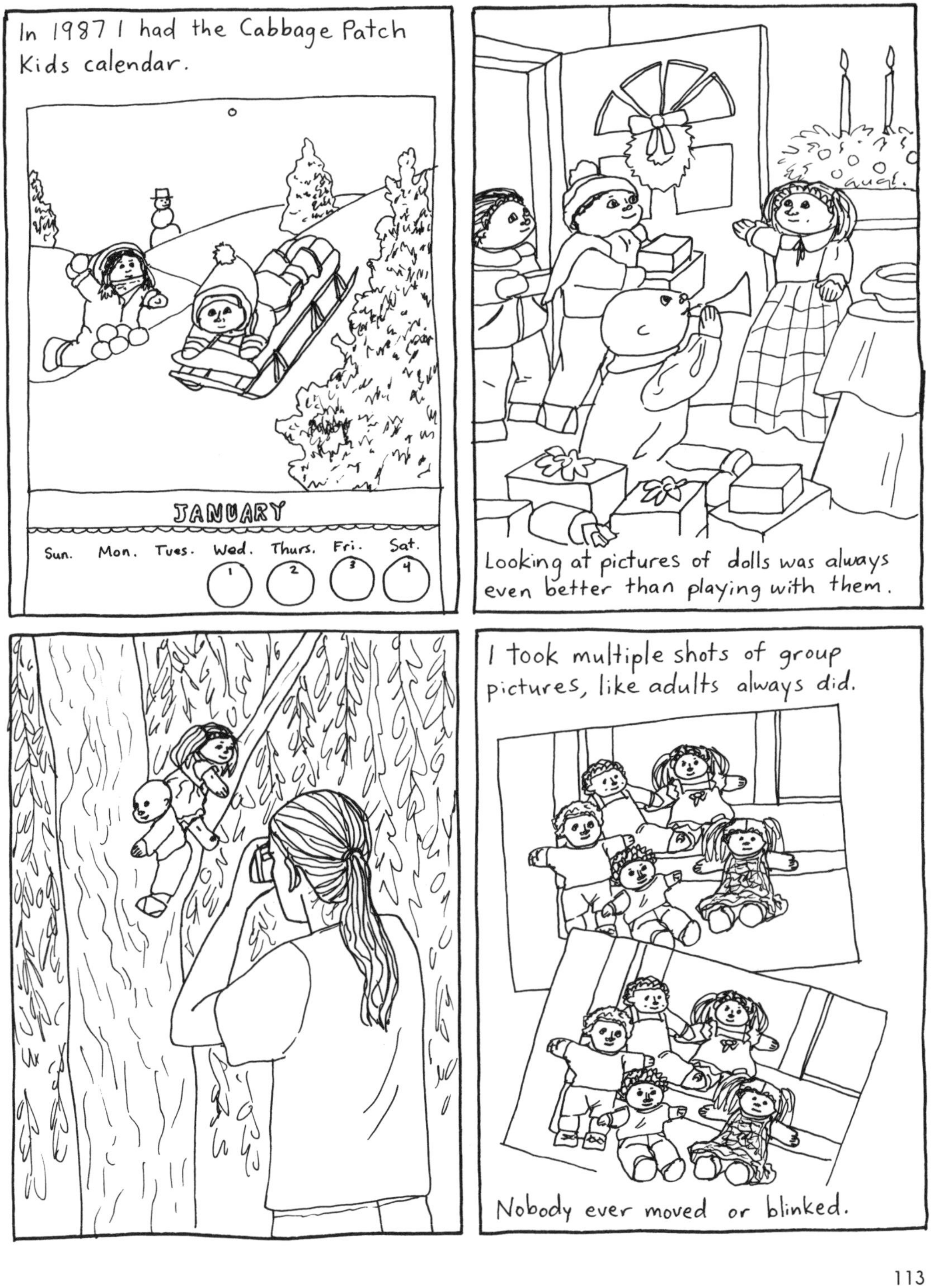
In 1987 I had the Cabbage Patch Kids calendar.
JANUARY
Sun. Mon. Tues. Wed. Thurs. Fri. Sat.
1 2 3 4
Looking at pictures of dolls was always even better than playing with them.
I took multiple shots of group pictures, like adults always did.
Nobody ever moved or blinked.

Twice I found dead hummingbirds outside and kept them in my freezer for years, hoping to learn how to stuff and mount them.

Both times I threw them out when I was thawing my freezer while preparing to move.

I painted a still life with the second hummingbird displayed in a sunglasses case. It looked like a little coffin.

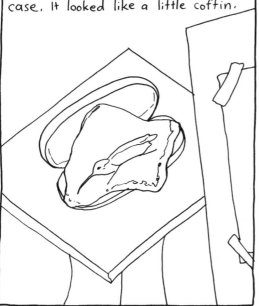

While I was painting, it thawed out and its long, pink tongue emerged from its beak. I'd never thought about their tongues before.

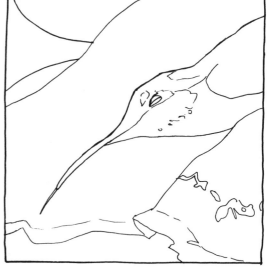

114

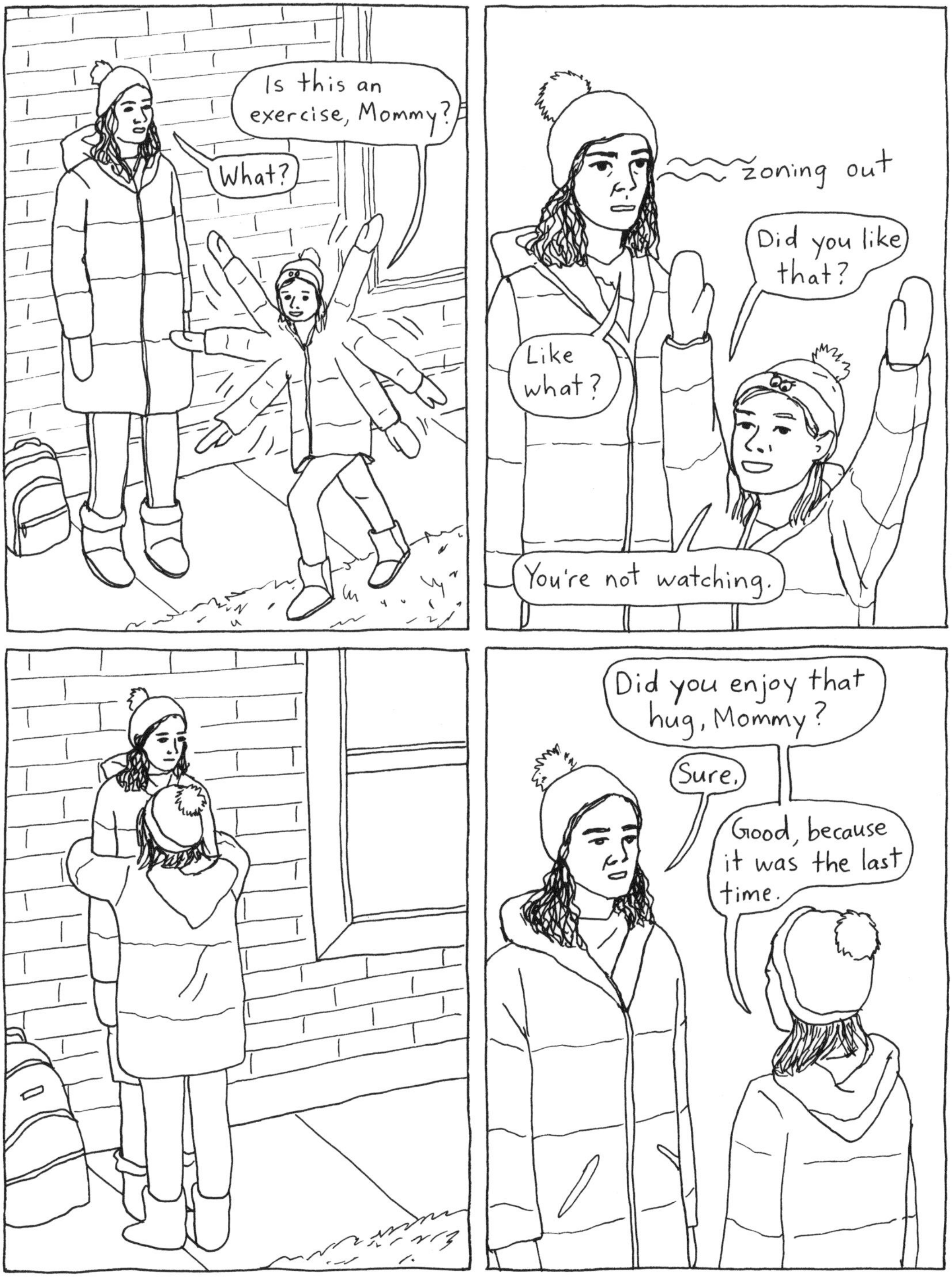

Is this an exercise, Mommy?
What?
zoning out
Did you like that?
Like what?
You're not watching.
Did you enjoy that hug, Mommy?
Sure.
Good, because it was the last time.

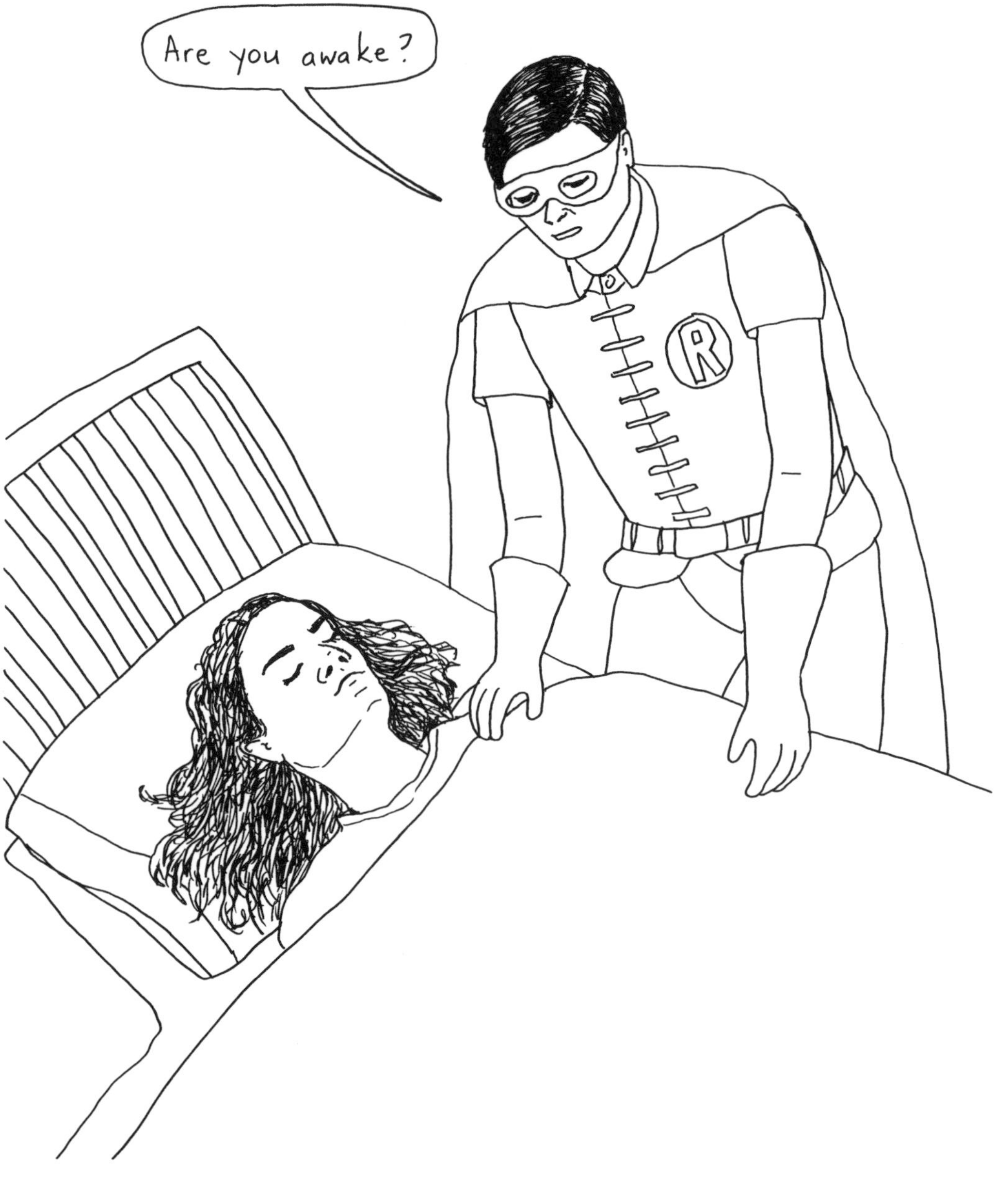
Are you awake?

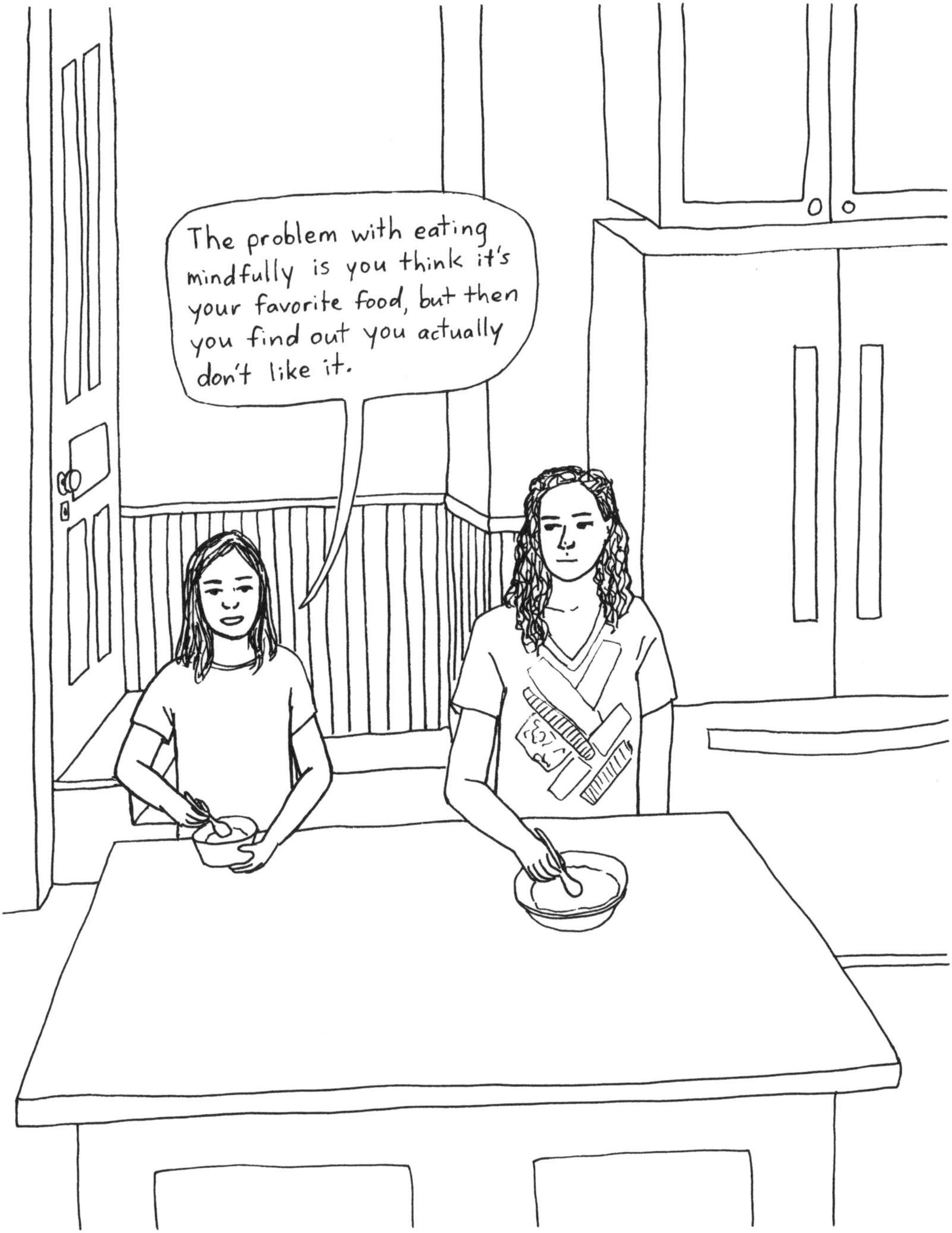
The problem with eating mindfully is you think it's your favorite food, but then you find out you actually don't like it.

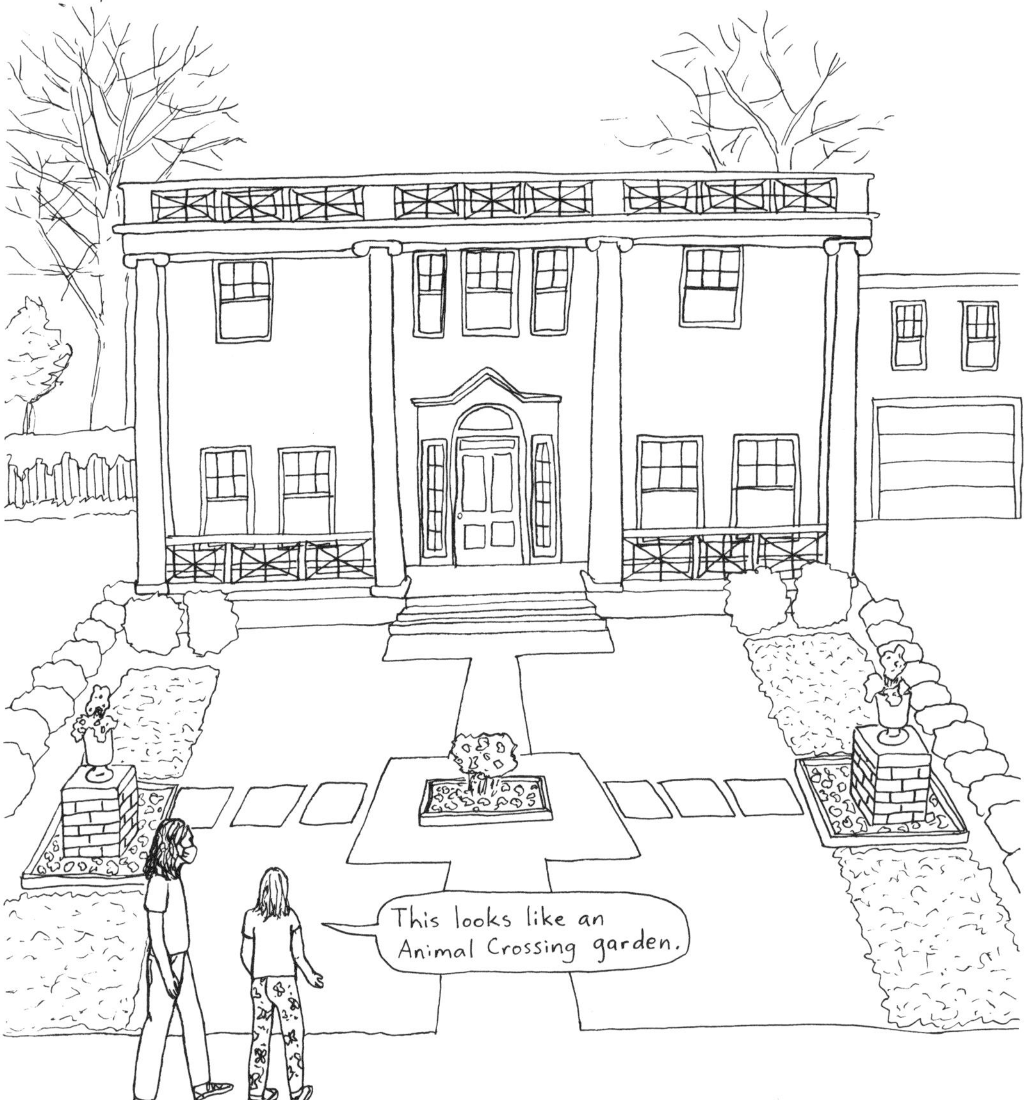
This looks like an Animal Crossing garden.

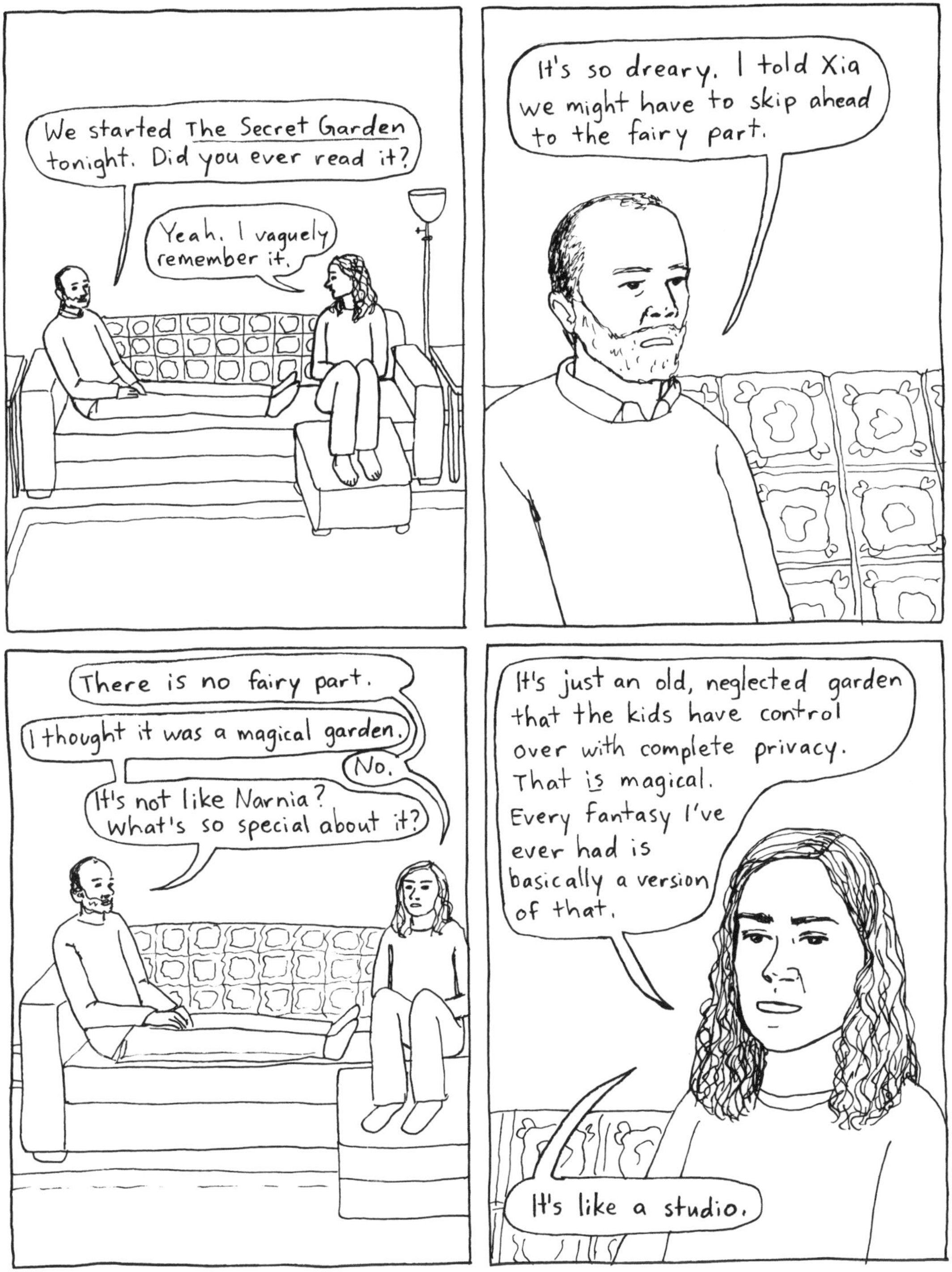
We started The Secret Garden tonight. Did you ever read it?
Yeah. I vaguely remember it.
It's so dreary. I told Xia we might have to skip ahead to the fairy part.
There is no fairy part.
I thought it was a magical garden.
No.
It's not like Narnia? What's so special about it?
It's just an old, neglected garden that the kids have control over with complete privacy. That is magical. Every fantasy I've ever had is basically a version of that.
It's like a studio.

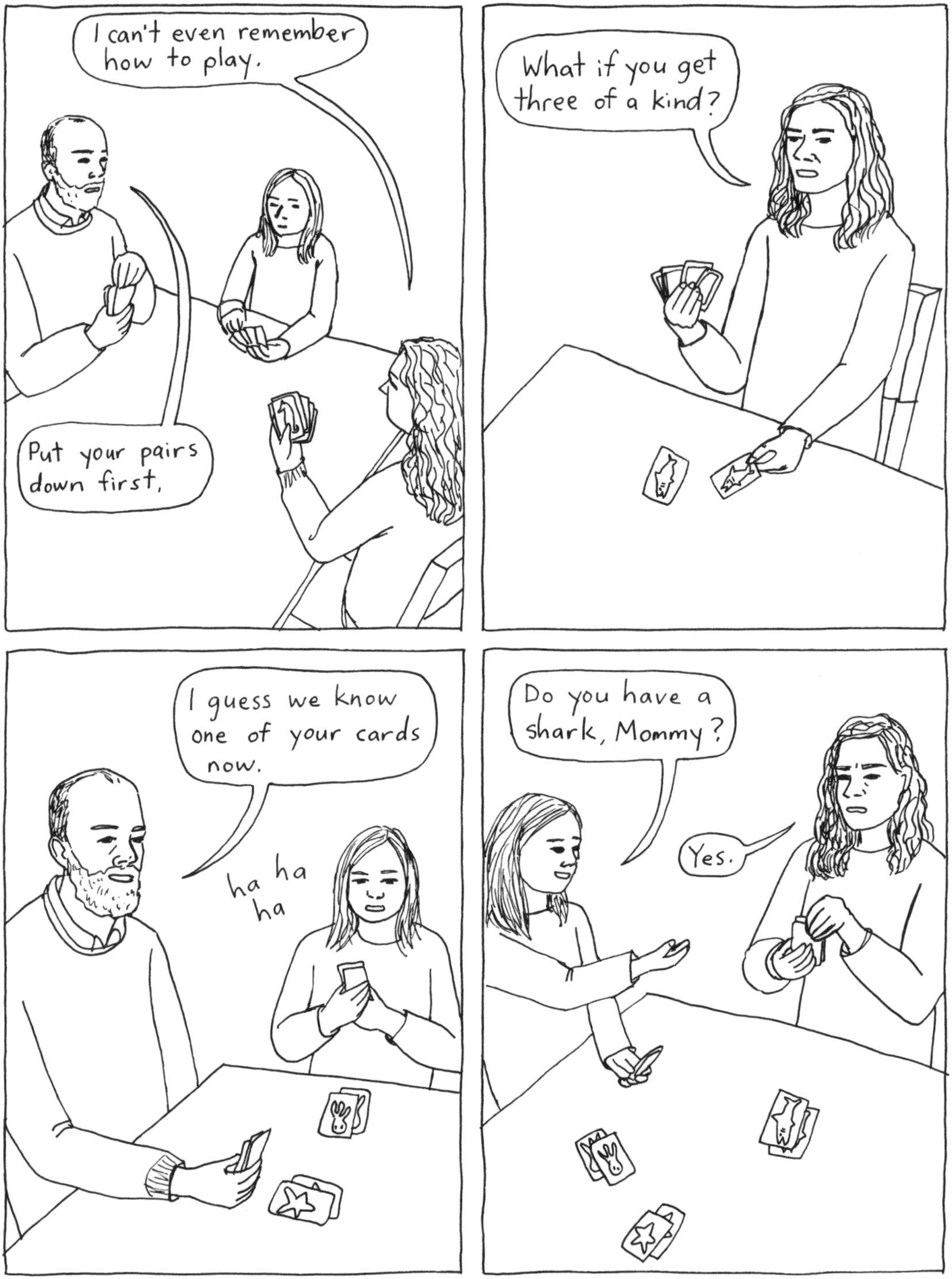
I can't even remember how to play.
Put your pairs down first.
What if you get three of a kind?
I guess we know one of your cards now.
ha ha ha
Do you have a shark, Mommy?
Yes.

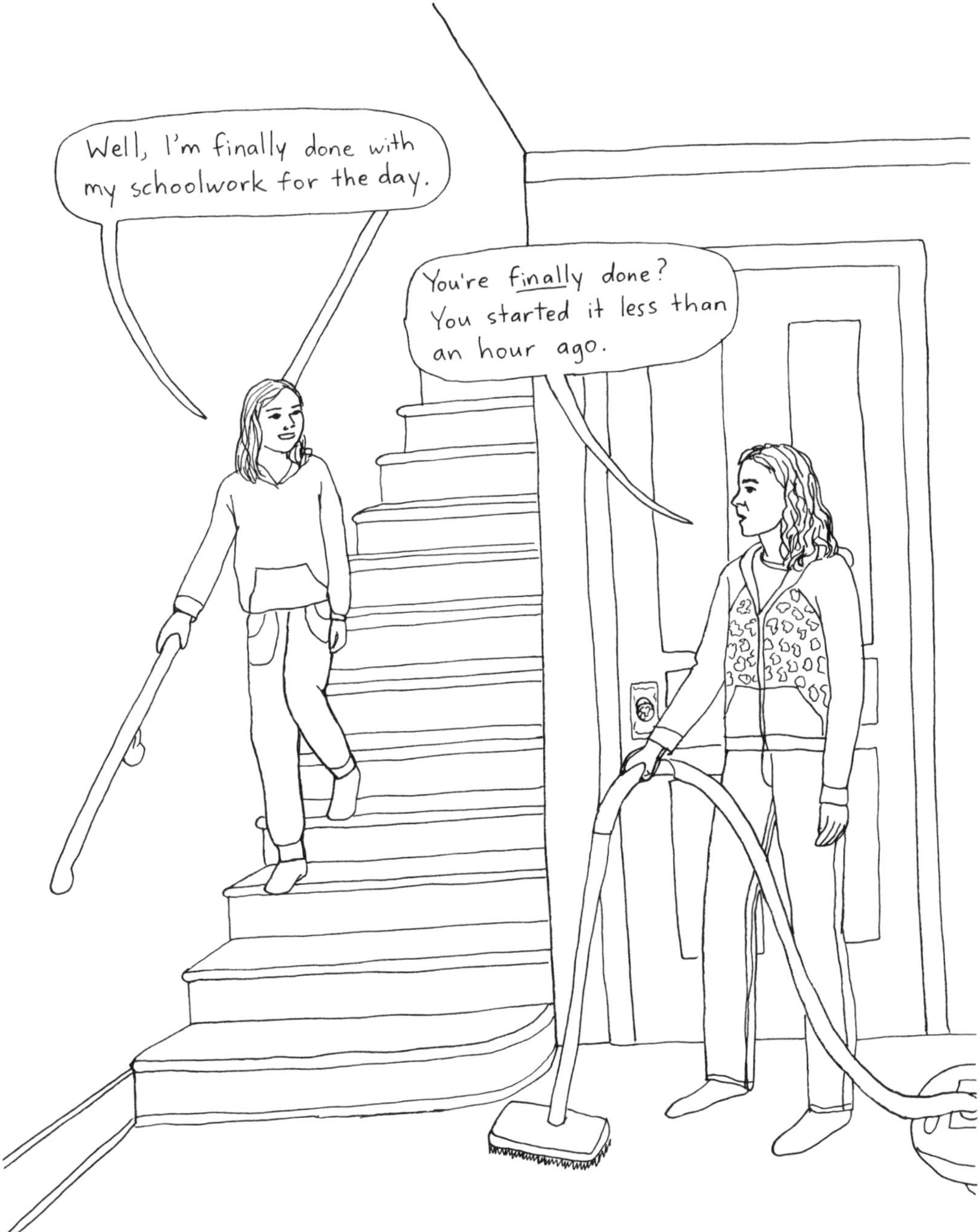
Well, I'm finally done with my schoolwork for the day.
You're finally done? You started it less than an hour ago.

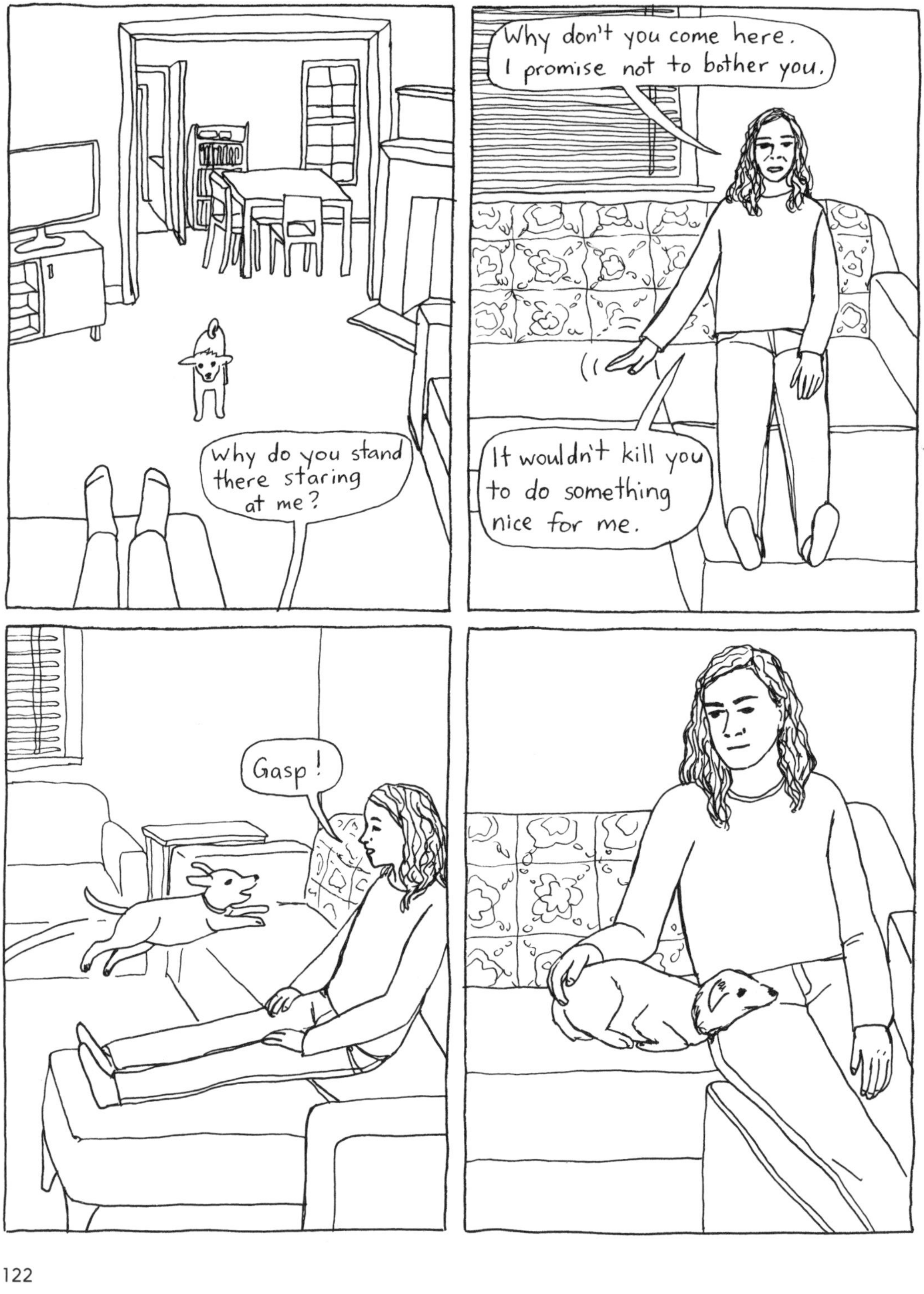
Why do you stand there staring at me?
Why don't you come here. I promise not to bother you.
It wouldn't kill you to do something nice for me.
Gasp!

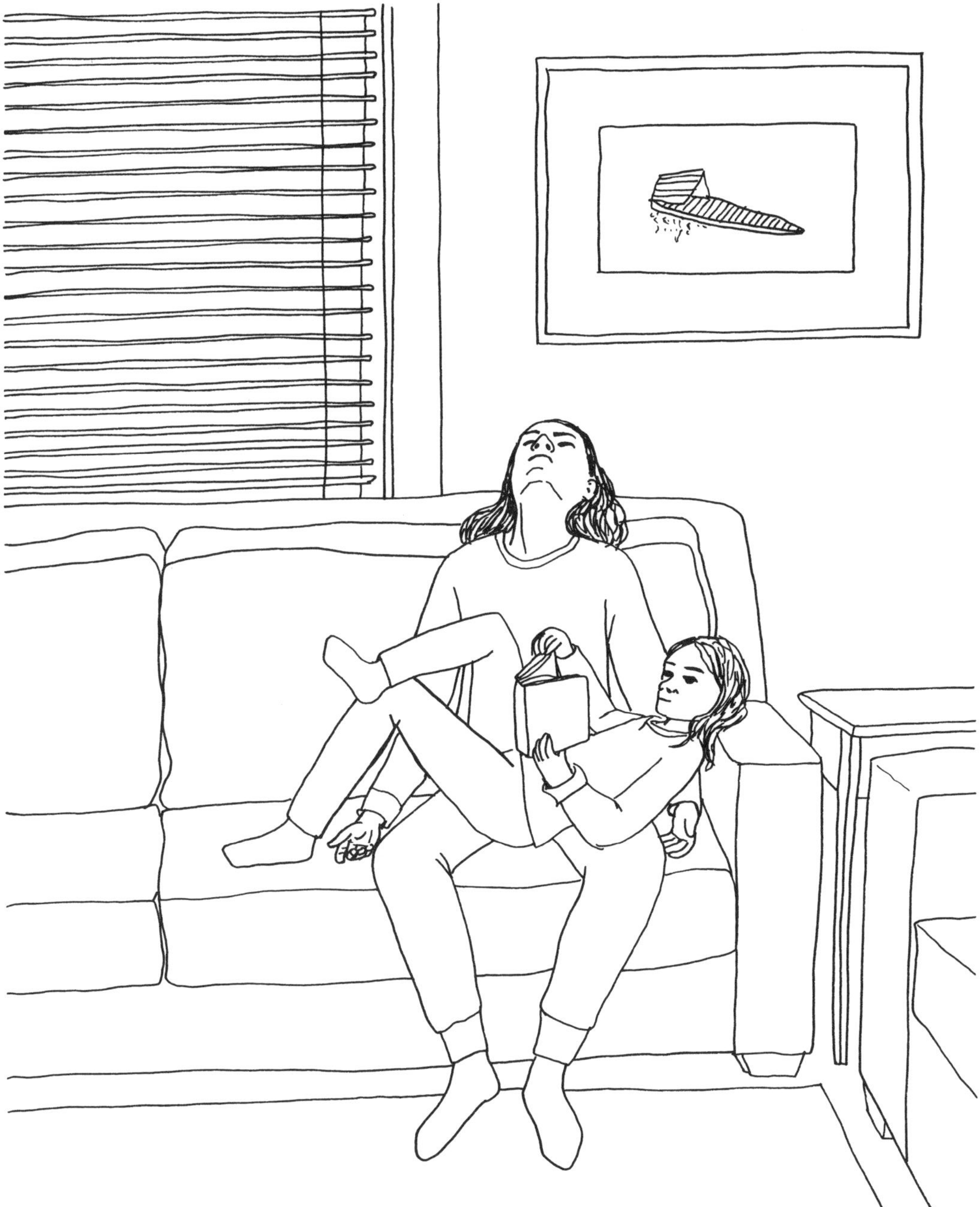

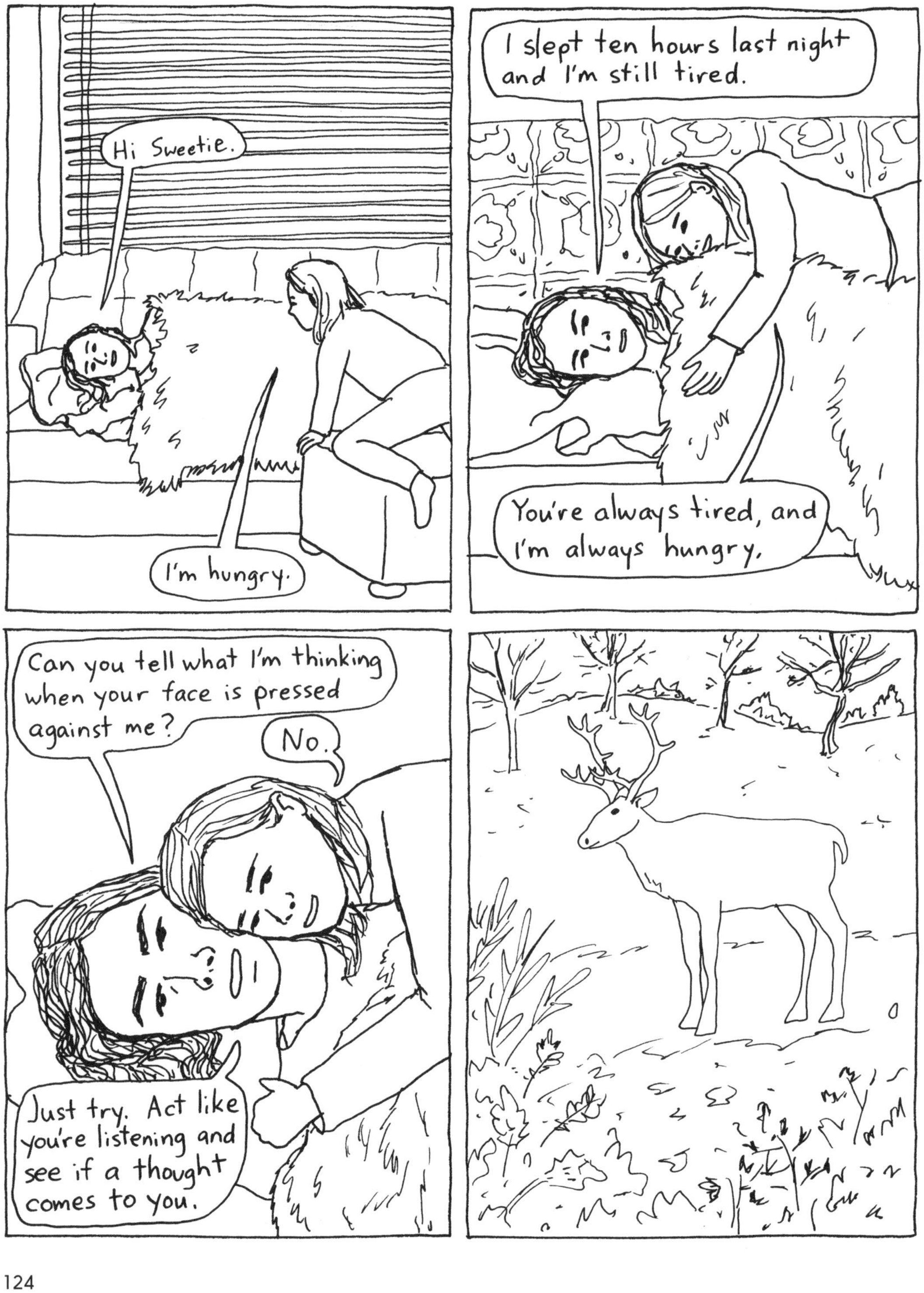
Hi Sweetie.
I'm hungry.
I slept ten hours last night and I'm still tired.
You're always tired, and I'm always hungry.
Can you tell what I'm thinking when your face is pressed against me?
No.
Just try. Act like you're listening and see if a thought comes to you.

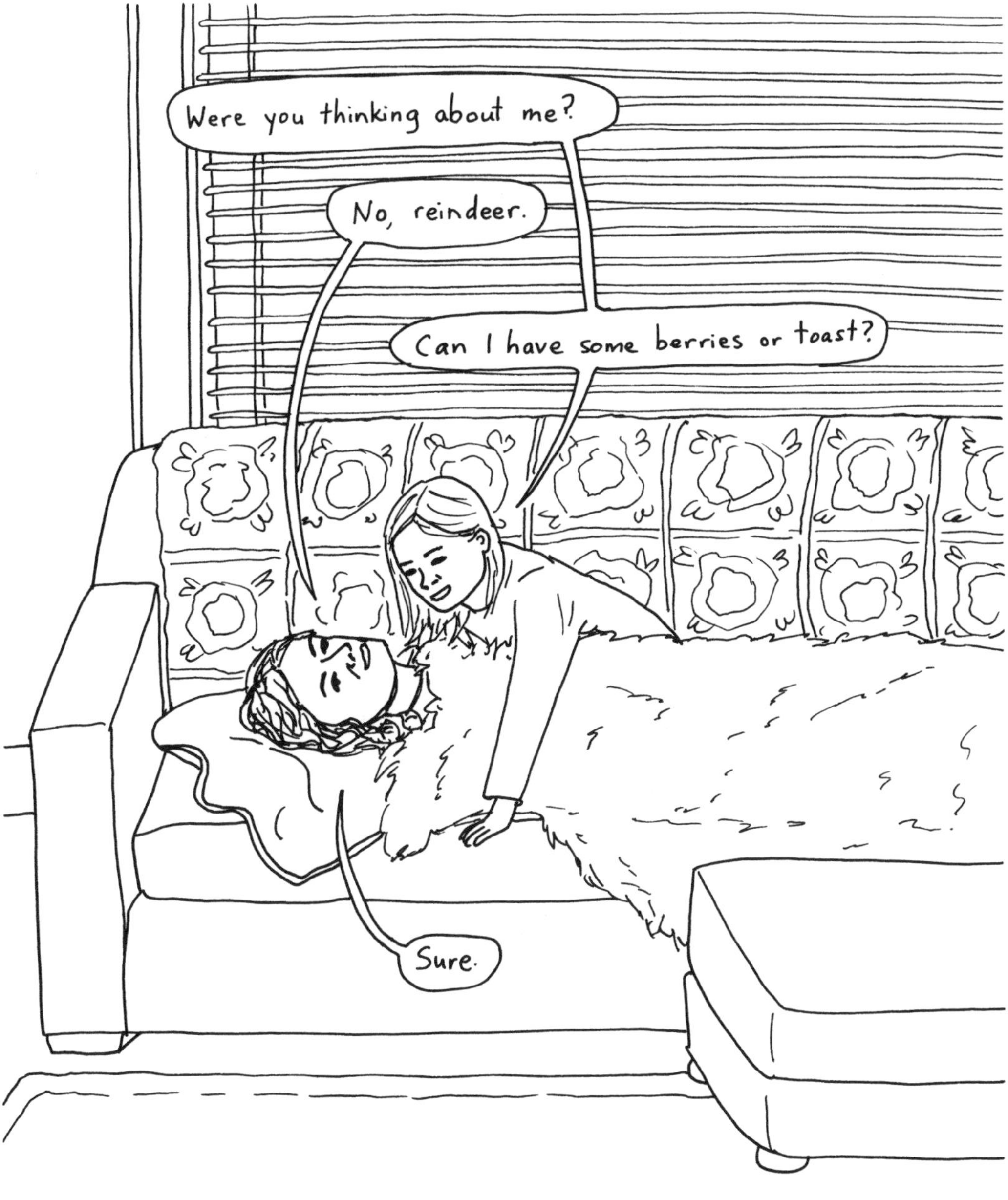
Were you thinking about me?
No, reindeer.
Can I have some berries or toast?
Sure.

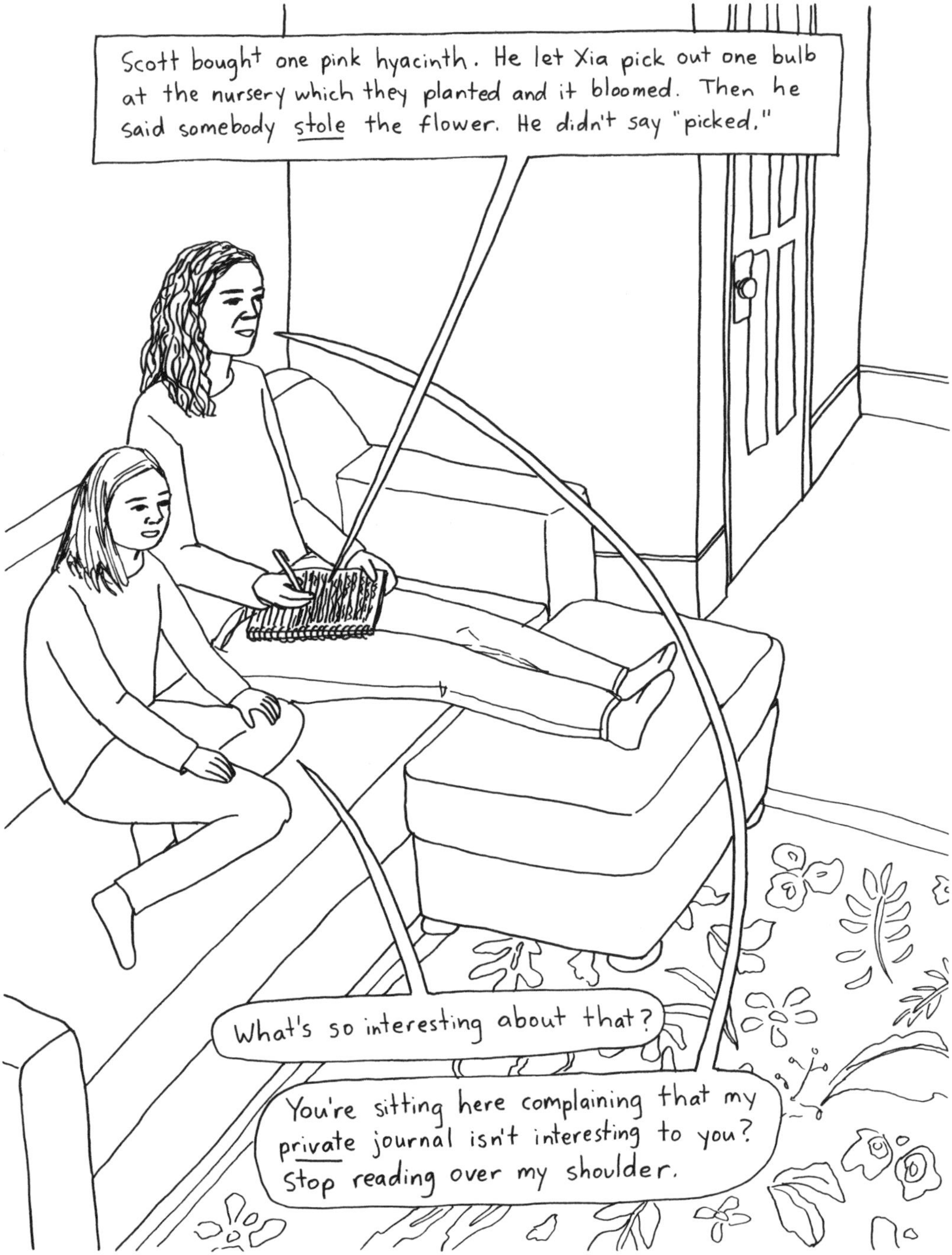
Scott bought one pink hyacinth. He let Xia pick out one bulb at the nursery which they planted and it bloomed. Then he said somebody stole the flower. He didn't say "picked."
What's so interesting about that?
You're sitting here complaining that my private journal isn't interesting to you? Stop reading over my shoulder.

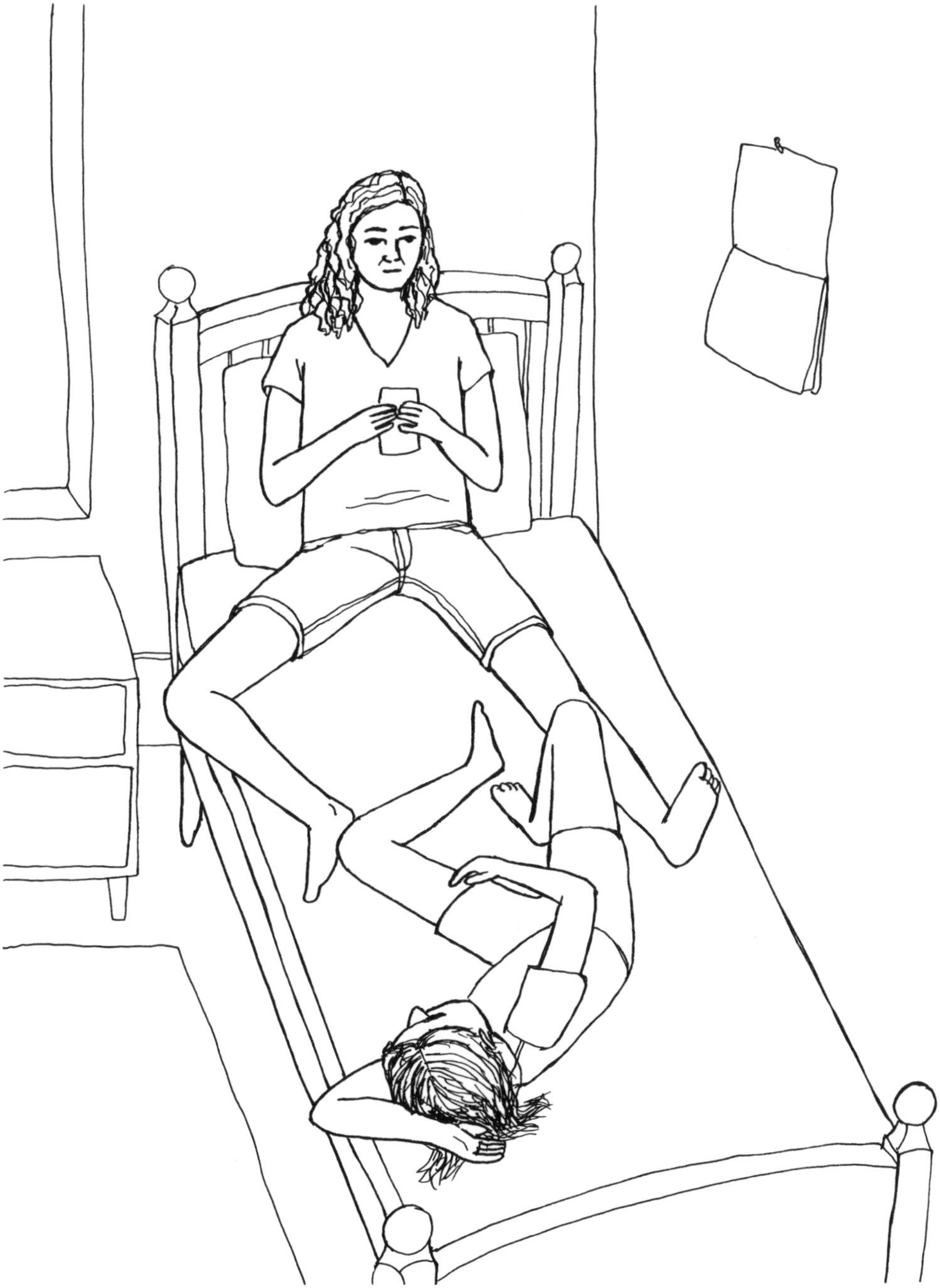

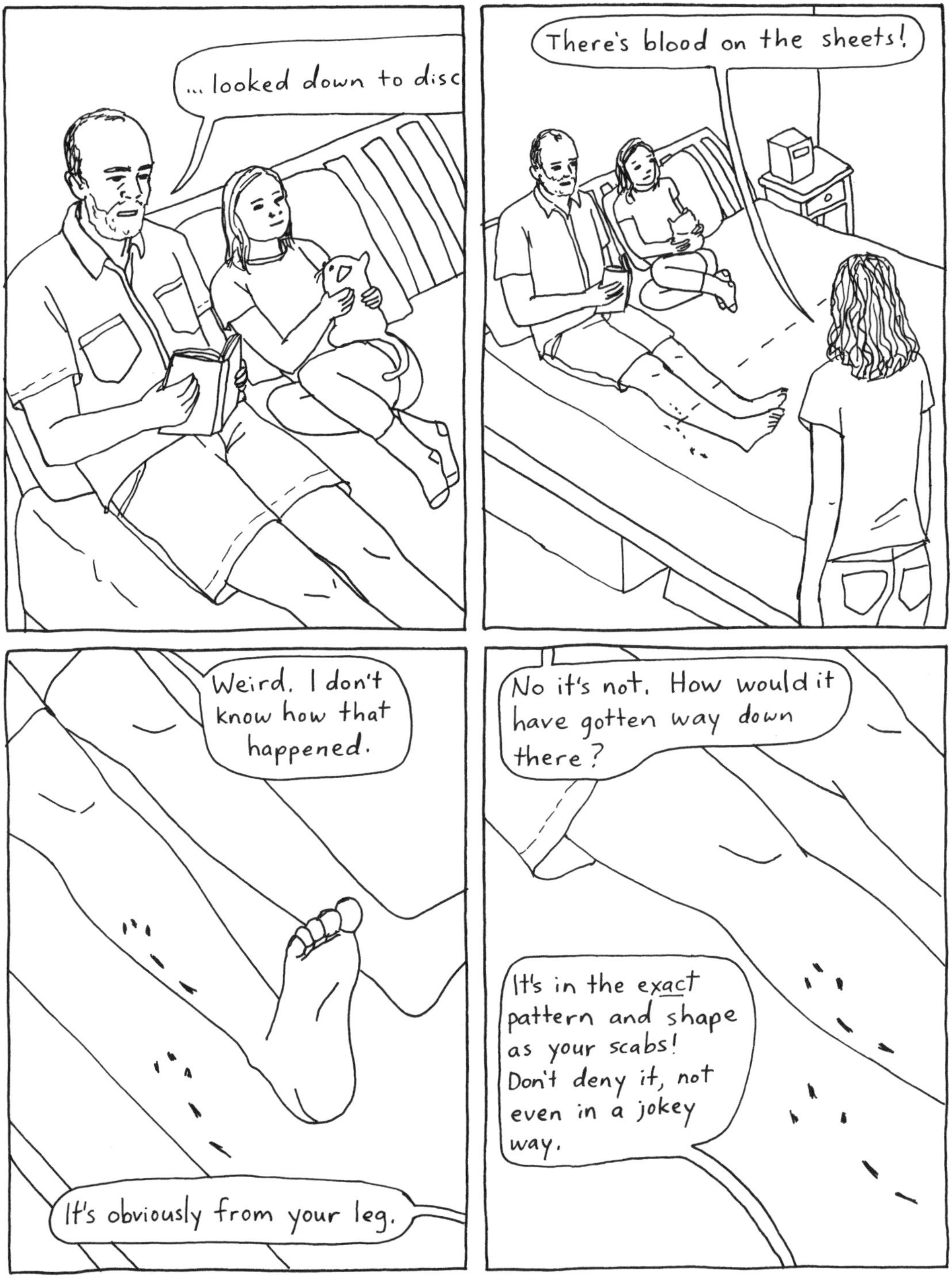
... looked down to disc
There's blood on the sheets!
Weird. I don't know how that happened.
It's obviously from your leg.
No it's not. How would it have gotten way down there?
It's in the exact pattern and shape as your scabs! Don't deny it, not even in a jokey way.

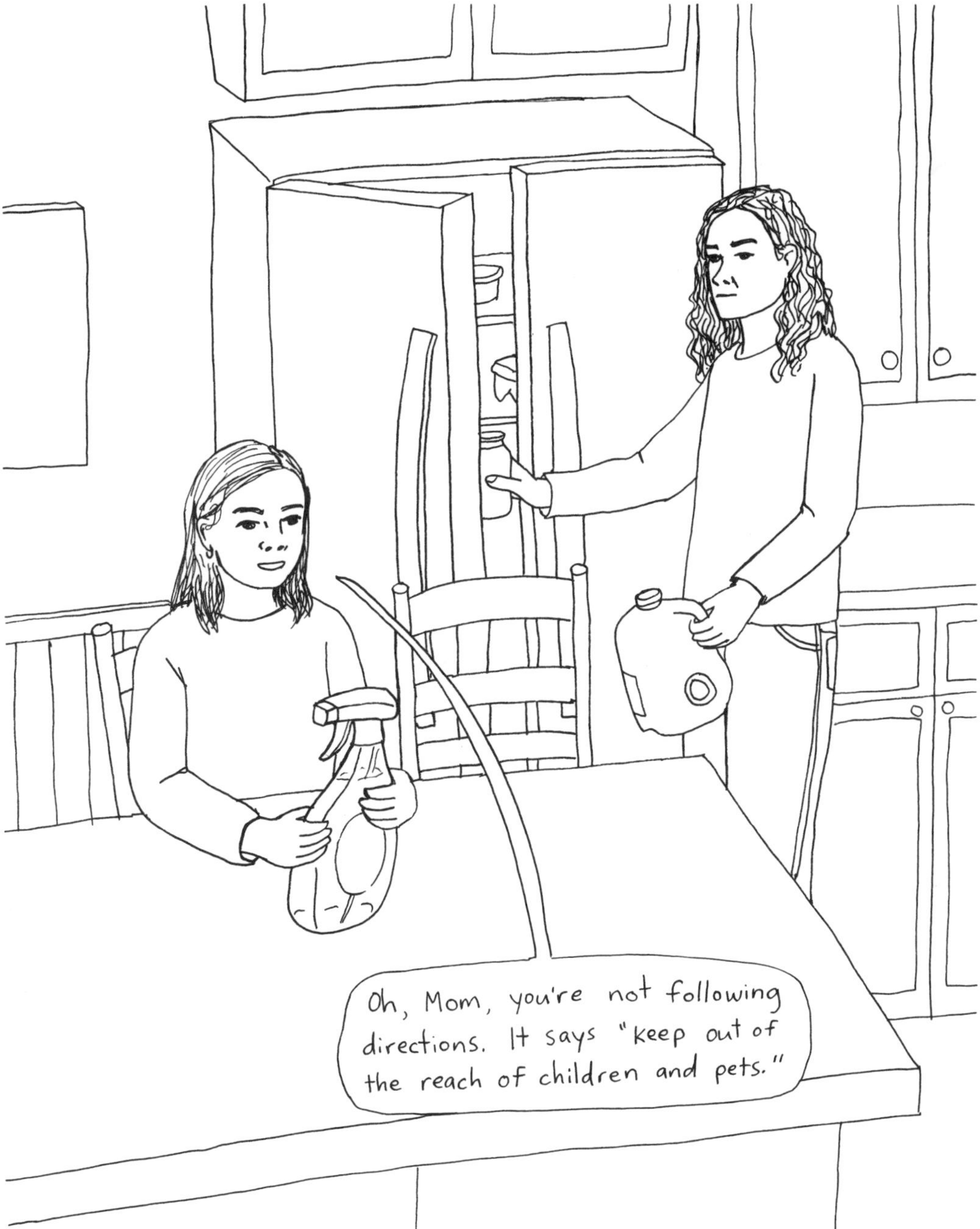
Oh, Mom, you're not following directions. It says "keep out of the reach of children and pets."

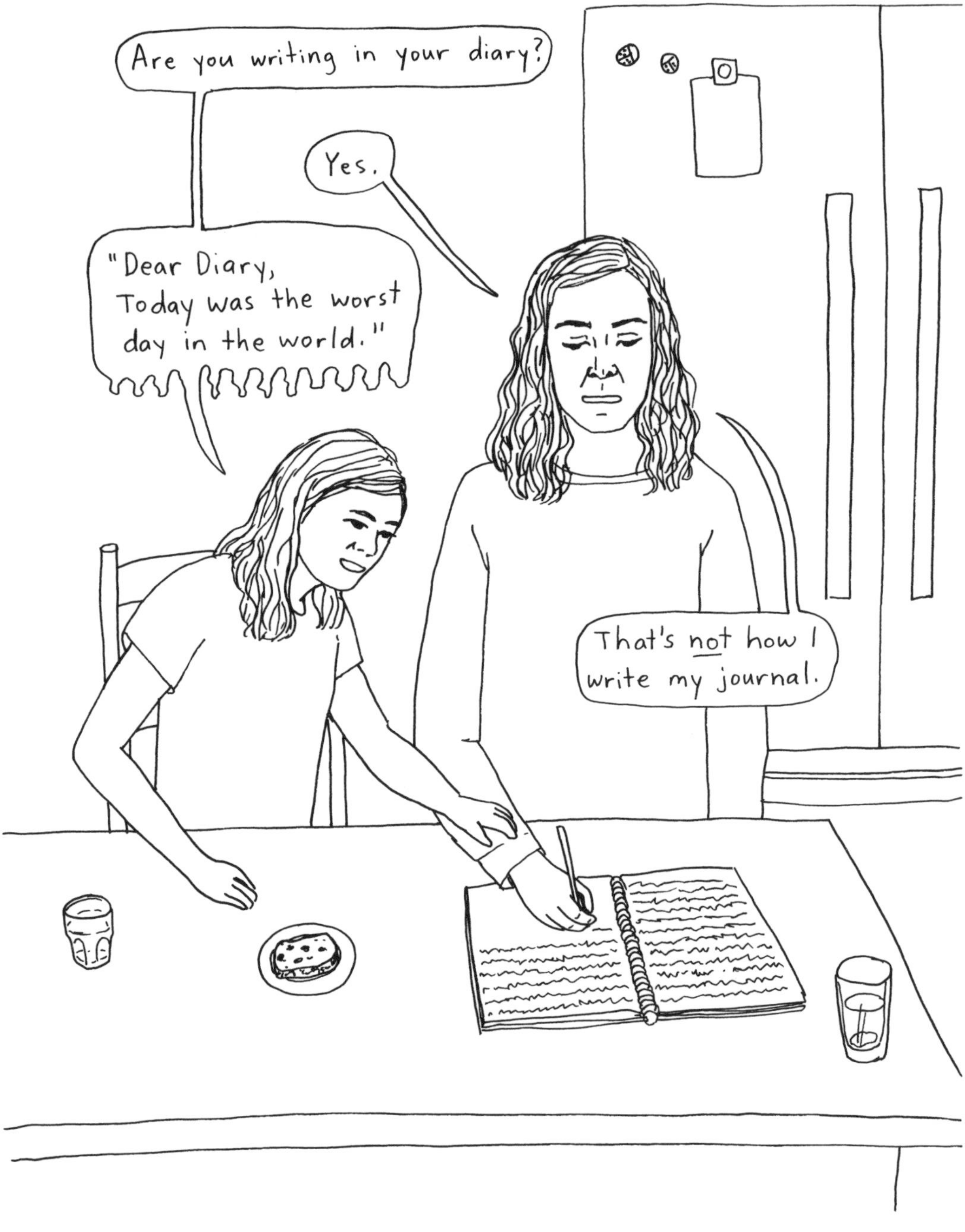
Are you writing in your diary?
Yes.
"Dear Diary,
Today was the worst
day in the world."
That's not how I
write my journal.

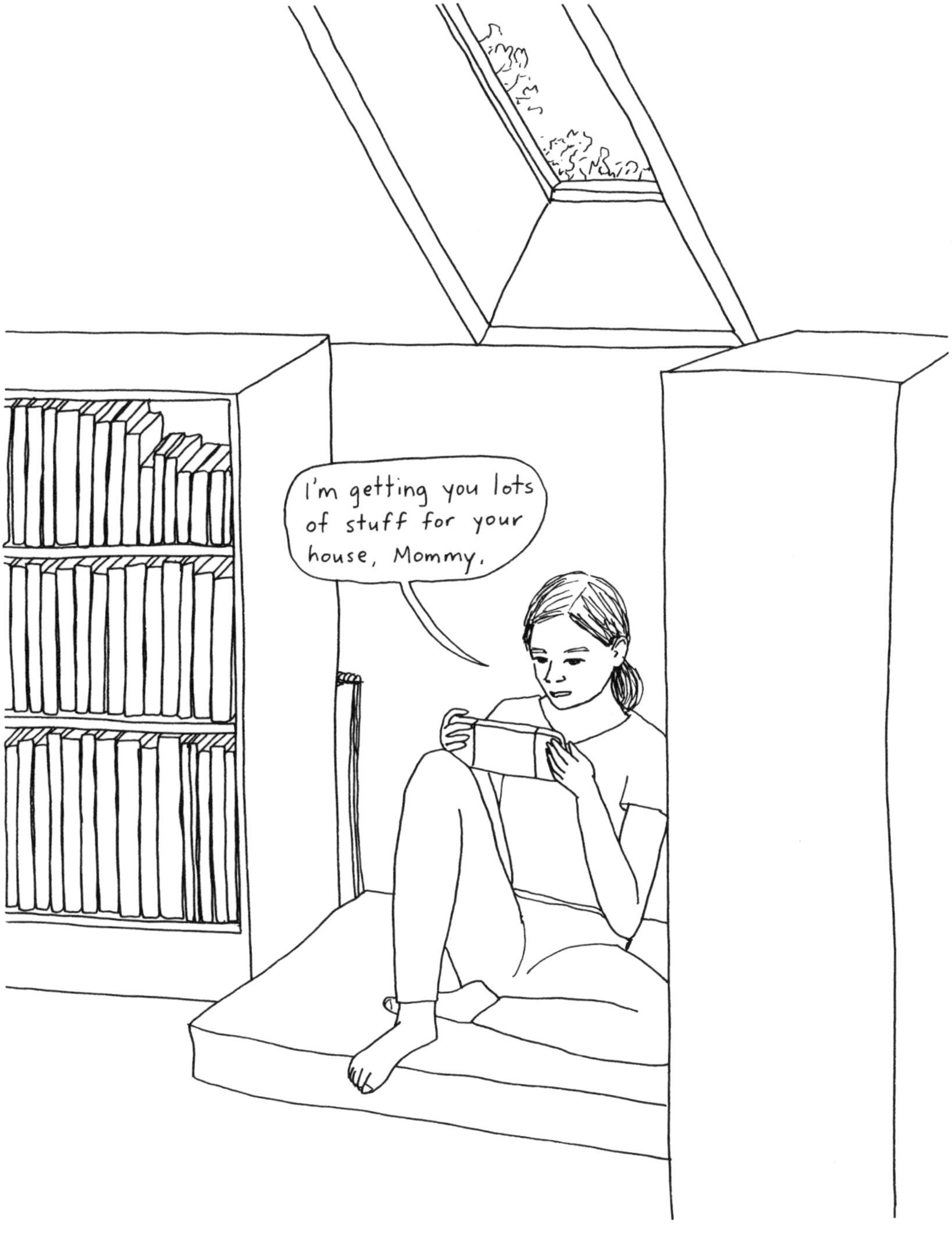
I'm getting you lots of stuff for your house, Mommy.

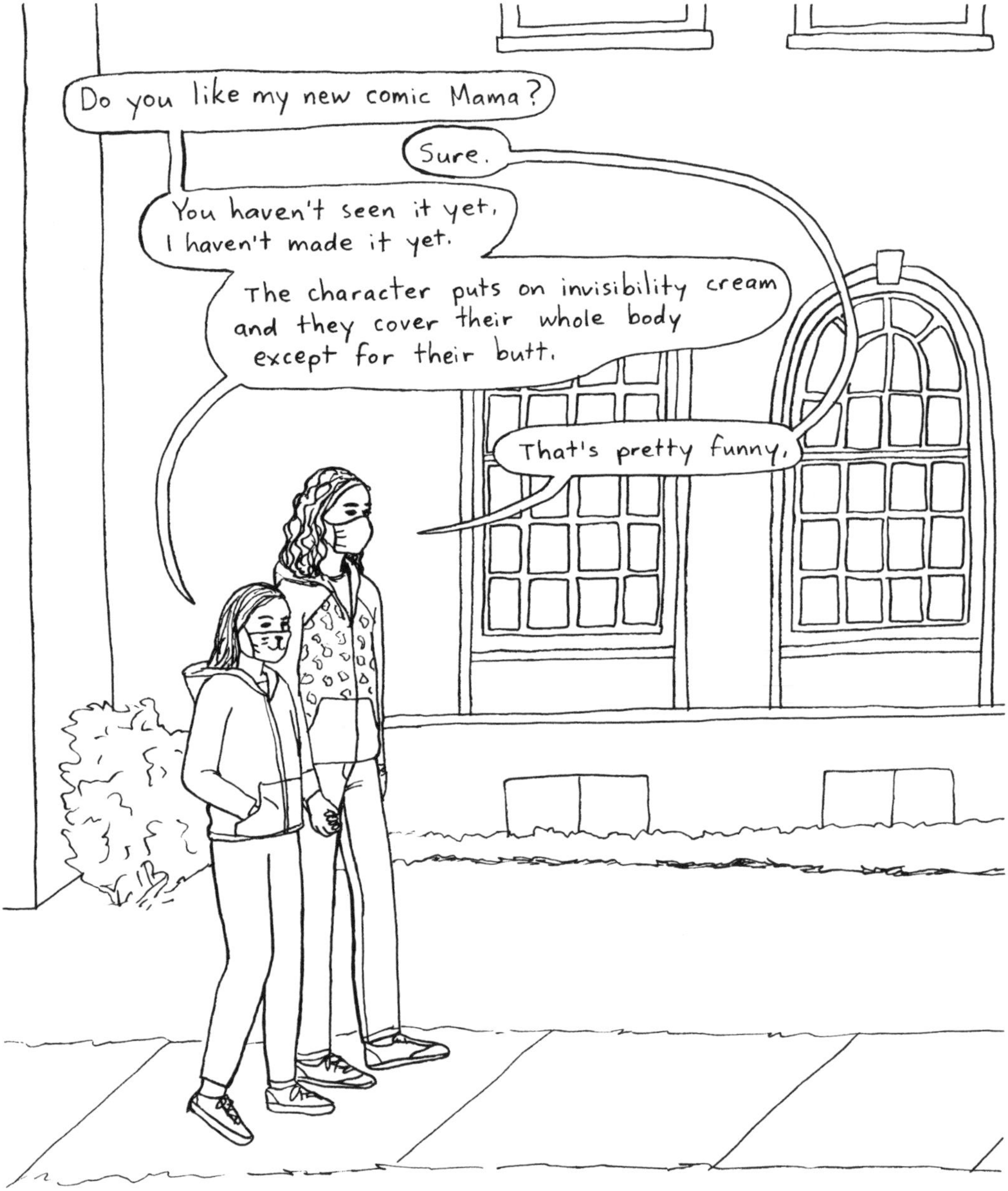
Do you like my new comic Mama?
Sure.
You haven't seen it yet, I haven't made it yet.
The character puts on invisibility cream and they cover their whole body except for their butt.
That's pretty funny.

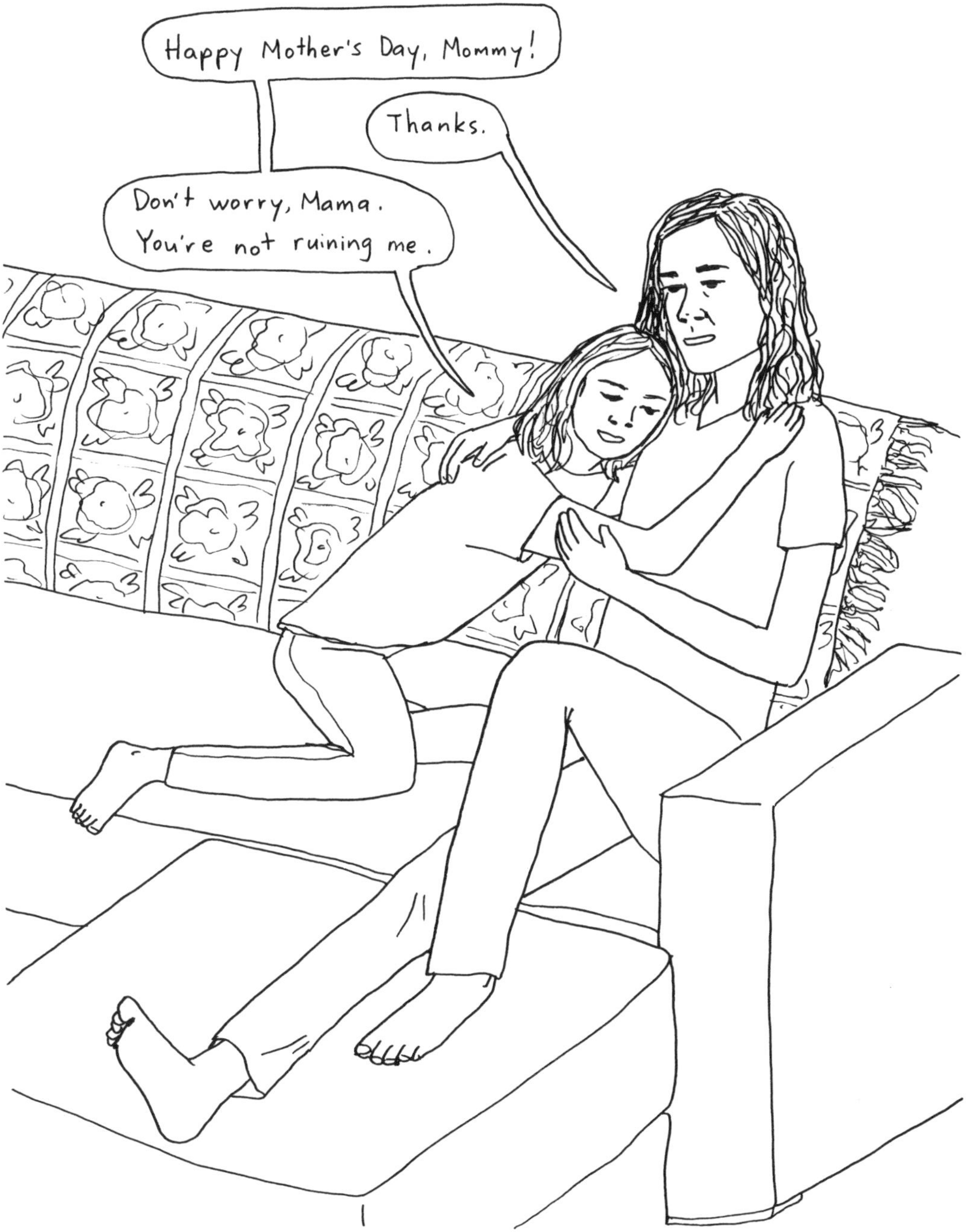
Happy Mother's Day, Mommy!
Thanks.
Don't worry, Mama. You're not ruining me.

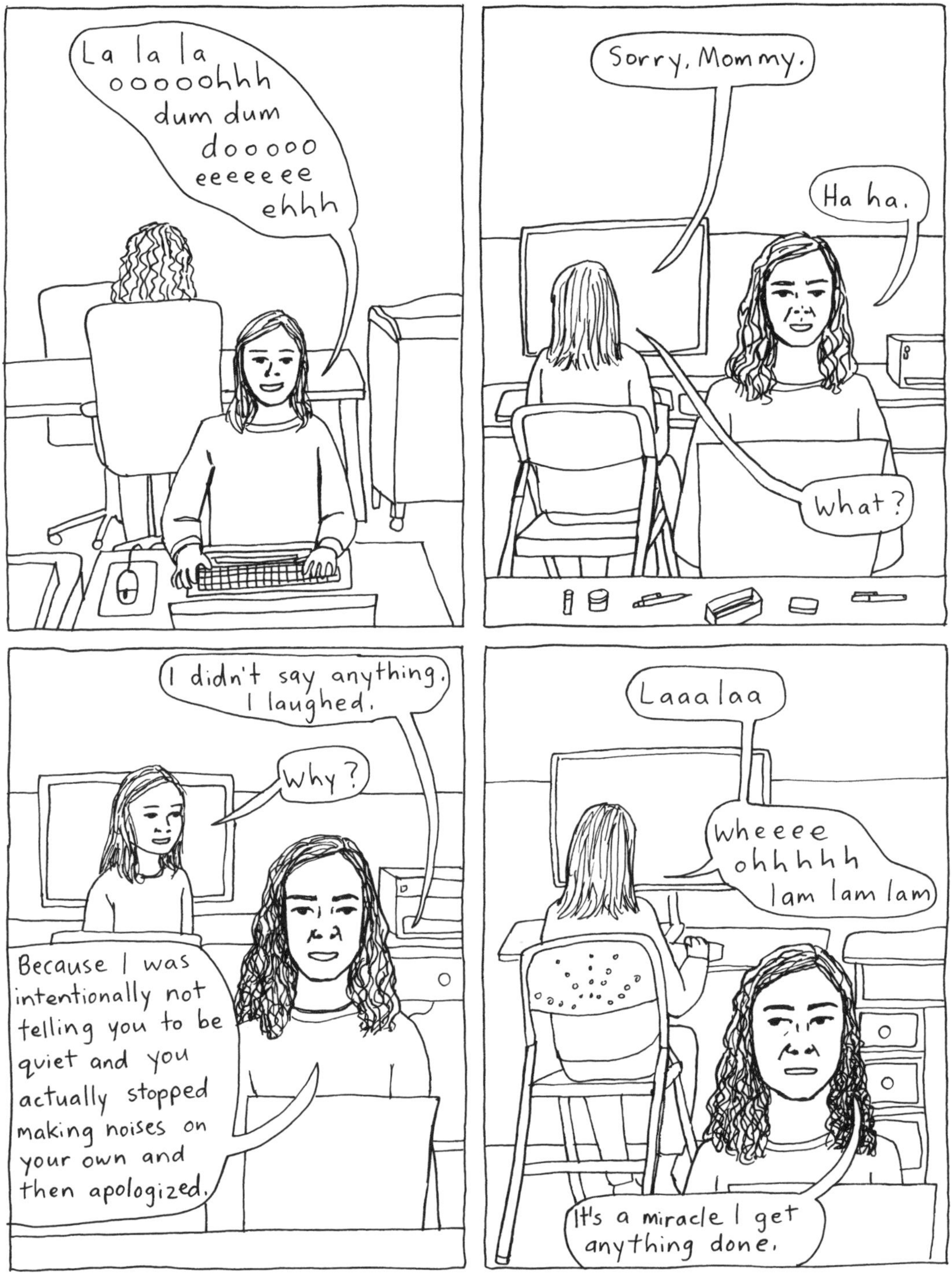
La la la oooochhh dum dum dooooo eeeeeee ehhh
Sorry, Mommy.
Ha ha.
What?
I didn't say anything. I laughed.
Why?
Because I was intentionally not telling you to be quiet and you actually stopped making noises on your own and then apologized.
Laaalaa
wheeee ohhhhh lam lam lam
It's a miracle I get anything done.

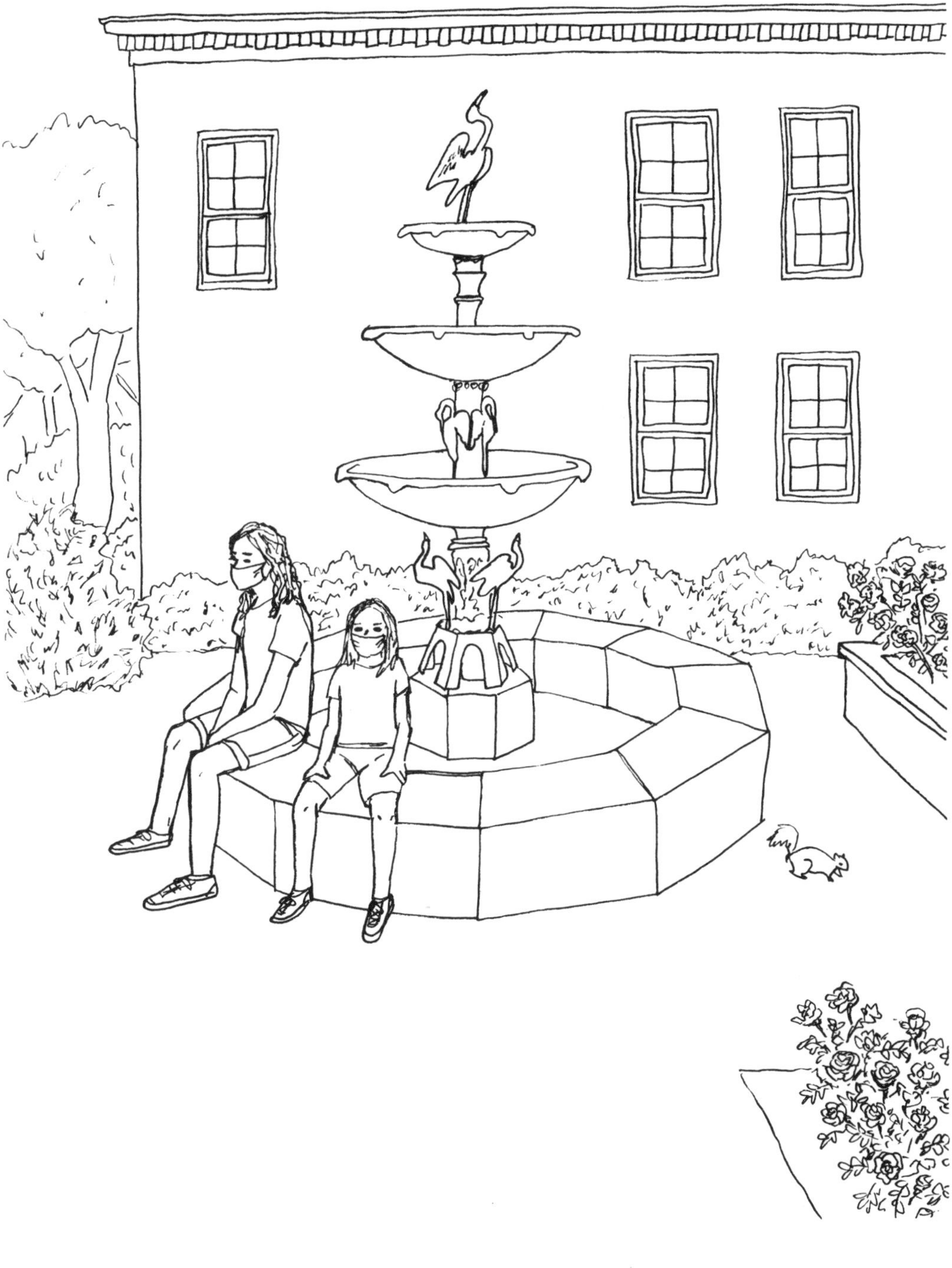

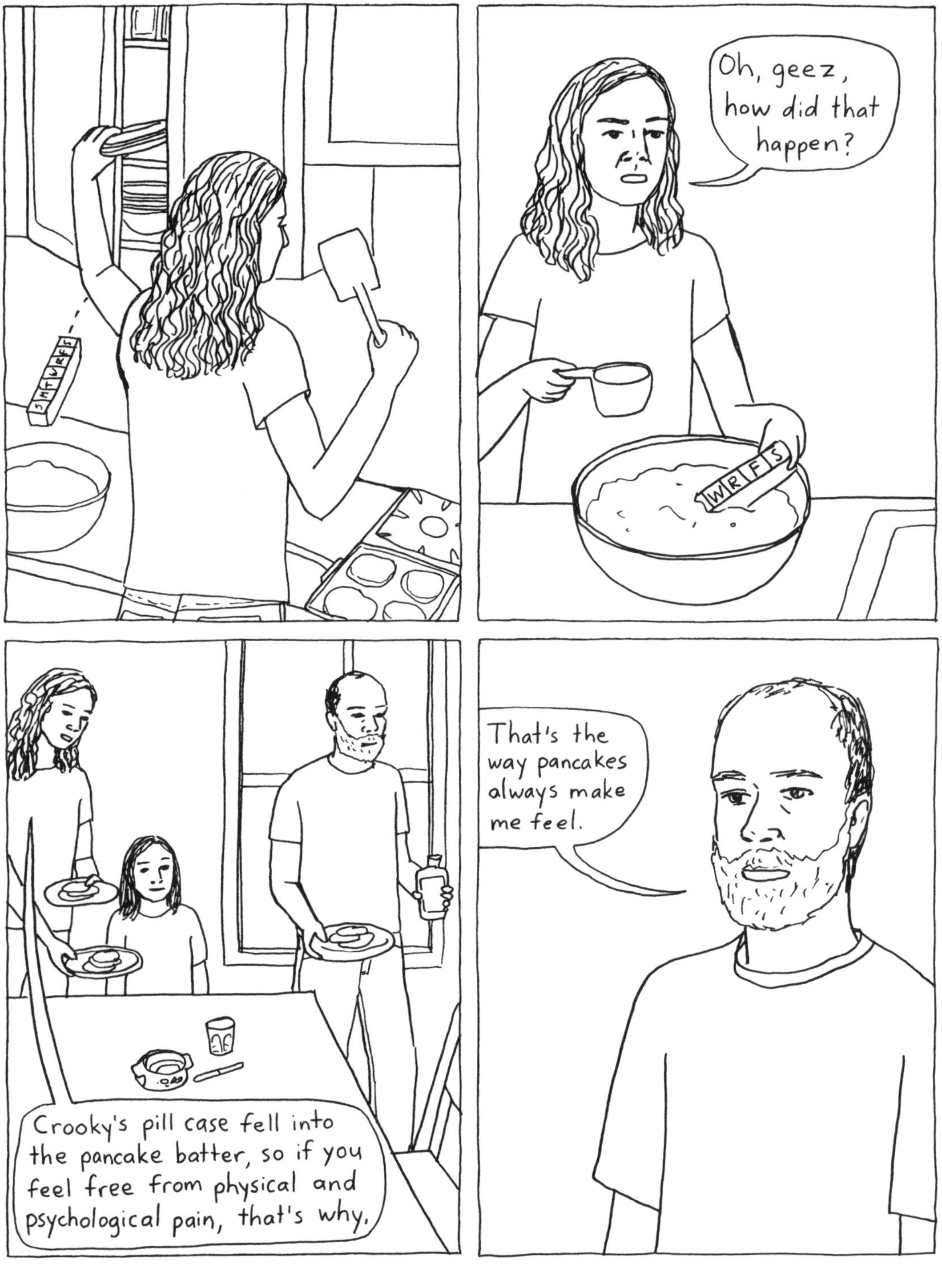
Oh, geez, how did that happen?
Crooky's pill case fell into the pancake batter, so if you feel free from physical and psychological pain, that's why.
That's the way pancakes always make me feel.

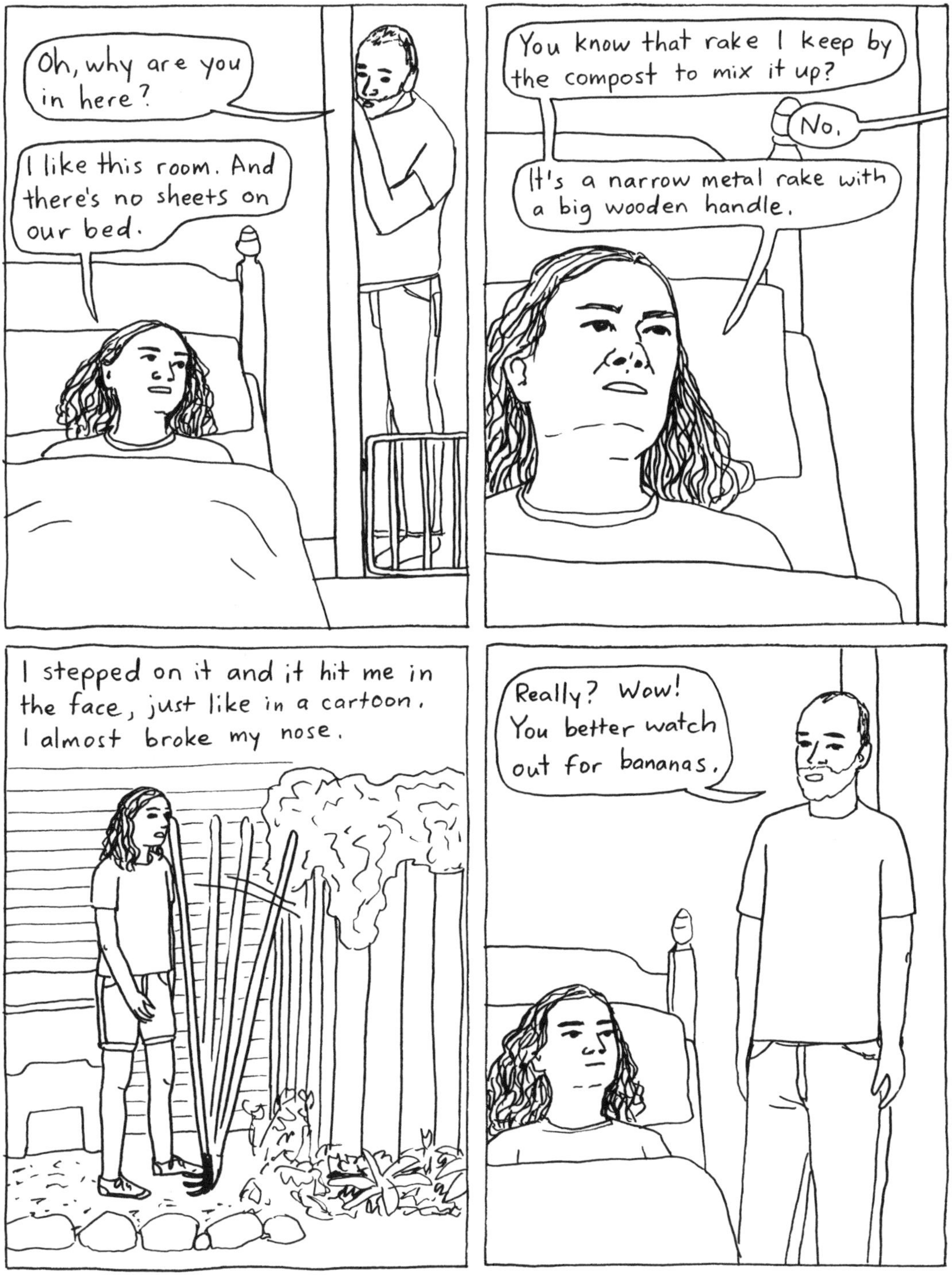
Oh, why are you in here?
I like this room. And there's no sheets on our bed.
You know that rake I keep by the compost to mix it up?
No.
It's a narrow metal rake with a big wooden handle.
I stepped on it and it hit me in the face, just like in a cartoon. I almost broke my nose.
Really? Wow! You better watch out for bananas.

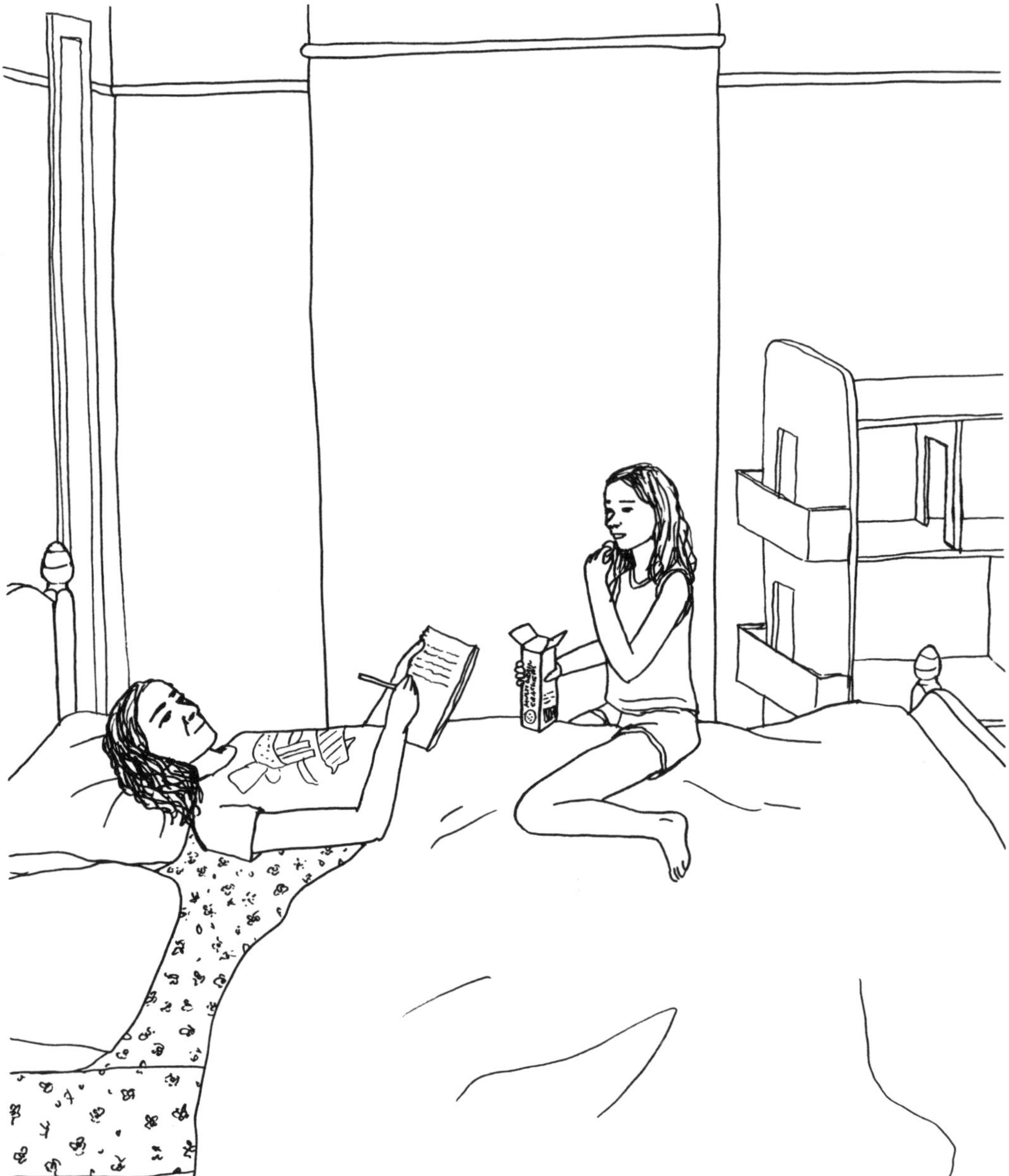

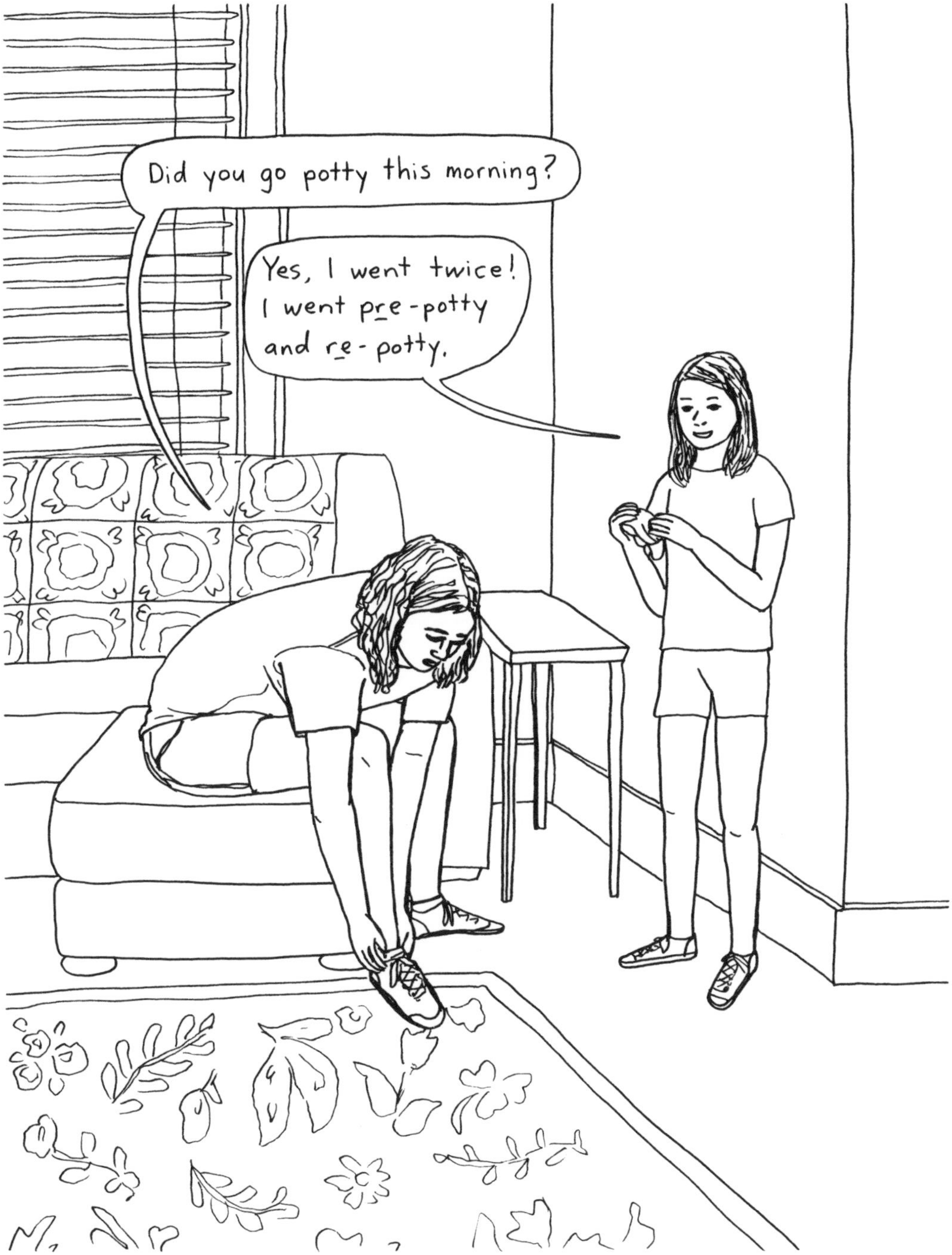
Did you go potty this morning?
Yes, I went twice! I went pre-potty and re-potty.

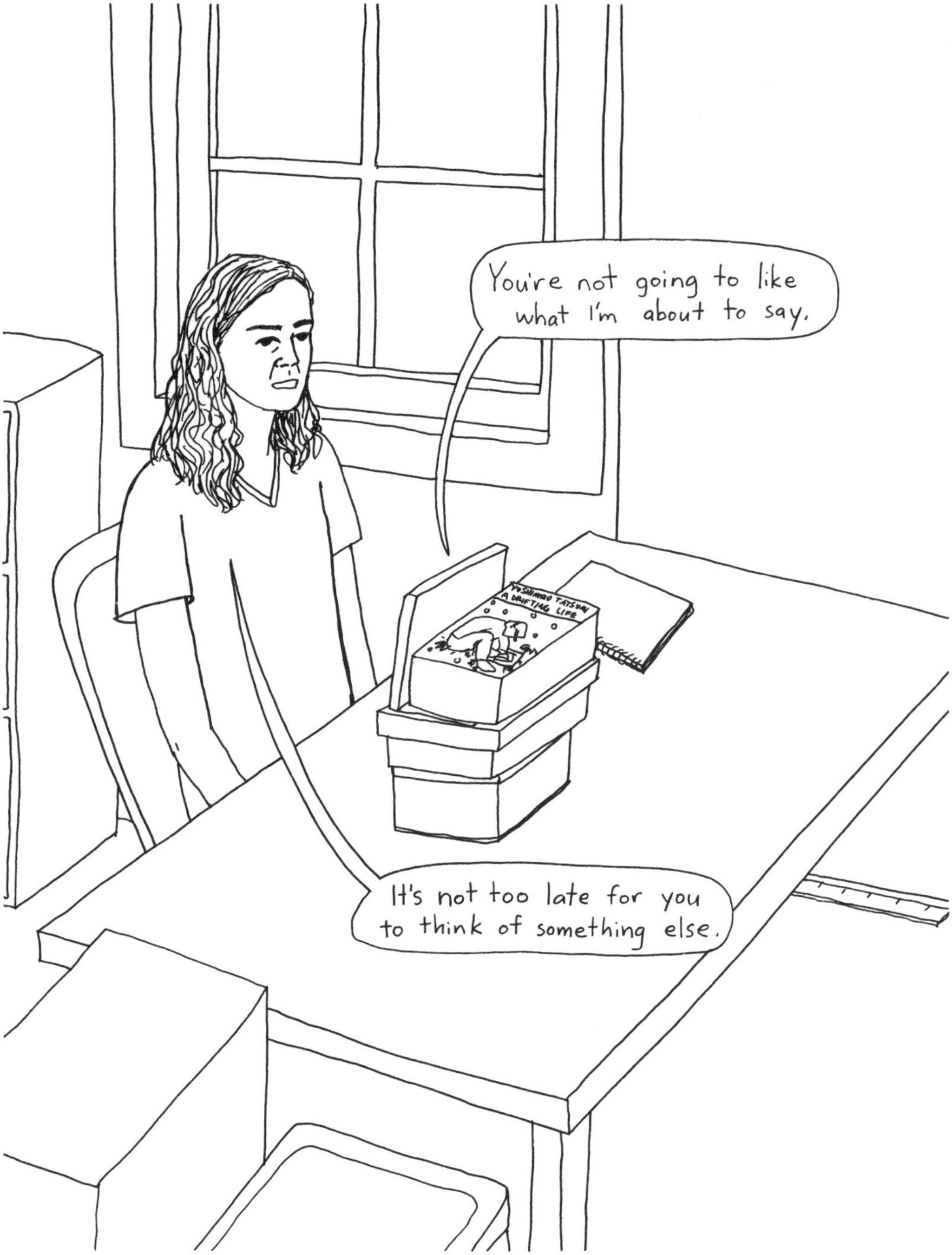
You're not going to like what I'm about to say.
YOSHIHIRO TATSUMI
A DRIFTING LIFE
It's not too late for you to think of something else.

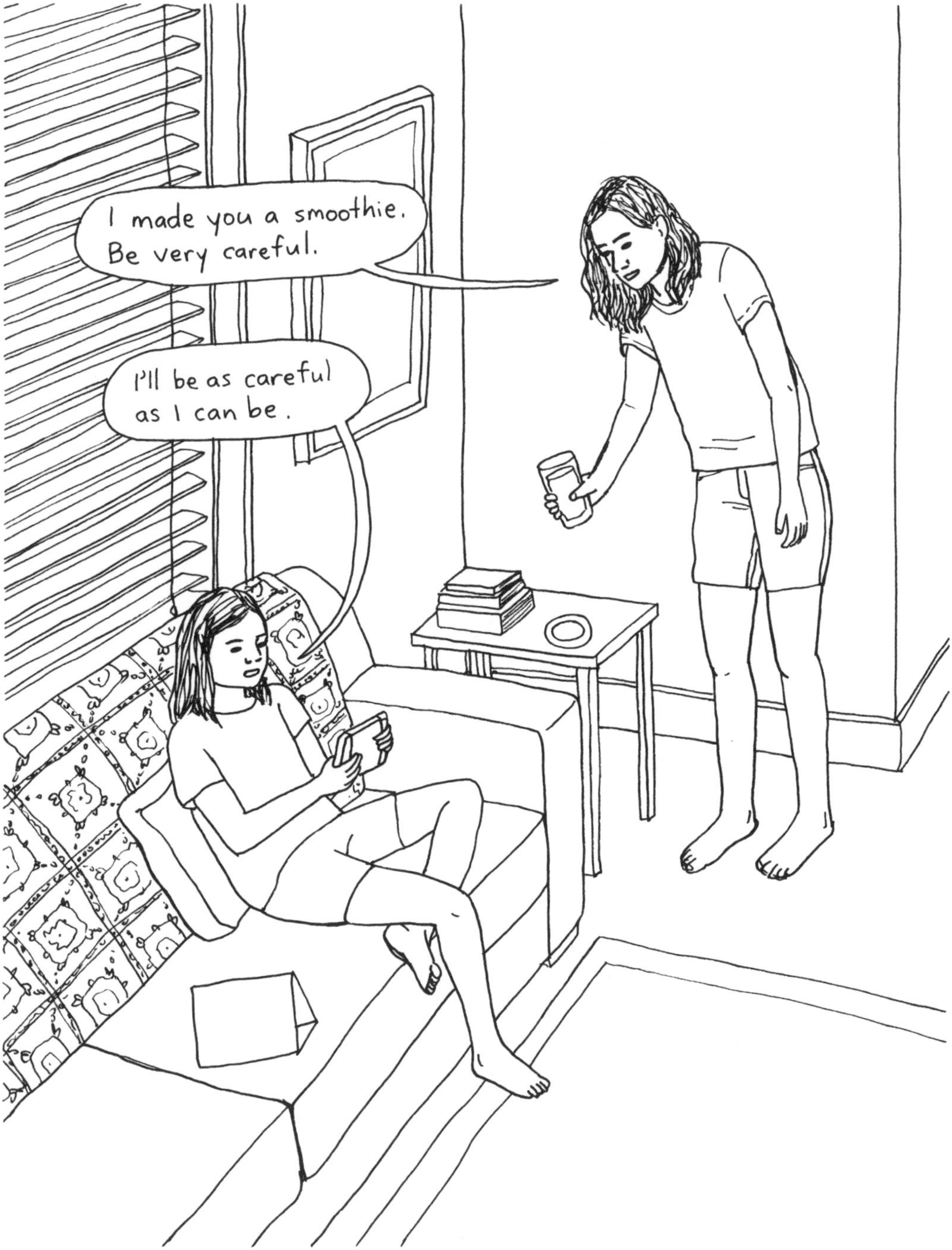
I made you a smoothie. Be very careful.
I'll be as careful as I can be.

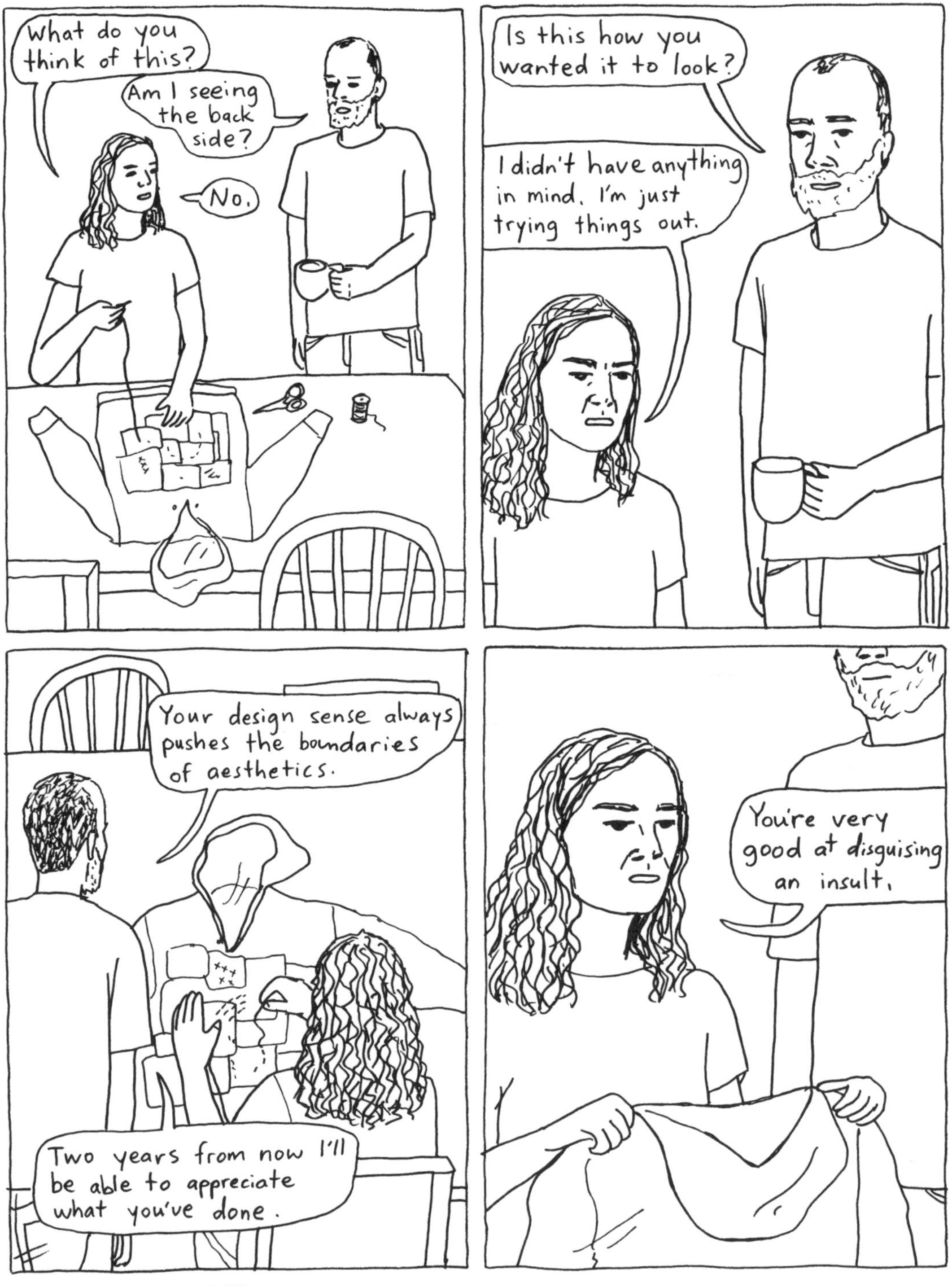
What do you think of this?
Am I seeing the back side?
No.
Is this how you wanted it to look?
I didn't have anything in mind. I'm just trying things out.
Your design sense always pushes the boundaries of aesthetics.
Two years from now I'll be able to appreciate what you've done.
You're very good at disguising an insult.

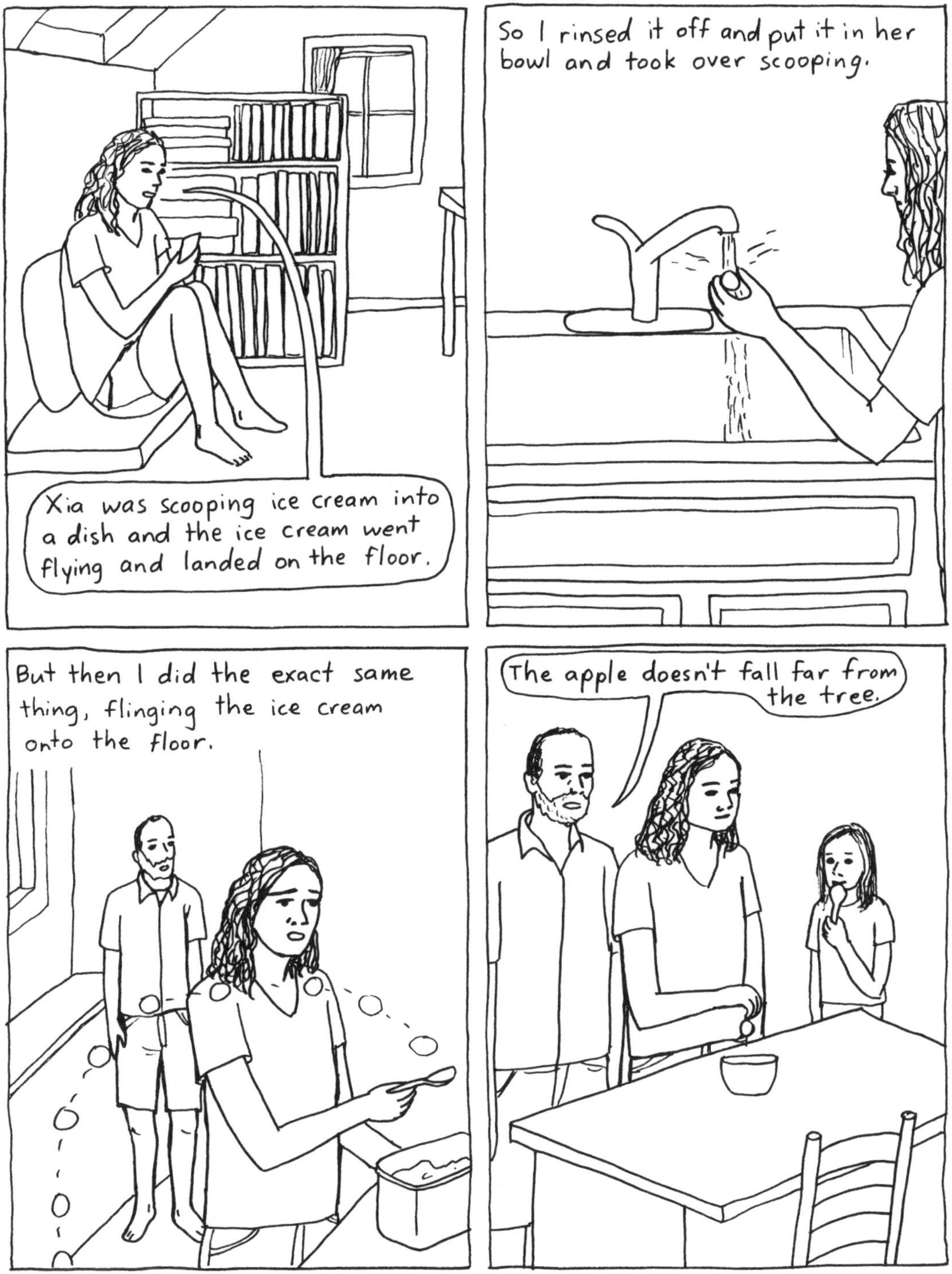
Xia was scooping ice cream into a dish and the ice cream went flying and landed on the floor.
So I rinsed it off and put it in her bowl and took over scooping.
But then I did the exact same thing, flinging the ice cream onto the floor.
The apple doesn't fall far from the tree.

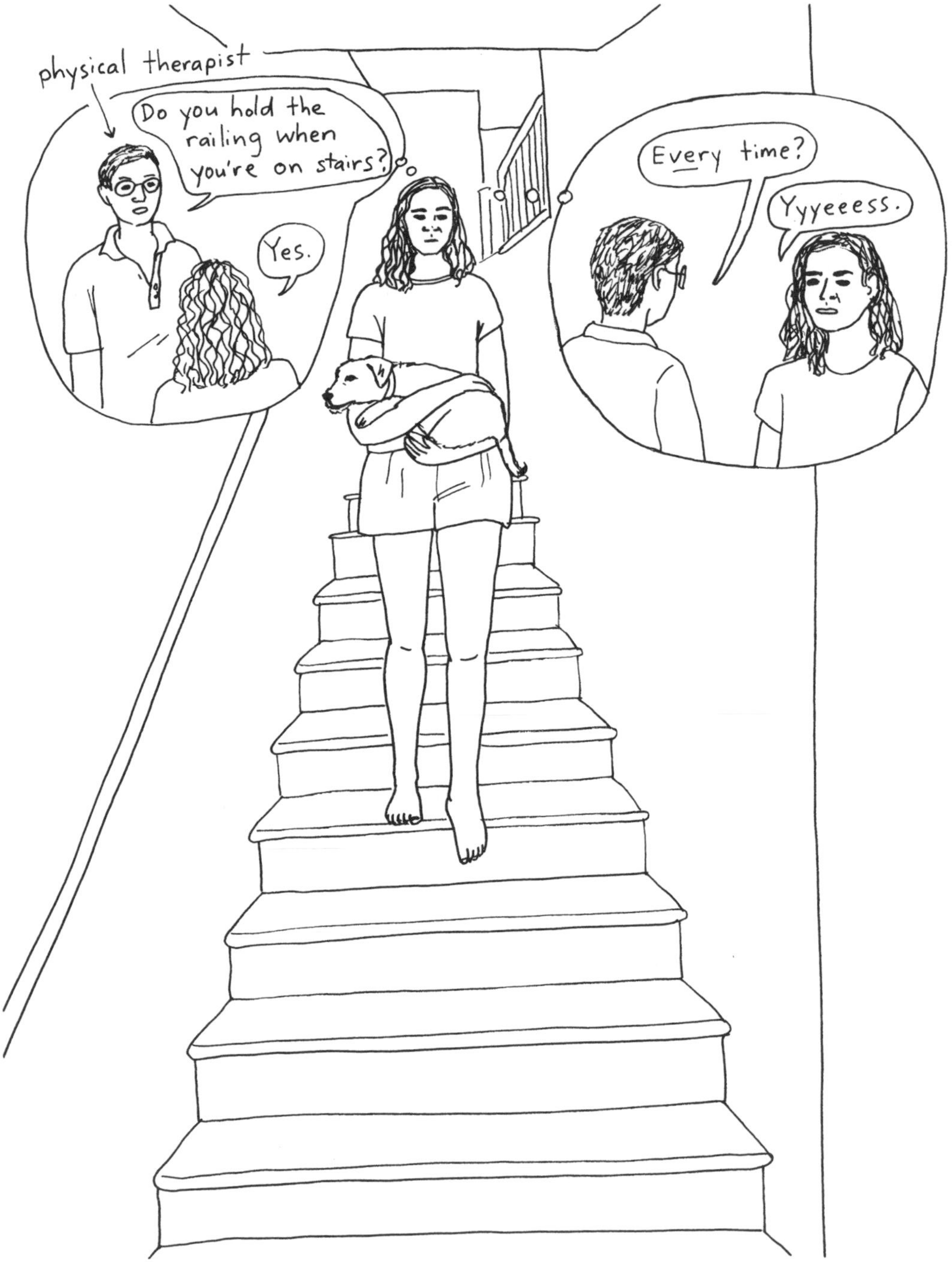
physical therapist
Do you hold the railing when you're on stairs?
Yes.
Every time?
Yyyeeess.

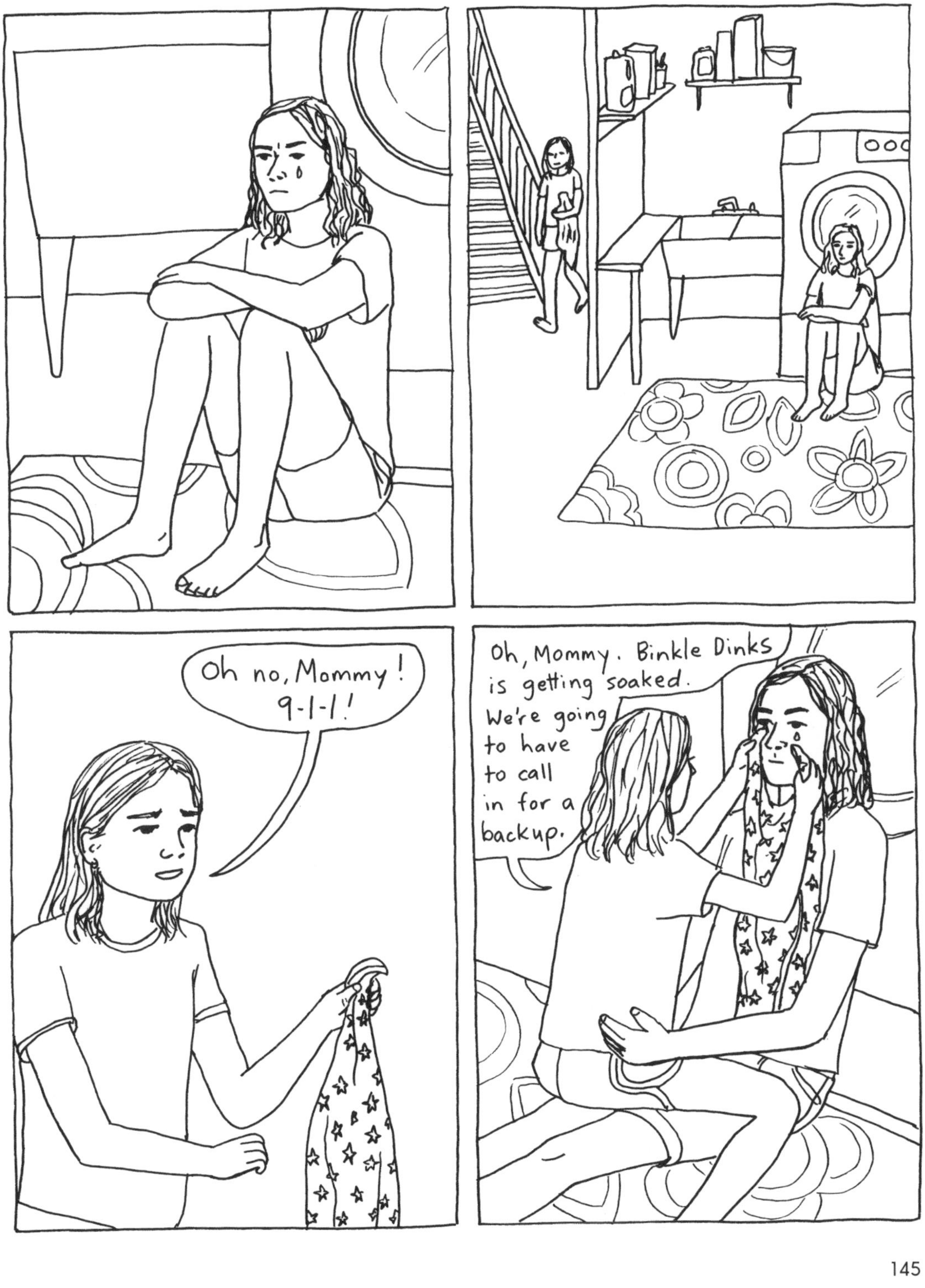
Oh no, Mommy!
9-1-1!
Oh, Mommy. Binkle Dinks is getting soaked. We're going to have to call in for a backup.

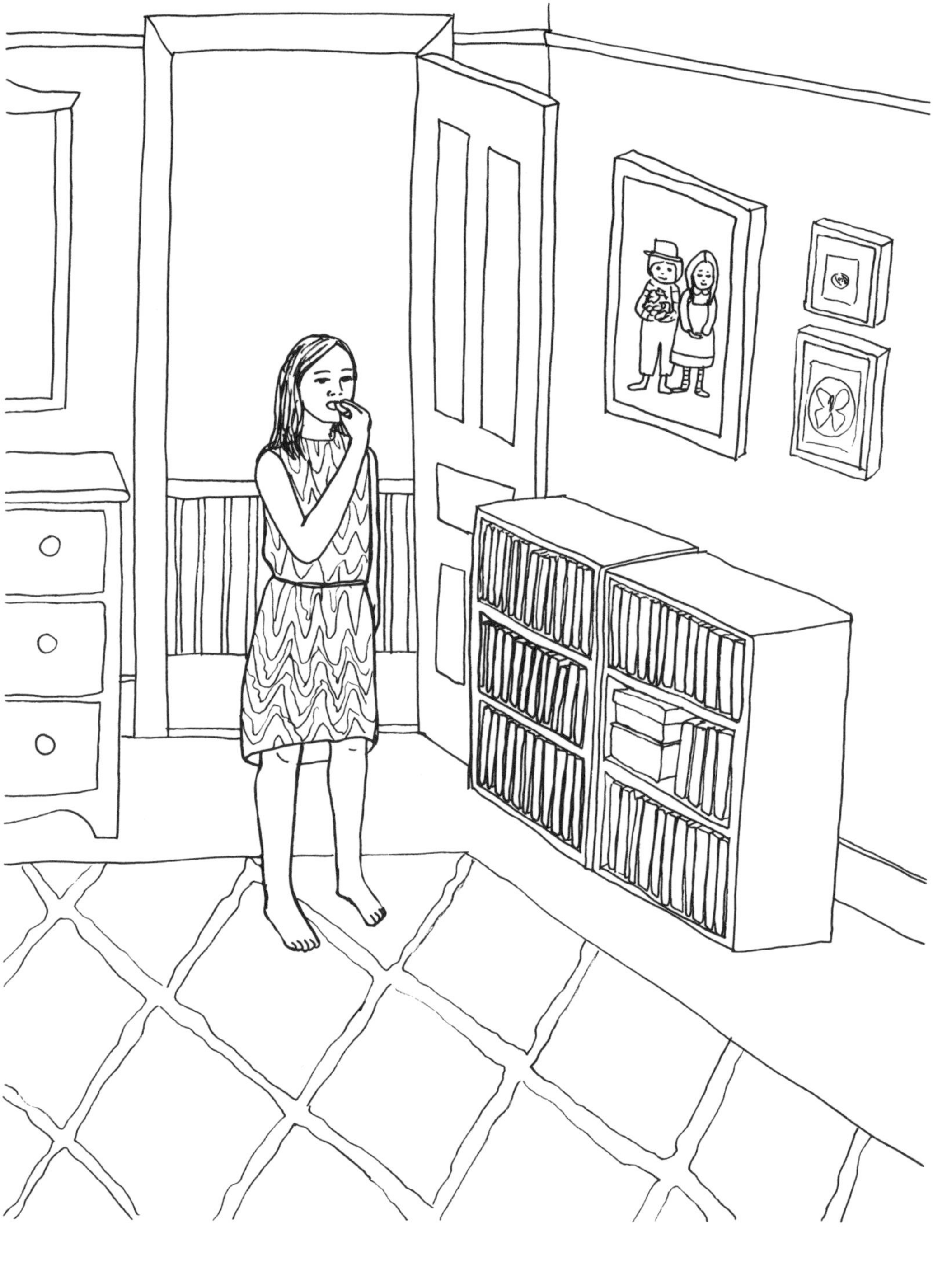

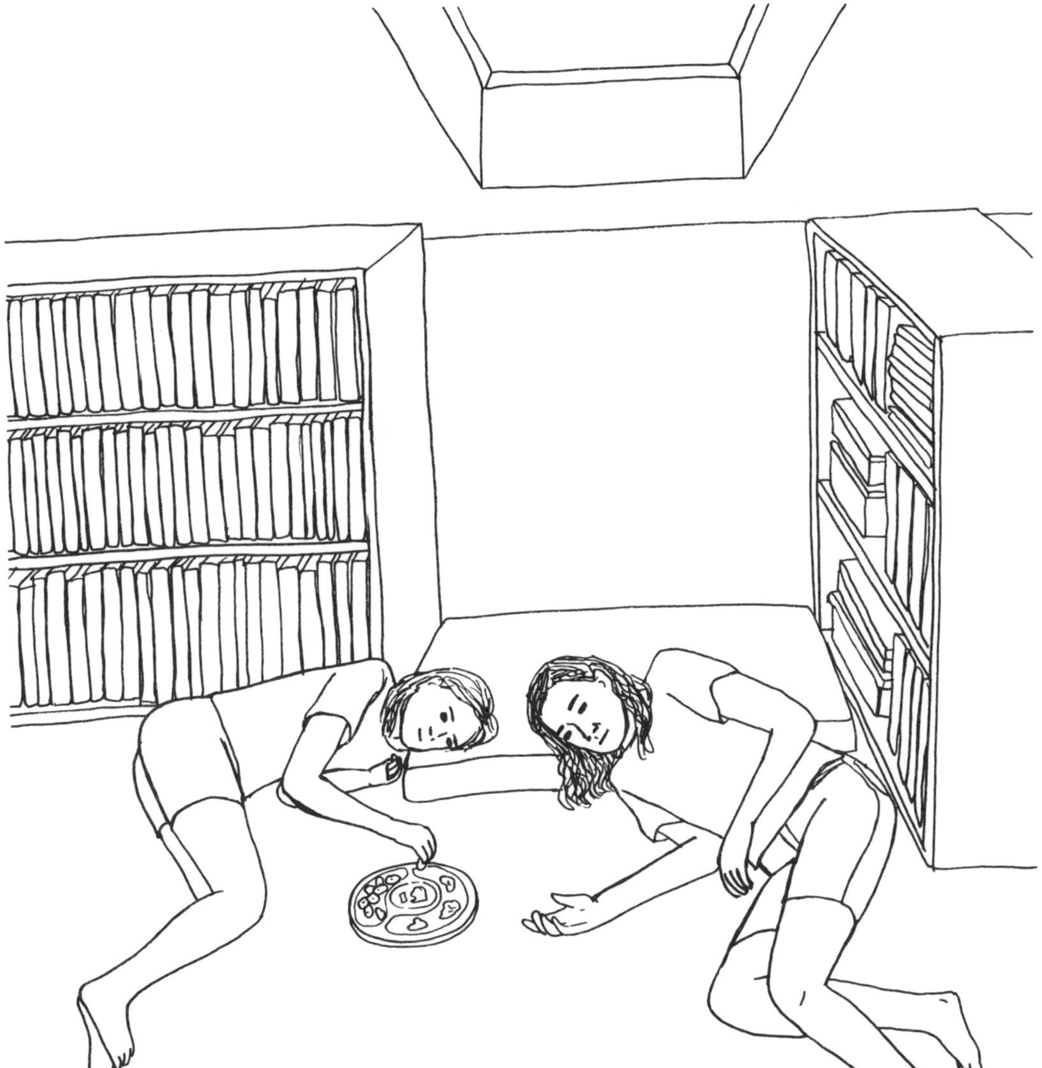

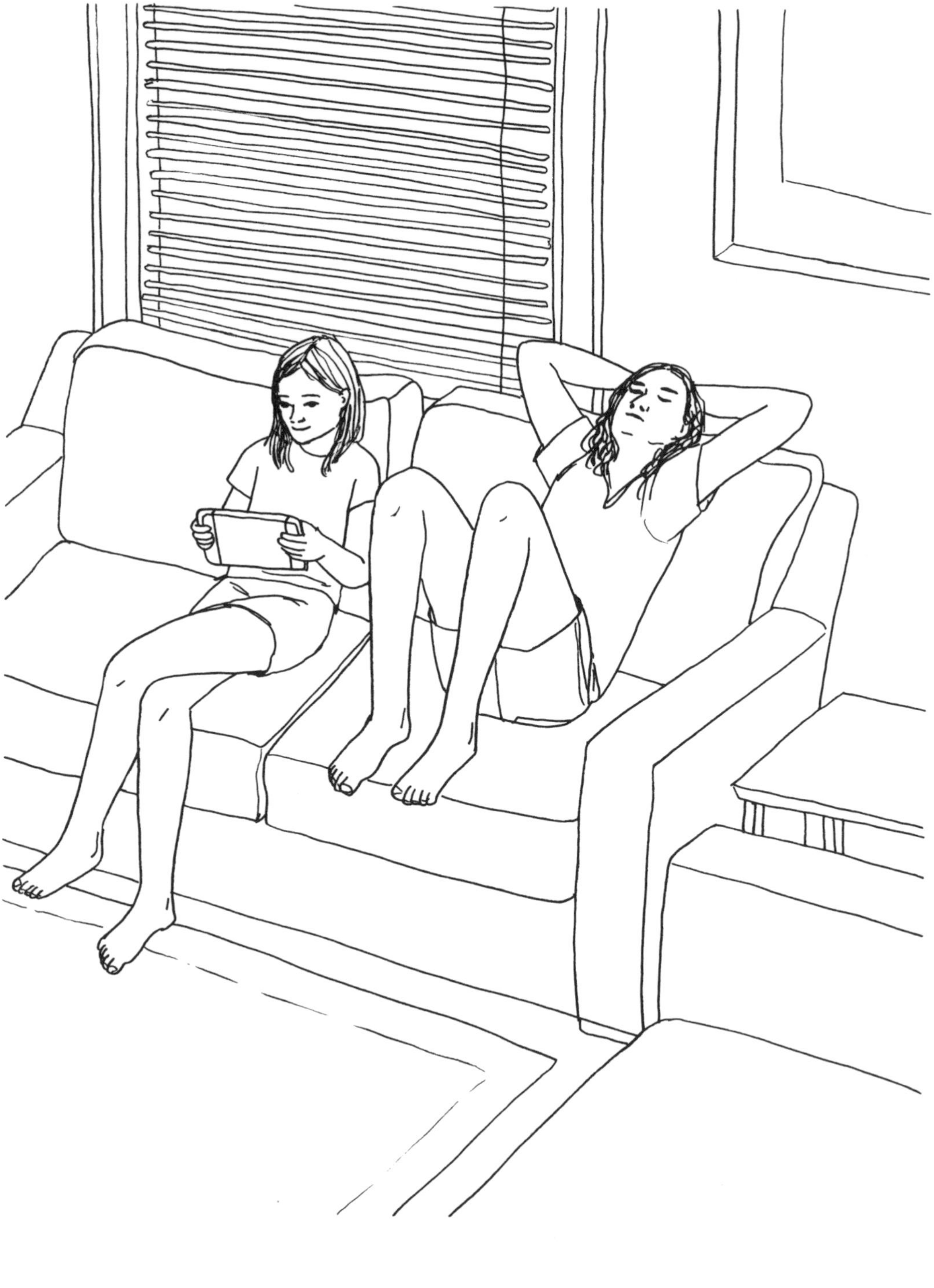

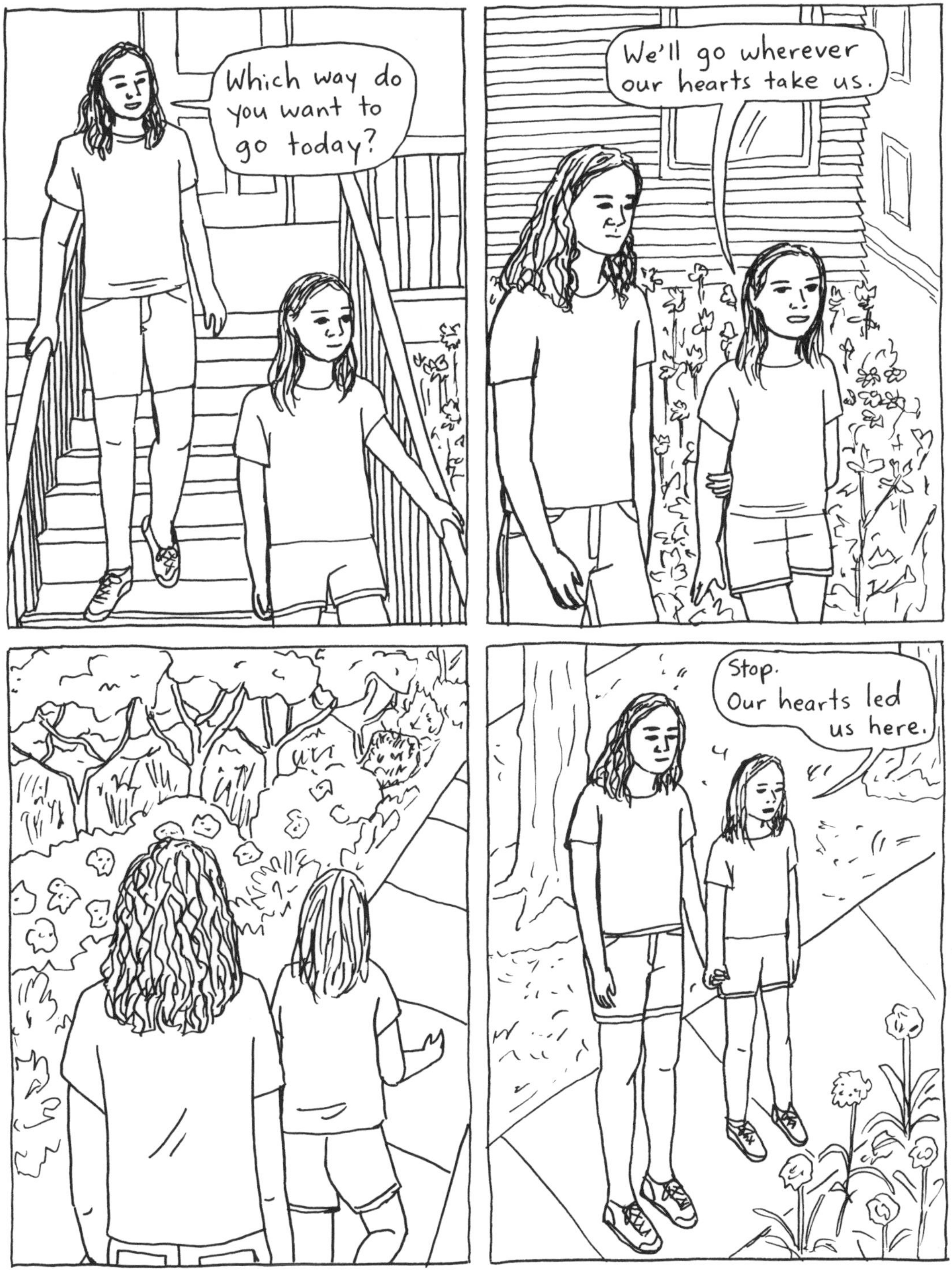
Which way do you want to go today?
We'll go wherever our hearts take us.
Stop. Our hearts led us here.

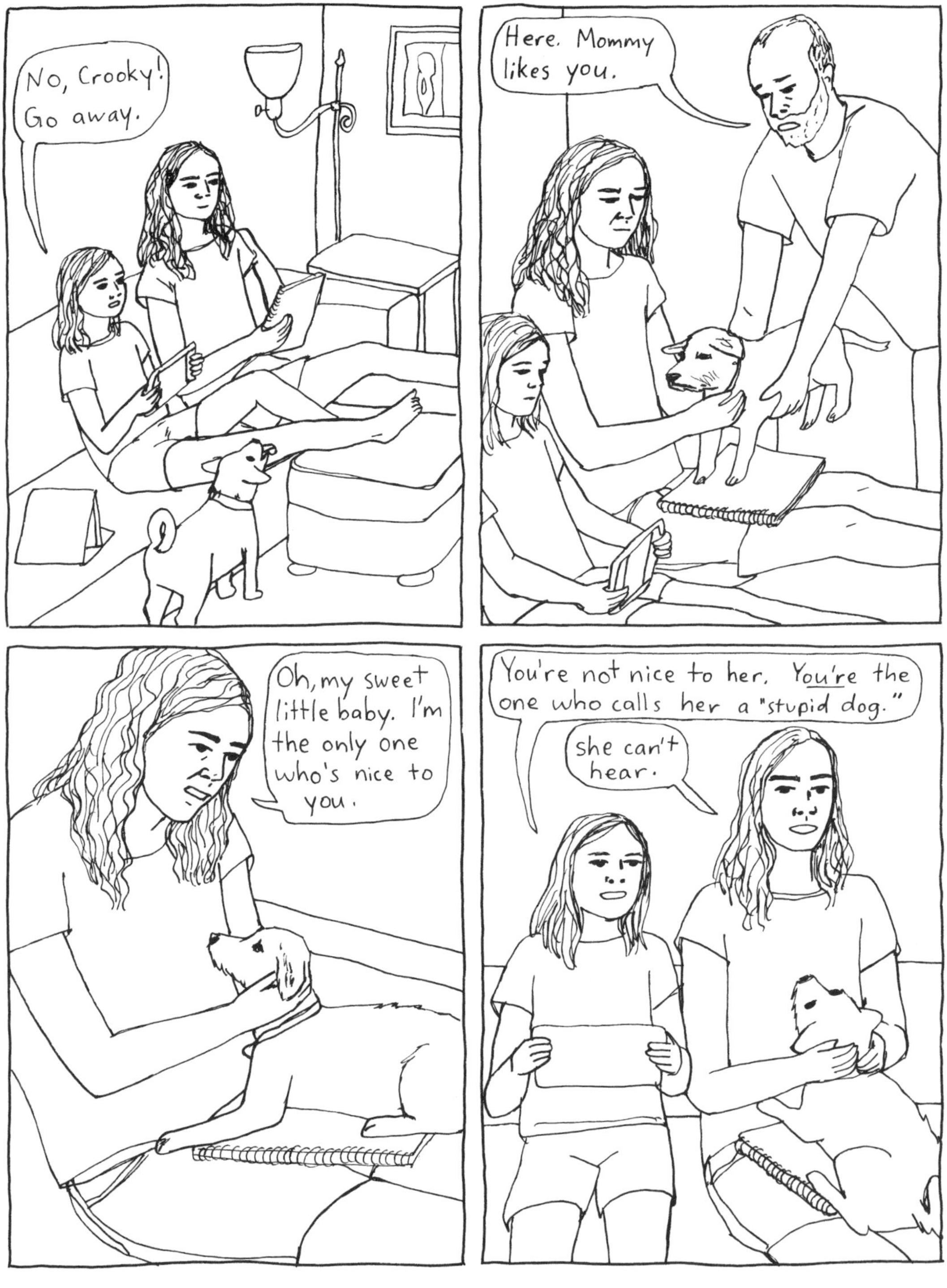
No, Crooky! Go away.
Here. Mommy likes you.
Oh, my sweet little baby. I'm the only one who's nice to you.
You're not nice to her. You're the one who calls her a "stupid dog."
She can't hear.

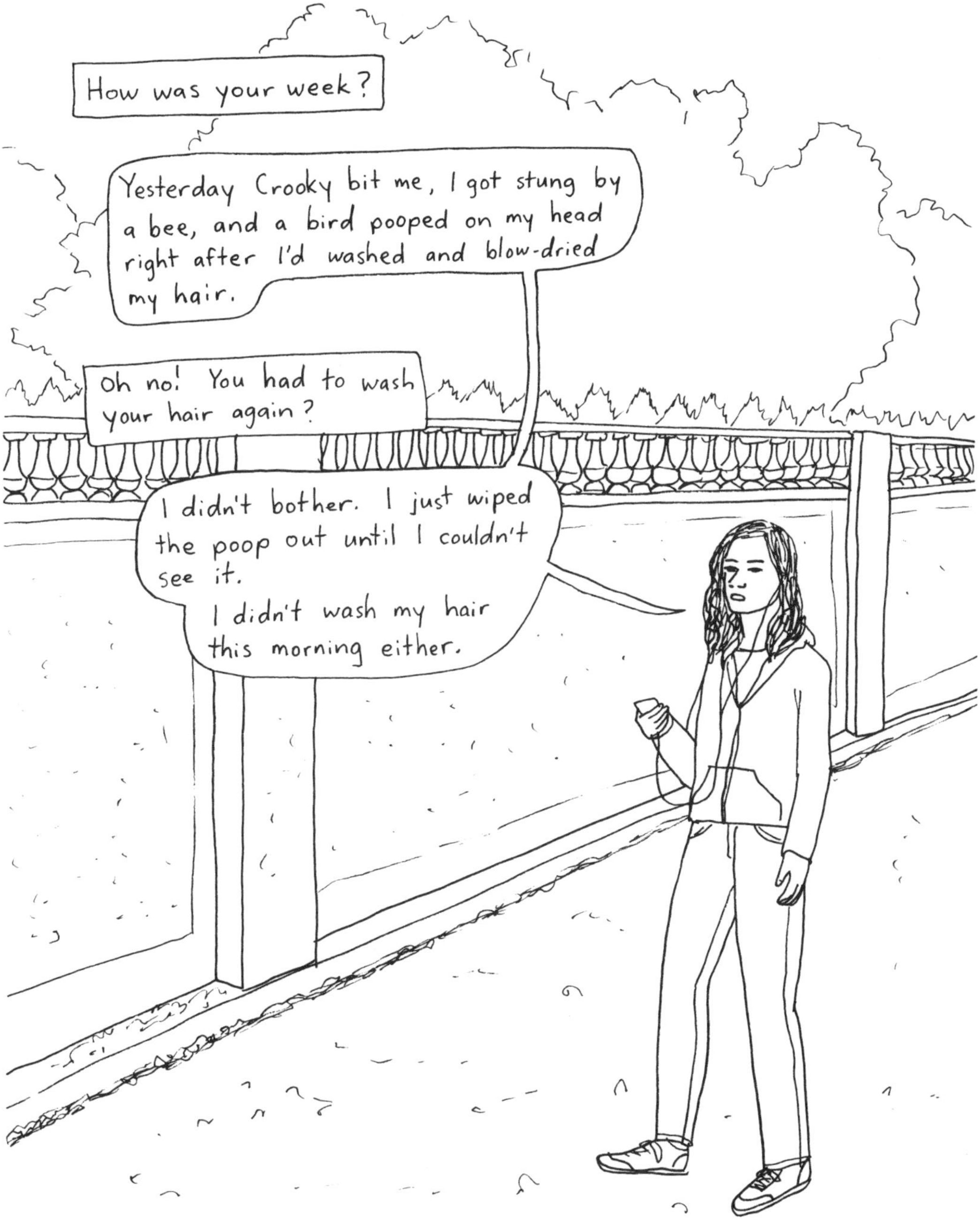
How was your week?
Yesterday Crooky bit me, I got stung by a bee, and a bird pooped on my head right after I'd washed and blow-dried my hair.
Oh no! You had to wash your hair again?
I didn't bother. I just wiped the poop out until I couldn't see it.
I didn't wash my hair this morning either.

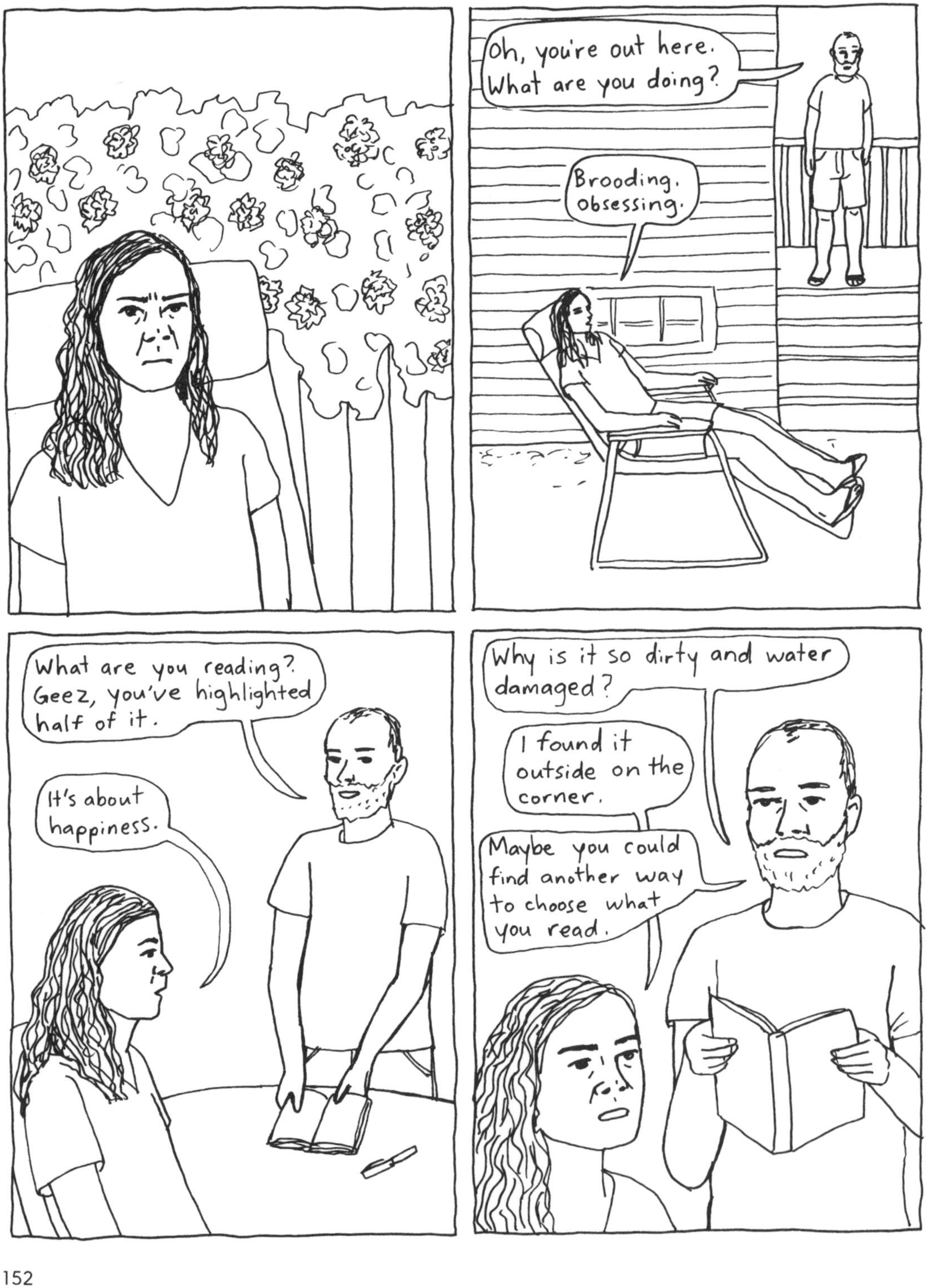

Oh, you're out here. What are you doing?
Brooding. obsessing.
What are you reading? Geez, you've highlighted half of it.
It's about happiness.
Why is it so dirty and water damaged?
I found it outside on the corner.
Maybe you could find another way to choose what you read.

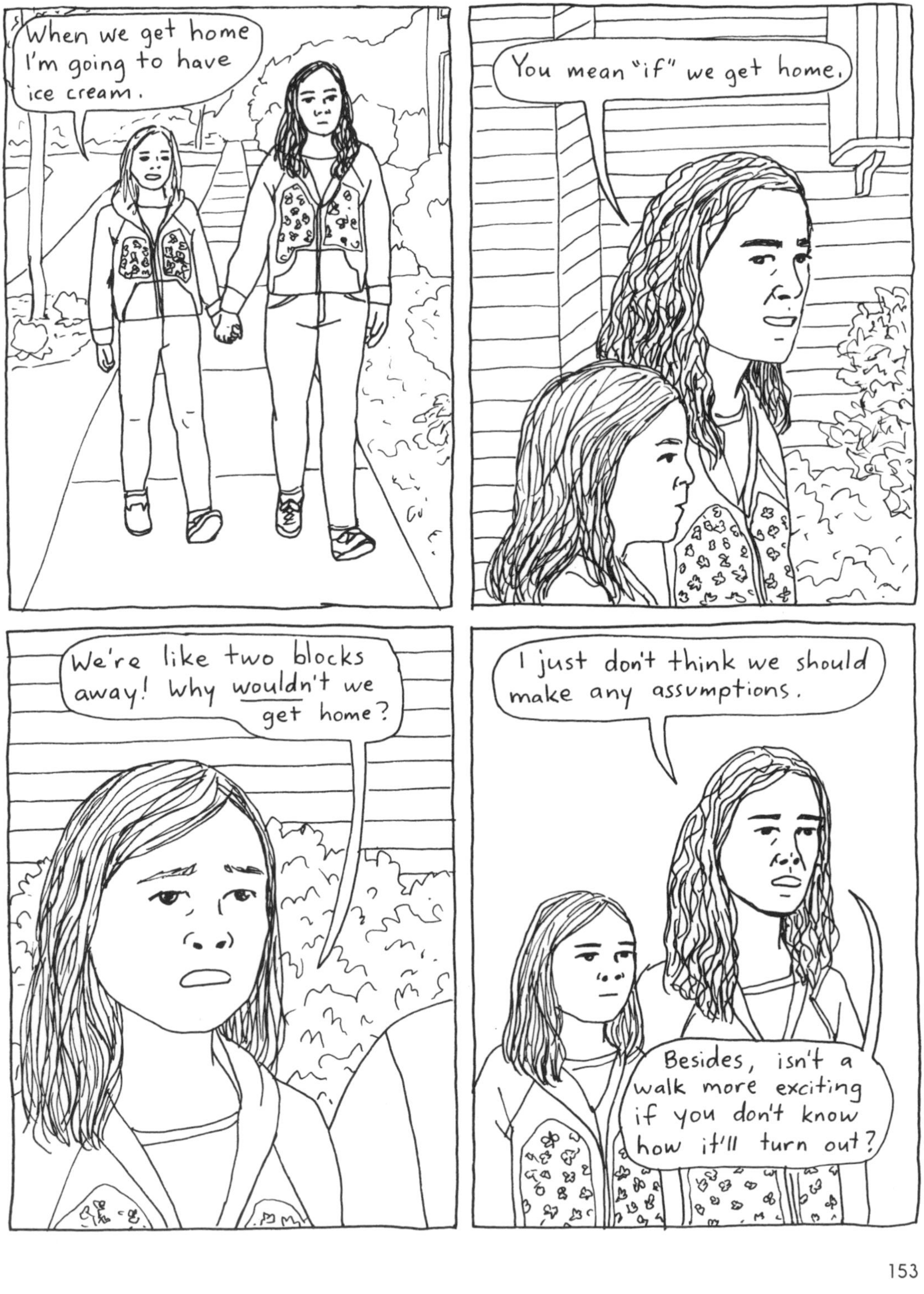
When we get home I'm going to have ice cream.
You mean "if" we get home.
We're like two blocks away! Why wouldn't we get home?
I just don't think we should make any assumptions.
Besides, isn't a walk more exciting if you don't know how it'll turn out?

name: Xia
City: Evanston

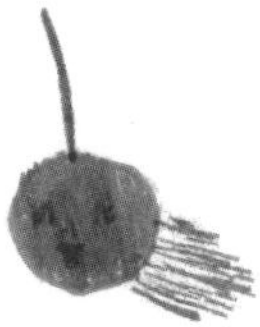

My Begging chart

	M	Tu	W	Th	F	Sa	Su	
No								I begged. yes/no
yes								I got my way. yes/no

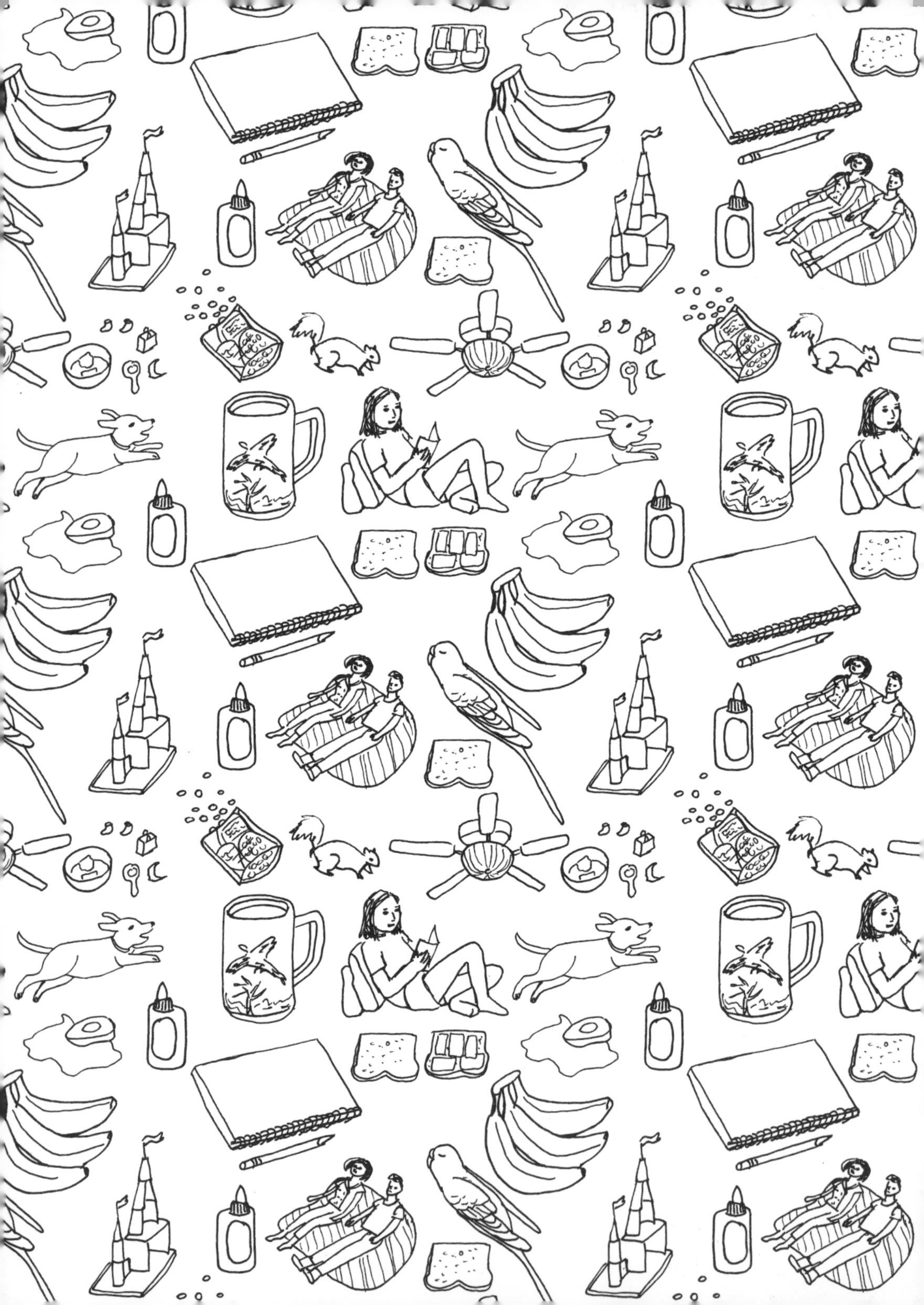